They Were Women, Too

They Were Women, Too

**A DAILY DEVOTIONAL
BASED ON THE WOMEN OF
THE OLD TESTAMENT**

BY

JOY JACOBS

CHRISTIAN PUBLICATIONS

CAMP HILL, PENNSYLVANIA

Christian Publications
Publishing House of The Christian and Missionary Alliance
3825 Hartzdale Drive, Camp Hill, PA 17011

The Mark of ✠ *Vibrant Faith*

Library of Congress Catalog Card Number: 01-67319
© 1981 by Christian Publications, Inc. All rights reserved
First printing 1981   Second printing 1985
ISBN: 0-87509-304-3

Printed in the United States of America

PREFACE

Have you ever found yourself in a predicament for which there seemed to be no definite guidelines in God's Word? Perhaps it was a situation in which even the question "What would Jesus do?" didn't bring a helpful answer. You searched the Bible but just couldn't seem to find what you needed. Maybe you were almost to the point of saying, "Well, it's a woman's problem—and the Bible was written by men!"

I think we women have been missing something all these years! I'm becoming more and more aware that the average Christian woman is largely unaware of facts given in the Bible about women like Shiphrah and Puah (who in the world were they?) . . . Zipporah (is that a brand name for zippers?) . . . the Deborahs (did you know there were two?) . . . Peninnah (Elkanah's *other* wife). Many Christian mothers—mine was an exception—have neglected to teach their daughters the stories of Dinah, Tamar, Michal, and Bashemath and Judith. True, some of these stories are rather sketchy, but certainly they have meanings relevant to today's world.

I believe in the inerrancy of the inspired Word of God. In studying Bible women, I have come to the conclusion that every woman whose story is given in Scripture was mentioned for a divine purpose.

As a matter of fact, I was amazed at the parallels between their lives and mine. We share the same frustrations, joys, and fears. Those mothers and daughters laughed, cried, loved, hated, and felt the same resentments and jealousies that we do today. Why not? They were women too!

Throughout the book, the studies are divided into weekly units. The opening page for each week (to be read on Sunday) introduces the character and theme and lists the Old Testament passages covered that week. Please don't skip over the sections reserved for prayer requests and answers to prayer! So often we forget to note the answers and thus miss a valuable part of our spiritual growth.

Sunday would also be a good day to read the poetry for the week at one sitting; you will find yourself becoming more personally involved with each woman in this way. Submerge yourself in each personality; realize that each woman has something to share with you.

Since we have been told so little about some women in the Word, I have taken the liberty of reconstructing parts of their lives that have remained a question mark over the years. Please keep in mind that the poetry section of each day is often fictional and reflects the feelings of each woman studied as *perceived by the author*. Please feel free to agree or disagree, and to use your own imagination!

Each daily reading (Monday through Saturday) contains a scriptural theme followed by an optional reading assignment—also Scripture. (I must warn you, however, that some of the less familiar stories will be difficult to follow unless you're doing your homework!)

Following each day's poetry are several paragraphs which clarify the poetry, provide historical background, fill in biblical information, and make a practical application of the scriptural theme. Each devotional concludes with a prayer and a thought for the day.

This book deals specifically with Old Testament women, and so there is something else you need to keep in mind. Eugenia Price has said it well: "Those people had far more reason to be unpleasant, impatient, evil, clannish, self-right-eous, and idolatrous, because Jesus Christ had not yet come to reveal the Father's true nature or to make possible the gift of the permanent, indwelling Holy Spirit."[1] From that point of view, today's women are truly blessed. It is my prayer that this study of women in the Word will help *you to become a woman in the Word.*

EVE: "AND BEHOLD, IT WAS VERY GOOD"

"And behold, it was very good." With these simple words God repeated and summarized His feelings of complete satisfaction about the products of His creation. God was happy with what He had brought into being.

You are probably familiar with the biblical account of creation as told in Genesis 1. (If not, please read it.) God had created life and everything that was needed to sustain life; then He created man to be the master of all living things.

In Plato's *Symposium* is found an interesting myth that tells of original humans who were round, with four arms, four legs, and two heads. They disobeyed their gods, and in punishment, the gods divided them, leaving frustrated, doomed people who spent their lives in search of their other halves, content only when complete.

The biblical account of creation also points out that man was incomplete without woman, but also includes that God forethought the potential beauty of the "one-flesh" union of mind, spirit, and body (Gen. 2:24), to be unsurpassed by any other earthly relationship. The second chapter of Genesis vividly describes the initial beginnings of that sacred union.

In chapter 3 we discover the concept of authority, and that God has intended it as a protective covering in our lives.[1] When we disregard the warnings of authorities, we lose out: "The authorities that exist have been established by God. Consequently, he who rebels against the authority is rebelling against what God has instituted, and those who do so will bring judgment on themselves" (Rom. 13:1-2, NIV). And that's exactly what happened in the story of Adam and Eve, the "couple who had everything."

O. T. PASSAGE THIS WEEK: Genesis 2:8—3:7

SPECIAL PRAYER NEEDS THIS WEEK:

ANSWERS TO PRAYER THIS WEEK:

IT ISN'T GOOD FOR MAN TO BE ALONE

I have created him for my glory (Isa. 43:7, KJV). I will make him an helpmeet for him (a helper suitable for him, NIV) (Gen. 2:18, KJV). Read Genesis 2:18-25.

> *"Wow!" Adam yelled when he woke up.*
> *"If this is Woman, she's worth waiting for!"*
> *My eyes met his, and we both knew*
> *That You had made us 'specially for each other.*
> *You had shaped me from his rib,*
> *Breathed life within,*
> *Then placed me by his side.*
> *How good the fresh air felt!*
> *I looked about me gratefully—*
> *God's world was good!*
> *And Adam needed me. . .Adam, my love.*
> *—Eve*

Woman—taken from an inner sanctum right next to man's heart, designed by her Creator to fill the spot left empty by the missing rib. Adam enjoyed the presence of God Himself, but still something was missing from his life—woman!

Someone has said that "woman was taken not from man's head to rule over him, nor from his feet to be trampled upon, but from his side, under his arm, to be protected, and closest to his heart, to be loved." It follows that since woman was formed from man's side, she was planned to be a help to him; he, in turn, owes her "the full protection and devoted shielding of his arm. The two beings make up the completed whole, the crown of creation."[2]

Father, I want to learn about Your plans for my life. I want what *You* want for me, whatever it is, whatever it takes. Thank You, Father, for the special place in life You have given me.

BLOOM WHERE YOU'RE PLANTED!

YOU MUST NOT EAT FROM ONE TREE

This is love for God: to obey his commands. And his commands are not burdensome. . . (1 John 5:3, NIV). Read Genesis 2:8-17.

The Garden You had given us to live in, love, explore,
Provided constant pleasure.
Such perfect beauty—and at our command!
We shared it with the animals, our delightful friends;
How we enjoyed them!
Each night of restful sleep prepared us for another day
Of further sampling Your provision for our needs.
In all the Garden there was only one tree banned.

Obedience to You was our protection from the evil one.
As long as I obeyed Your rules
Your love umbrella sheltered me.
There was no fear of harm;
Your love casts out all fear.
Obedience and trust go hand in hand.

—*Eve*

Imagine yourself as a child going out into a heavy rainstorm—but you aren't getting wet because your father is beside you, holding a large umbrella directly over your head. You feel safe and warm and protected. But what happens if you dart out from under the umbrella to investigate the intensity of the storm? You get wet, drenched, soaked to the bone—and the next morning you wake up with a sore throat. Your father had told you to stay under the umbrella. Was his command unreasonable? But did you realize that at the time?

Father, thank You for Your love. Help me to learn from Eve's story that Your laws are not restrictions on my freedom, but safeguards for my protection. Help me to search out Your rules of life for me in Your Word, and please help me to obey the ones I already know, especially this one: _____ .

AN UMBRELLA CAN PROTECT YOU ONLY IF YOU STAY UNDER IT!

IS THAT *REALLY* WHAT GOD SAID?

No temptation has seized you except what is common to man (1 Cor. 10:13, NIV). Read Genesis 3:1-3, 6.

"Did God really say that?
You must not eat from any tree?
Perhaps you heard Him wrong,
Misunderstood His meaning."
The serpent's words penetrated,
Confused my mind, beguiled my thoughts.
What had God really said?
Surely His rules were flexible.
This situation is different.
God will understand.

        —Eve

Wait a minute! What's happening here? God had told Adam very definitely, "You *must not* eat from the tree of the knowledge of good and evil" (Gen. 2:17, NIV). Obviously Eve was aware of the rules—yet here she is, questioning the meaning of God's words. Why? Because she had listened to the serpent, and now she wanted that luscious-looking piece of fruit, wanted it more than anything in the world. Why? Because it was the one thing in the world she couldn't have!

"The grass is always greener on the other side of the fence" isn't true only for cows! Isn't it just as true of us women? Had Eve realized the extent of the serpent's persuasive powers, she might not have been silly enough to discuss God's rules with him. Once he had drawn her into a discussion, her resistance crumbled and she could think only of how delicious that forbidden fruit would taste.

Father, thank You for this lesson on the danger of listening to Satan's arguments. I realize that he's too powerful for me to fight on my own. Thank you that You have promised that You will not allow me to be tempted beyond what I can bear (1 Cor. 10:13).

HOLDING A CONFERENCE WITH THE DEVIL IS ALWAYS DANGEROUS!

WHEN YOU EAT YOUR EYES WILL BE OPENED

You said in your heart. . .'I will make myself like the Most High.' But you are brought down to the grave (Isa. 14:13-15, NIV). Read Genesis 3:4-6.

"Like gods," he said, "You'll be like gods!"
And suddenly a strange desire
Became an overpowering urge.
I'd never felt this way before in my young life.
It frightened me, this strange new urge,
Yet fascinated, drew me on.
I wanted to be powerful, to be like God.
I wanted to control my life—and Adam's too.

—Eve

It's so easy to succumb to that contagious desire for importance, for power, for significance in life. Lawrence Crabb points out that *"true* significance depends upon understanding who I am in Christ. I will come to feel significant as I have an eternal impact on people around me by ministering to them."[3] What does it mean to minister to people? Isn't that the pastor's job?

Jesus said, "Whoever wants to become great among you must be your servant, and whoever wants to be first must be slave of all. For even the Son of Man [Jesus] did not come to be served, but to serve, and to give his life as a ransom for many" (Mark 10:43-45, NIV).

Father, if I'm honest, I don't like to serve others, at least not some people. I don't have a servant's spirit—but I'm beginning to realize that You want me to have one, just as You did when You were here on Planet Earth. My spirit is proud, Father, but I'm willing to be humbled. Help me especially in this area: _____
and with this person: _____ .

"TRUE SIGNIFICANCE DEPENDS UPON UNDERSTANDING WHO I AM IN CHRIST!"

THE POWER OF A WOMAN!

A wife of noble character who can find? She is worth far more than rubies. Her husband has full confidence in her. . . . She brings him good, not harm, all the days of her life (Prov. 31:10-12, NIV). Read Genesis 3:6-7.

I couldn't be content to disobey alone.
My guilt cried out in panic
To share its burden.
And so, my Adam, I spoke softly, sweetly,
Of how delicious was the taste
Of the forbidden fruit.
Sly Satan couldn't have won without my help.
Debate or logic couldn't have changed your mind,
But so persuasive was my touch
You yielded quietly, without a fight.

—Eve

"The woman saw. . .took. . .ate. . .gave" (Gen. 3:6, NIV). The action verbs tell the story vividly to us, the understanding readers. We can understand Eve because we too experience self-deception when we rationalize that what we want is good for us.

And there's something else to consider. Make a mental list of the men in your life: husband, father, brothers, nephews, friends, men you work with, neighbors. Now try to visualize what effect *your* life has on them. (You might be surprised at how closely they watch you!) When they spend time with you, are they aware that you're a Christian? Does your influence make them want to draw closer to the Lord? Or do you "turn them off" on spiritual things? What do they think when they look at you?

Father, help me to be concerned more about inner beauty than outward beauty. Help me to have a positive influence on the men and other women around me, as I encourage them to think about things that are true and pure (Phil. 4:8). **HOW DO YOU INFLUENCE OTHER PEOPLE—FOR RIGHT OR FOR WRONG?**

FREEDOM OF CHOICE!

Choose for yourselves this day whom you will serve (Josh. 24:15, NIV). Read Psalm 119:105-112.

The choice was ours!
Adam and I did not hang from strings,
Manipulated by a giant hand.
We had a choice!
And when we chose to disobey,
Reject love's kind umbrella,
You let us walk away from You
Into the storms of life,
Although Your heart was sorely grieved.
You knew our future well—
If only we had known!

—Eve

If you've experienced the hurt that results when your child or a friend rejects your love and concern and goes stubbornly on his way, a path that will lead to certain problems—drugs, immorality, a clash with the law—then you understand a little of what God must have felt when Adam and Eve disobeyed His clear command, then hid from Him in guilt and shame. And how we must grieve Him when we disobey His guidelines for our lives and ignore His presence!

Am I able to say, along with the psalmist, "I have chosen your precepts. . .your law is my delight" (Ps. 119:173-174, NIV)? David says further that he is sustained or given support by God's laws. God's "love letter" to us is designed for our nourishment and protection!

Father, thank You for the guidelines You have provided in Your Word. Help me to spend time in Your Word on a regular, daily basis, so that it becomes alive in my life. Help me, too, to share it with others, especially _____
GOD GIVES YOU FREEDOM OF CHOICE!

EVE: OUT FROM UNDER THE UMBRELLA

Nancy Tischler writes: "Perhaps. . .adventuresomeness of the mind is simply a natural part of woman's equipment. While man may venture physically across the sea or engage in battle, woman's biology usually traps her into a more limited physical sphere with less vigorous activity. Therefore, she may well compensate by being mentally adventurous, seeking her excitement in danger and in change, even though she may thereby jeopardize her safety and peace of mind. . . . We will gamble Eden for excitement."[1]

Disobedience to God's rules can look *so* exciting! It certainly did to Eve. The choice she—and later, Adam—made is the prime example of the paradoxical nature of human freedom. Our freedom to choose our own way leads to enslavement by our own desires and a loss of the greater freedom to follow God's will.

Until we learn to give our will back to God, we can never know the joy of true freedom. "If the Son therefore shall make you free, ye shall be free indeed" (John 8:36, KJV).

The story of the Fall also points out that sin can never be a completely independent act. "Sin is like a spiderweb; touch it and watch with wonder as the sticky threads lead outward in all directions."[2] Yet sin is also lonely; even a sin shared with someone else eventually drives a wedge between the partners, as we see in Adam and Eve's relationship.

God is good—but He is also just. His divine system of judgment required punishment: dual punishment for dual sins. Man was given a kind of "travail" just as woman was; what each had formerly enjoyed now became painful. Adam's new enmity with nature made his work a curse

O. T. PASSAGE THIS WEEK: Genesis 3:8—4:1

SPECIAL PRAYER NEEDS THIS WEEK:

ANSWERS TO PRAYER THIS WEEK:

HIDING IN THE TREES

After desire has conceived, it gives birth to sin (James 1:15, NIV).
Read Genesis 3:8-13.

> *How terrible—the sudden realization of our wrong!*
> *"Who told you you were naked?" God had asked,*
> *When fig leaves failed to cover guilt and shame.*
> *He knew, of course, that we had disobeyed.*
>
> *My Adam failed to take responsibility*
> *For what we had done—*
> *He blamed it all on me.*
> *I passed the buck and blamed the serpent.*
> *"The devil made me do it!"*
> *I begged for leniency.*
> *I could not face the blame for sin.*
>
> *—Eve*

Almost as soon as a child learns to talk he learns to blame others for the problems in his life. "I didn't do it, Mommy—it's all his fault!" or "He made me do it!" are familiar words in any home with children.

Bill Gothard says: "It is our natural inclination to find other people or circumstances which are to blame for what we have done in order to justify or excuse our offenses. The greater our guilt, the more we must blame. The resulting bitterness and guilt are devastating to our mental and emotional balance."[3]

Father, I need to learn to take full responsibility for my actions. Help me to realize the effect my environment has on me in the sense that I learn to run from temptation, but correct me when I blame people or things other than myself for my sin.

"THE GREATER OUR GUILT, THE MORE WE MUST BLAME!"

YOU'LL EAT DUST
ALL THE DAYS OF YOUR LIFE

He ₍Jesus₎ replied, 'I saw Satan fall like lightning from heaven' (Luke 10:18, NIV). The God of peace will soon crush Satan under your feet (Rom. 16:20, NIV). Read Genesis 3:14-15.

Then God turned to the snake in wrath.
"This is your punishment," God said:
"From all inhabitants of the earth
You are singled out!
You sly and crafty one, you are cursed!
You will crawl upon your belly evermore
And be the enemy of the one you tricked.
And as you grovel daily in the dust,
Remember that the future brings a day
When a descendant of the woman Eve
Will bruise your head,
And you will bruise His heel."

—Eve

Since Satan fell, he's been super-busy. His major goal? To build his kingdom. In order for his kingdom to grow, he needs to include as many people as possible. That means you and I are prime candidates for what, on the surface, appear to be very attractive, top-notch positions. What "apple" is he dangling in front of your nose right now? Beware of the lures Satan uses—in a short time apples rot.

Father, help me to be aware of the way in which Satan strikes for my weakest spot, my "Achilles heel." Help me to remember that he is too powerful for me to argue with on my own. Help me to turn my back on him and walk away after I have rebuked him in Your name. Thank You for the assurance You have given us that You will crush Satan under Your feet. **EVEN BEAUTIFUL APPLES ROT IN A SHORT TIME!**

YOUR LIFE WILL CHANGE

Submit to one another out of reverence for Christ (Eph. 5:21, NIV).
Read Genesis 3:16.

> *Then God spoke softly, sadness in His eyes:*
> *"Dear Eve, my child, why didn't you obey?*
> *Your needs were met, but greedy hands*
> *Reached out for more—yes, always more!*
> *So now all is changed, and pain invades your life.*
> *Your children will be born in labor so intense*
> *Your body will be wracked with pain,*
> *And pain will follow them, and strife.*
> *Yet even so, you'll welcome Adam's touch,*
> *No longer as a child with some new toy*
> *But as a wife who knows her husband's call.*
> *You couldn't be held accountable for equal power,*
> *So now, my child, submit to Adam's leadership."*
>
> —*Eve*

Howard Hendricks writes: "Submission is not the exclusive responsibility of the woman. Submission is the life style of the Christian. . . . The question is, are you willing to submit yourself. . .to the Lord's plan for your functioning in marital relationship?"[4]

Father, teach me the true meaning of submission. Thank You for Your patience with me—submission is a difficult lesson to learn. I need the "unfading beauty of a gentle and quiet spirit" (1 Pet. 3:4, NIV), and it's so hard to achieve that in today's world. I can't achieve it on my own, Father—it must be a gift from You. But thank You for the knowledge that You're in control just as much today as You were yesterday. Please help me today in this area of submission: _____ .

"SUBMISSION IS THE LIFE STYLE OF THE CHRISTIAN."

TO DUST YOU WILL RETURN

He. . .must work, doing something useful with his own hands, that he may have something to share with those in need (Eph. 4:28, NIV). Read Genesis 3:17-19.

I cringed as God stared Adam down.
My husband seemed to shrink as God's voice spoke:
"I have cursed the ground because you disobeyed.
What once was fertile must be coaxed to bear
The fruit that yesterday fell thickly to the ground,
But thorns and thistles are in great supply.
You will eat your food while trying to relax
From each day's tiring, sweaty work.
O, Adam, my creation, from the ground you came
And to the same ground you will return."
                                        —Eve

Work must have seemed unbearable those first few days to Adam and Eve, compared with their former schedule of pleasure and fellowship with God. The cruel thistles must have torn their uncalloused hands and feet, and their bodies must have ached by the end of each day.

But as those bodies toughened and responded to their new responsibilities, I believe their souls responded in a new way to their Creator. Just as we begin to appreciate how much our parents have done for us when we ourselves become parents, so Adam and Eve began to realize more and more what they had originally taken for granted—God's untiring love and concern for His children.

Thank You, Lord, that because You love me, You chasten me. Thank You for the lessons I have learned through chastening. Help me not to repeat the same mistakes, but to profit by them. Looking back over the past, I can remember a chastening experience, and I thank You for it now: _____ .

THE LORD DISCIPLINES THOSE HE LOVES!

BANISHED FROM THE GARDEN!

*For I acknowledge my transgressions: and my sin is ever before me. . .
Cast me not away from thy presence. . . (Ps. 51:3, 11, KJV). Read Genesis
3:21-24.*

> *Then in great kindness our God covered us*
> *With garments that we didn't know how to make,*
> *And though He banished us, His love*
> *Reached out anew in His great plan*
> *To draw two sinning humans to Himself—*
> *And many more who would follow through the years.*
> *He could not take a chance that we who sinned*
> *Might disobey His laws a second time,*
> *And having eaten of the Tree of Life,*
> *Live on eternally in pain and strife.*
> *As always, He was thinking of our good.*
>
> *—Eve*

If you have ever been separated for an extended time from someone you loved, you can verify the truth of the old saying: "Absence makes the heart grow fonder." You may take someone's presence for granted before a separation, but how you recognize that person's importance to you while he or she is gone!

And so Adam and Eve, who had been created with a void that could be filled only through fellowship with their Creator, must have realized in a new way their need of Him as they left the warm shelter of their garden home.

Father, I thank You so much for the security of Your love—a love from which nothing can separate me (Rom. 8:38-39). I am so totally dependent on You for life and everything that is important in it. I have been holding back this one little portion of my life, Lord, just one little corner, but here it is today: _____ .

WE ARE CREATED WITH A VOID THAT CAN BE FILLED ONLY BY FELLOWSHIP WITH OUR CREATOR.

TO WORK THE GROUND
FROM WHICH HE HAD BEEN TAKEN

Man goes out to his work, to his labor until evening (Ps. 104:23, NIV). Read Genesis 3:20; 4:1.

How life changed! My lust for power
Produced a servant's life instead.
God's words were true, and life was hard—
And yet our work had its rewards;
To see the earth responding to our care,
To see it bringing forth increase at last.

My body was responding, too, to life within.
Our first child was already on its way—
A first for mankind!
I had no one to tell me what to do, how to prepare,
What to expect in this child's birth,
Except the words of God: "There will be pain."
What did He mean? What kind of pain?

—Eve

Can you imagine what it must have been like to be Eve at this point in her life? No doctors, no hospitals—not even a midwife or another woman! Every day of her pregnancy was a brand-new experience. During these months of new discoveries Eve must have realized anew her dependence on the Creator who had breathed life into the bodies of her husband and herself—and now into their child.

Father, I thank You for the miracle of new life. Thank You for the children in my life—my own, my nieces and nephews, my neighbors. Children were precious to You, Lord, when You were here on earth. Help me to realize their potential and to be patient with them, especially in these formative years. Help me especially, Father, to show love to this child: _____

CHILDREN ARE THE RAW MATERIALS OF THE FUTURE!

NOAH'S WIFE: THE RESULTS OF SIN—
A DRENCHING

In *The Legacy of Eve*, Nancy Tischler describes the effect of the Fall on the relationship between man and woman: "Man was meant to have dominion over nature, but after the Fall, man found nature his enemy as often as his friend, and dominion no easy thing to establish. (Ask any gardener.) Woman was to be fruitful and multiply; she was created to be flesh of man's flesh. That 'good' creation, distorted in her fall, confuses the beauty of her body with the shame of her nakedness. Until the Fall, her sexuality was an innocent party to their mutual delight, her nudity a source of aesthetic pleasure. After the Fall, her body became a possession to be coveted, and she learned to use man's desire as a weapon against him. The harmony was thereby converted into a veiled and recurrent war between the sexes.

"The story of the Fall expands this image of woman to show us:

In her being is a potential for evil as well as for good.
She sins for psychological, physical, and philosophic
    reasons.
She involves others in her evil.
She tries to shift the blame.
She turns God's blessing into woman's curse."[1]

I felt sad as I read these thoughts. I felt sorry for Eve and for all of us as women as I contemplated those golden days in Eden that were forever lost: the thrill of having all the animals as friends; the close harmony with nature that required no protection, clothing, or labor; the completely open fellowship with God and one's mate in the cool of the morning.

O. T. PASSAGE THIS WEEK: Genesis 4, 6-9

SPECIAL PRAYER NEEDS THIS WEEK:

ANSWERS TO PRAYER THIS WEEK:

I'VE BROUGHT FORTH A MAN

How often have I longed to gather your children together, as a hen gathers her chicks under her wings (Matt. 23:37, NIV). Read Genesis 4.

So many years, it's been since Cain was born
And Abel shortly afterward. If I had known
The pain that would result from those two boys,
I couldn't have borne it!
As God had said, I suffered pain in childbirth,
But how much greater anguish Abel's death
Brought to my life—my own dear son
Killed by his brother Cain.
I searched my heart for reasons why.
Had I failed as a mother? Adam, too, as a father?
Had our God punished them for our misdeeds?

But God is a God of justice. . .and of love.
He knows Cain's heart the same way He knows ours.
He is in control!
He has a plan—He must!

And God sent Seth to fill the void that Abel left.
—Eve

Just as Eve's pregnancy and the excitement of a child were "firsts" for her and for God's world, so the trials of parenthood were brand new experiences as well. Eve must have grieved over the inevitable sibling rivalry as her little boys competed with each other with the usual "brotherly shoves." She must have been brokenhearted as the disagreements continued and grew more threatening in Cain and Abel's early adult years. The result must have almost killed her as well.

Father, there are times when the problems in our family tear me apart. Help me to depend on You, moment by moment, for wisdom to face each new situation.

"GOD IS OUR REFUGE AND STRENGTH, A VERY PRESENT HELP IN TROUBLE" (Ps. 46:1, KJV).

GOD'S HEART WAS FILLED WITH PAIN

As it was in the days of Noah, so it will be at the coming of the Son of Man (Matt. 24:37, NIV). Read Genesis 6:1-13.

When God's word came to Noah, we both trembled.
I know my husband is a righteous man. . .
And yet—to talk with God! To hear His words!
I know that Eve and Adam
Talked to Him each morn and night—
But here's my husband *talking to the Lord!*

And what a message Noah brings
Of doom to humankind—
They have grieved God's heart, caused Him great pain.
But Noah has found favor in His sight.
—Noah's wife

Noah's wife is not given a name in Scripture, but we can use our imagination just enough to imagine how she must have felt when God came to Noah with the message of destruction. There is no biblical record that God talked to any man between the time Adam and Eve were exiled from the Garden of Eden and the first time He spoke to Noah.

Noah was a very special man, the only man on earth at that time who tried to live his life according to God's will. The Living Bible says that Noah was "a pleasure to the Lord" (Gen. 6:8). What a beautiful description of one man's life in the midst of corruption!

Father, I thank You for the examples You have given me in Your Word. I pray, Lord, that these same words could be said of me, that my life would be a pleasure to You. Help me to search out the principles of right living that You have laid out in Your Word, the foot-lamps that give me just light enough for one step at a time.

DOES MY LIFE GIVE PLEASURE TO THE LORD?

BUILD A BOAT
450 FEET LONG AND 45 FEET HIGH!

For in the days before the flood, people were eating and drinking, marrying and giving in marriage, up to the day Noah entered the ark (Matt. 24:38, NIV). Read Genesis 6:14-22.

The building orders God has given—
I've never heard such plans!
What will our neighbors say?
They will think we have gone insane!
Sometimes I wonder too. . .
Although I trust my Noah.
He's been so good to me and to our boys.
There is no doubt that he believes all this—
And yet it seems so strange, so different from
The normal life we have lived so long.
Oh, Noah's God, forgive my doubts!
Help me to trust as Noah does.

—Noah's wife

The people of Noah's day just did not care. They did not care that breaking God's rules was causing God's heart to be filled with pain. They didn't care that their sinful ways were an offense in the eyes of a holy God.

Oswald Chambers warns: "Beware of the pleasant view of the Fatherhood of God—God is so kind and loving that of course He will forgive us. . . . The only ground on which God can forgive us is the tremendous tragedy of the Cross of Christ. . . . Forgiveness, which is so easy for us to accept, cost the agony of Calvary. . . . When once you realize all that it cost God to forgive you, you will be held as in a vice [vise], constrained by the love of God."[2]

Forgive me, Father, when I take Your forgiveness for granted. Help me to see sin through Your eyes for the loathsome thing it really is.

"FORGIVENESS, WHICH IS SO EASY FOR US TO ACCEPT, COST THE AGONY OF CALVARY."

GOD SHUT THE DOOR

And they knew nothing about what would happen until the flood came and took them all away. That is how it will be at the coming of the Son of Man (Matt. 24:39, NIV). Read Genesis 7.

> *So here it starts—our strange new life.*
> *We're saved from death, but saved for what?*
> *What will we find when that day comes*
> *When we can leave this ark at last—*
> *This floating zoo, with all its sounds and smells?*
> *Oh, keep my stomach right-side-up, dear God,*
> *So I can help my husband feed our growing family!*
> *This task that You have given to us*
> *Is overwhelming. . .yet I feel a strange new faith.*
> *Please help me through these long dark days.*
> *—Noah's wife*

Noah's neighbors probably laughed as his family walked into the ark and the door was shut—but they stopped laughing when the rain began to flood the floors of their homes. Disaster sobered them very quickly.

In many ways our world situation today is very similar to that of Noah's time. Bill Bright, of Campus Crusade for Christ, points out that the "forces of evil are gathering momentum everywhere in the world. This is an hour of destiny—a time of unprecedented opportunity for Christians. . . . You can help as you change the world by introducing men to Jesus Christ, the only One who can change men from within."[3]

Father, I want to help change this world, but I feel so small and insignificant. I need the power of Your Holy Spirit in my life. I have confessed every known sin, and I ask You to fill me with Your Spirit. I'm claiming Your promise in 1 John 5:14-15.

"THIS IS AN HOUR OF DESTINY—A TIME OF UNPRECEDENTED OPPORTUNITY FOR CHRISTIANS."

TIME TO LEAVE!

Therefore keep watch, because you do not know on what day your Lord will come (Matt. 24:42, NIV). *Read Genesis 8.*

> *The time has come! A breath of air—*
> *Of fresh clean air—is all I've had in months!*
> *And now I'm free to fill my lungs*
> *And breathe again. . .again!*
> *I've grown to love the animals, though,*
> *And they love us in such a special way.*
> *Our family, too, has grown so close.*
> *The knowledge that we're all that's left.*
> *He's sobered us, made us forget our petty fights.*
> *The things that once annoyed me I don't mind—*
> *They were swept away by forty days of rain.*
> *—Noah's wife*

Did you ever notice what petty little things families fight about? Listen to children arguing and you wonder how they can possibly get so upset about such a little thing. Then listen to Mom and Dad having a "discussion" sometime and you wonder the same thing! Permanent family feuds have resulted from ridiculously small disagreements.

The realization that we are living in the last days should shake us out of our petty problems. To quote Bill Bright again: "A spiritual revolution will not and cannot become a reality until millions of Christians reexamine their priorities, commit themselves to be trained in discipleship and evangelism and become part of a mighty movement of God's Spirit. We should say with C. T. Studd. . .'If Jesus Christ be God and died for me, then no sacrifice can be too great for me to make for Him.'"[4]

Father, forgive me for being so involved in my own little world. Shake me out of my "backyard" lethargy. Help me to be concerned about the issues that really count. Break my heart with the things that break Your heart. Make me a channel of Your love today, especially: _____ .

"IF JESUS CHRIST BE GOD AND DIED FOR ME, THEN NO SACRIFICE CAN BE TOO GREAT FOR ME TO MAKE FOR HIM."

THE FIRST RAINBOW

So you also must be ready, because the Son of Man will come at an hour when you do not expect him (Matt. 24:44, NIV). Read Genesis 9:1-17.

A rainbow! Such a thing of beauty!
A special promise from our God to us
That never will a flood occur again
To wipe all humankind from Planet Earth.

And as it crosses the serene blue sky,
In brilliant colors from Jehovah's mighty brush,
I see, through tears, He cares so much for us.
He has brought us through earth's punishment for sin,
And then, in reassurance and in love,
He has arched His promise through the tears of life.
— Noah's wife

The rainbow was God's promise that the earth would never again be destroyed by a flood, and God has kept that promise. But there will come another day of destruction for those who have not accepted Jesus Christ as Savior and Lord of their lives. That day will come "like a thief in the night, while people are saying, 'Peace and safety'" (1 Thess. 5:2-3, NIV). Are you ready for that day?

Perhaps you are ready, but what about the people you see every day who are *not* ready? Your neighbor, your milkman, your Avon lady, your boss at work, your son's baseball coach—make your own list: _____ .

Father, give me a burden for these people. Help me to see those popular, witty, attractive people (around whom I'm so tongue-tied) as lost souls in need of You. Please give me compassion for the average-Joe people whom I just take for granted or ignore. Make me a channel of Your love today.
"AM I WISE ENOUGH IN GOD'S SIGHT, AND FOOLISH ENOUGH ACCORDING TO THE WORLD, TO BANK ON WHAT JESUS CHRIST HAS SAID?"[5]

SARAH: FOLLOW ME

Jehovah still desired to raise up a people who would carry out His will on the earth, and in Noah, God had made a new start. It becomes evident that on this "new" earth God's chosen people must recognize His orders and His direct leadership, and in Genesis 12 Abram begins to emerge from the line of Shem (Noah's son) as Jehovah's chosen representative. On Abram would be placed the full responsibility of receiving and carrying on God's revelation.

Why Abram? He heard God's call while in his hometown of Ur, a thriving commercial city with unusually high cultural standards. The inhabitants of Ur—and perhaps Abram as well—worshiped the moon-god Sin. Abram was commanded "(a) to renounce the certainties of the past, (b) to face the uncertainties of the future, (c) to look for and follow the directions of Jehovah's will."[1] Abram obeyed!

This week you'll be meeting Sarai (her name was later changed to Sarah), a woman famous for her beauty who gave up her home, family, and everything that spelled security in order to obey the command God had given to her husband. Have you ever stopped to think about the loneliness, frustrations, and doubts—not to mention the agony of her barrenness—that Sarai experienced as she trekked across the desert with her businessman-turned-nomad husband?

The Bible doesn't tell us how Sarai felt toward her niece by marriage, Lot's wife. Were they friends or were they at odds? Did Sarai pass on her doubts to the younger woman or did she keep them to herself? As you read their story, draw your own conclusions. And ask yourself how *you* are influencing other women around you.

O. T. PASSAGE THIS WEEK: Genesis 11:26—14:16

SPECIAL PRAYER NEEDS THIS WEEK:

ANSWERS TO PRAYER THIS WEEK:

LEAVE YOUR COUNTRY AND YOUR FAMILY

Abraham believed God, and it was credited to him as righteousness (Rom. 4:3, NIV). Read Genesis 11:26-32; 12:1-5. See also Genesis 20:12.

"Believe, my love—you must believe!" he says.
Would he believe if this strange God
Had spoken to me instead?
It's all so hard to understand.
How can I know that it was God who spoke,
And not some strange nightmare?

To me it's been a nightmare.
At sixty-five
I had to give away or sell
Possessions dearest to my heart.
Our home is gone—sold too—
Our dear ancestral home that Terah loved.

Ah, Terah—father to us both, Abram and I,
Though born to different mothers—
Terah believed too,
And yet we left his body in a far-off grave
And traveled on to find that promised land.
                                                    —Sarai

Abram and Sarai (their original names) were born in the highly civilized city of Ur. Sarai probably lived in a two-storied, balconied house, with servants to dress her, prepare her food, and clean her thick, silky oriental rugs.[2] She left a life of luxury for a life of packing and unpacking, of gypsy-like traveling across an almost trackless, semidesert land.

Are You telling me through the story of Sarai, Father, that my possessions are too important to me? Please show me if I'm holding on to them too tightly.

"IT IS THE THINGS THAT ARE RIGHT AND NOBLE AND GOOD FROM THE NATURAL STANDPOINT THAT KEEP US BACK FROM GOD'S BEST."[3]

TRUST ME!

My God shall supply all your need according to his riches in glory by Christ Jesus (Phil. 4:19, KJV). Read Genesis 12:6-16.

Then God appeared again—so Abram said—
And promised: "I will give this place
To your descendants." (What descendants?)
"Your nation will be great!"
Yet still we had no rest,
For there was famine in the land—
The land of promise?

Abram said, "Yet farther south in Egypt
We'll find food."
But Abram feared,
For I was beautiful.
They would kill him to get me.
"It's not a lie," he urged,
"That you're my sister. Tell them that
And save our lives."

—Sarai

Nomads had no way of storing food against a time of famine, and famines were frequent. Abram saw a move to Egypt as the only alternative to starvation; the Nile River would furnish water for crops and cattle until the famine had ended and the group could return to Canaan.

But fear clutched Abram's heart as he and his beautiful wife neared the palace. Certainly the Pharaoh would want Sarai as a member of his harem—and then Abram's life would be in danger. So Abram, instead of reaching out to God, used the homemade "life preserver" of a half-truth to keep his family safe.

Father, I realize my lack of trust in You. Forgive me for rushing ahead of You so often. Thank You, Father, that You still love me in spite of my childish impatience. Teach me to wait, knowing that You are in control.

THE END DOES *NOT* JUSTIFY THE MEANS!

THE MASTER TEACHER

No man can serve two masters: for either he will hate the one, and love the other; or else he will hold to the one, and despise the other (Matt. 6:24, KJV). Read Genesis 12:17-20; 1 Peter 3:1-6.

Pharaoh soon discovered Abram's trick
And sent us from his land in haste.
With us we brought back a slave
Whose name is Hagar.
Somehow I seem to trust her
Even though she's dark.
She's very helpful, Hagar. . . .
It's good to have a trusted servant girl.

—*Sarai*

The Bible does not tell us that Hagar was acquired during Abram's sojourn in Egypt, but she *was* Egyptian, and so it is quite possible to surmise that Hagar came back to Canaan with the nomadic group. (See what can happen when we are out of the Lord's will, as Abram was in Egypt?)

It's important to remember, however, that God teaches us through our failures. By trying to become someone else's conscience (my husband's, for example), I may be keeping that person from learning a valuable lesson. God is more interested in my developing Christlike character and responses than He is in my earthly "success"!

Father, help me to be quiet so that *You* can teach the lessons that need to be taught—to myself and to others. Please take away the "I-told-you-so!" spirit within me. Help me to give myself and others room to fail. Thank You for loving me just as I am.

"A MAN IS ALWAYS FIGHTING HIS CONSCIENCE. IF YOU BECOME HIS CONSCIENCE HE WILL FIGHT YOU!"[4]

I'D BE HAPPY IF. . .

But godliness with contentment is great gain. For we brought nothing into this world, and it is certain we can carry nothing out. And having food and raiment let us be therewith content (1 Tim. 6:6-8, KJV). Read Genesis 13:1-7.

I've heard those legendary tales
Of Uncle Abram's faith so long—
I'm rather tired of hearing them!
Just tell me how it's profited him?
He still lives in a goat's-hair tent—
No proper home to call his own.
And Sarai's waiting for that child!
She has waited for him all her life!
If Lot and I are given a chance,
We will certainly take another path!

—Mrs. Lot

I'd be happy if we had a home like that. . .if I could get a new car. . .if I just had some really nice clothes to wear. . .if we could move away from this small-town gossip. I'd be happy *if*—but would I?

True happiness does not consist in accumulating possessions, going places, or being someone important. Real joy is a state of mind and heart that goes with us no matter what we are doing or where we go. The Apostle Paul wrote from a dark prison cell: "I have learned the secret of being content in any and every situation" (Phil. 4:12, NIV).

Father, I need to understand that secret. Teach me to rejoice when things are going just the opposite of how I think they should. I'll start out by thanking You for this problem in my life today: _____ .

HAPPINESS IS KNOWING JESUS CHRIST!

TEMPTATION AND A TRAP

People who want to get rich fall into temptation and a trap and into many foolish and harmful desires that plunge men into ruin and destruction. For the love of money is a root of all kinds of evil (1 Tim. 6:9-10, NIV). Read Genesis 13:8-13.

> *Old Abram was so foolish—*
> *Perhaps a little senile, at his age—*
> *To give us such a choice, indeed!*
> *There was no doubt in my Lot's mind*
> *Which land to take!*
> *Now all the plain of Jordan is ours,*
> *And I can hardly wait*
> *To see the sights of Sodom,*
> *To get some clothes, to make new friends,*
> *Perhaps to buy a home!*
> *—Mrs. Lot*

Although the Bible doesn't give us any background information on Lot's wife, we can be fairly sure that a great part of her life was spent wishing for and accumulating the earthly treasures that she found it so difficult to leave behind later in her life. She must have enjoyed the sensual, materialistic life she and Lot found in Sodom, or she would have prevailed upon her husband to raise their two daughters elsewhere.

Genesis 19 relates the disastrous results of Sodom's influence on Lot's daughters: lack of parental respect, familiarity with drunkenness, incest. What a powerful effect the environment we provide for our children has on their lives! What forces are you bringing to bear on the children in your life? What do they see as most important to you?

Thank You, Jesus, that You gave up the riches and glory of heaven to come to earth and die for me. Help me to think more about the enormity of Your sacrifice, and help me to get my priorities in order.

"BETTER IS LITTLE WITH THE FEAR OF THE LORD THAN GREAT TREASURE AND TROUBLE THEREWITH" (Prov. 15:16, KJV).

FAMILIARITY BREEDS CONTEMPT

Respect those who work hard among you, who are over you in the Lord and who admonish you. Hold them in the highest regard in love (1 Thess. 5:12-13, NIV). Read Genesis 14:8-16.

Well, Uncle Abram has saved our lives.
I guess we should be grateful to him.
We are—and yet why does it seem
He always manages to be so right?
We want to live our own lives,
Go our own way, do our own thing.
Why is he always there, smiling patiently,
And waiting on his God?
This waiting business drives me crazy.
I want the best in life—right now!

—Mrs. Lot

Here was the perfect opportunity for Lot and family to break away from the powerful hold Sodom exercised over their lives. They had been taken captive in a war between the kings of the area, and good ol' Uncle Abram had come to bail them out. Had Lot stayed out of Sodom, he probably would not have been involved in the war.

Imagine Lot's chagrin when Uncle Abram came to his rescue! But at this point Lot would not admit that he had been wrong in his choice of a home for his growing family; so back to the doomed Sodom he went, probably with very little thanks for Abram's good deed.

Father, forgive me for ignoring some of the good advice I've been given in the past. Forgive me, too, for the many times I've lacked respect in the way I've reacted to people who wanted the best for me. Teach me the meaning of gratefulness. . .and help me to show it.

LIVE IN AN ATTITUDE OF GRATITUDE.

SARAH: FAITH OR FOLLY?

Now Sarai, Abram's wife, had borne him no children. But she had an Egyptian maidservant named Hagar; so she said to Abram, 'The Lord has kept me from having children. Go, sleep with my maidservant; perhaps I can build a family through her.'

Abram agreed to what Sarai said. So after Abram had been living in Canaan ten years, Sarai his wife took her Egyptian maidservant Hagar and gave her to her husband to be his wife (Gen. 16:1-3, NIV).

There was no doubt about it; Jehovah had unmistakably promised an heir to Abram and Sarai. But as the years rolled by, the discrepancy between the promise and the expected product of that promise became more and more frustrating. To be barren was a calamity and a disgrace for any Hebrew wife, and even more so for the wife of Abram!

Both husband and wife must have been aware that to take a concubine was a violation of the "one-flesh" principle set forth in Genesis 2:24, yet Sarai was willing to ignore the divine standard in hopes of building a family. Instead, a tragedy began that has continued for centuries.

Sarai's beauty, as we have discussed, was so striking that it created problems for her! Twice in their life together Abram asked her to pose as his sister (She *was* his half-sister; see Genesis 20:12.) so that his life would not be put in danger by men who wanted her. Yet Sarai probably would have traded her beauty in a minute for the fertility of the slave girl Hagar.

As you read chapter 16 of Genesis and think about the relationship between Sarai and her servant girl, take time to examine and pray about the relationships in your life. Are they what God wants them to be?

O. T. PASSAGE THIS WEEK: Genesis 16

SPECIAL PRAYER NEEDS THIS WEEK:

ANSWERS TO PRAYER THIS WEEK:

FAITH OR FAILURE?

Now faith is being sure of what we hope for and certain of what we do not see (Heb. 11:1, NIV). Read Genesis 16:1-3; James 1:1-8.

We have been here ten long years.
There's nothing in this goat's-hair tent
To make it feel like home.
Oh, how I long for Ur!
Who is this terrible God
Who has brought us forth into this land
And left us stranded here without our promised son?

"Wait," Abram says, "believe and wait!"
I have waited ten long years
And many more before God's promise.
It seems my husband's God could use some help.
The marriage contract I signed long ago
Contained a promise I'd provide my husband with a
*   son.*
It is custom for a barren wife
To give life through a slave.
This aged body will never live again.
*   —Sarai*

Poor Sarai! It must have seemed to her at this point in her life that she had given up so much for so little. We're told the name "Sarai" means "contentious"—and since at that time children were often named in their teenage years, this was probably true of her personality.[1] Sarai was contentious, impatient, chafing at the bit. Does that sound familiar?

Father, I often rush ahead of You too—and I have Your Word to teach me trust in You, an advantage Sarai didn't have. Thank You for all the times that You've proved You're more than worthy of my trust. Teach me to rely on You completely.

TEACH ME, LORD, TO WAIT.

GLORIOUS FREEDOM!

It is for freedom that Christ has set us free. Stand firm, then, and do not let yourselves be burdened again by a yoke of slavery (Gal. 5:1, NIV). Read Galatians 5:13-26.

Was it my choice to leave my home in Egypt
And come to live with them?
No, I was given to them by the king
As an exchange for Sarai's beauty.

Sarai! For myself, I cannot see
What is so beautiful about her.
It seems to me she's aging fast.
I've heard it said she has never borne a child.
She treats me well. I wonder why
I catch her watching me so closely,
Almost as if measuring me
To see if I could handle some awesome task.

—*Hagar*

Yes, Hagar, Sarai does have a task in mind for you! You are her slave, and you must do whatever your mistress commands—even to the point of bearing a son for her.

Unbelievable, we say, that one person should have so much power over another! Yet many people in today's world are enslaved just as firmly: enslaved by greed for material possessions, by sexual desires, by addiction of many kinds. They don't realize that Jesus Christ came to Planet Earth to bring us freedom!

Thank You, Father, for setting me free through Your Son's atonement for my sins. Thank You that I don't need to depend on obeying laws and on my good works to make me right with You. Thank You that Your justification makes me just-as-if-I'd-never-sinned. Help me to share the joy of Your freedom with others.

THE TRUTH WILL SET YOU FREE!

I WAS A STRANGER

Keep on loving each other as brothers. Do not forget to entertain strangers (Heb. 13:1-2, NIV). Read Genesis 15.

Sarai's the only one who treats me well.
The other women shun me because I don't belong to
Their "chosen" nation.
They talk of some great God
Who promised them possession of this land.
Their rituals strike deep fear into my heart.

And who will lead them after Abram's gone?
He's also getting up in years.
It seems to me this little group in goat's-hair tents
Are all a bunch of fools.
Oh, how I long for Egypt—my homeland!
　　　　　　　　　　　　　—Hagar

The Egyptian maid Hagar must have felt very lonely as the nomadic group of which she had become a part traveled farther and farther away from her home. If God's message was difficult for Sarai to believe, imagine how ridiculous it must have seemed to Hagar as she looked at her aging mistress! And we can imagine how the other women must have shunned this dark-skinned Egyptian who worshiped the deities of the sun and moon.

Are you "turned off" on those who do not believe as you do? How do you feel toward the refugee family who has just moved into your neighborhood (whose children are unaccustomed to the idea of frequent showers and whose crowded apartment reeks of strange odors)? Are you prepared to invite them into your home as well as to your church?

Father, I need Your compassion for certain people in my life—people who confuse me, irritate me, make me feel uncomfortable. I recognize that You've brought us together for a purpose. Make me a channel of Your love, especially to:

_____ .

YOU CAN GIVE WITHOUT LOVING BUT YOU CANNOT LOVE WITHOUT GIVING.

THE LITTLE FOXES SPOIL THE GRAPES

Love is strong as death and jealousy is as cruel as Sheol (Song of Sol. 8:6, LB). Read Genesis 16:4; 1 Timothy 6:1, 2.

I have conceived! My body holds new life,
And that new life is heir to Abram's wealth!
I must make sure my son
Receives his rightful share.
My barren mistress
Already shows her jealousy.
I must beware.
She brought this on herself—
Why should I care about her?

—Hagar

Sarai's plan of action backfired! Having talked her husband into agreement with her idea, now, as she watched the slave-girl's belly swell with the coveted new life, Sarai found herself the victim of unexpected and uncontrollable jealousy. Beautiful Sarai had been outdone—and by a lowly slave girl! The slave girl, however, no longer thought of herself as lowly; she now despised her mistress.

Jealousy creeps in so subtly that it is often overlooked. . . until suddenly it strikes viciously, as cruelly as Sheol (the Hebrew word for death). But between the time of entry and the time it is recognized, jealousy is never at a standstill. It grows rapidly, using as fuel for its raging fire any offense, real or imagined.

Father, help me to recognize jealousy for what it is—sin. Tear it up by the roots before it develops into bitterness and hatred. Create in me a clean heart, oh God. . . .

JEALOUSY IS A FORERUNNER OF HATRED.

JEALOUSY TURNS TO BITTERNESS

So if you are standing before the altar. . .and suddenly remember that a friend has something against you, leave your sacrifice. . .and be reconciled to him, and then come and offer your sacrifice to God (Matt. 5:23-24, LB). Read Genesis 16:5-6; 1 Thessalonians 5:14-22.

> *She despises me, that arrogant slave,*
> *Now that she has felt the life God promised me!*
> *Oh, why did Abram listen when I told him*
> *That she could take my place?*
> *Her dark Egyptian eyes look with contempt*
> *On my old body!*
> *This "man of faith" has let me down again—*
> *Why didn't he wait upon his God the way he told me to?*
> *And yet I know he tried to please me—I'm to blame.*
> *But I can't bear to have her here*
> *Reminding me she bears his seed.*
>
> *—Sarai*

We are warned in Hebrews 12:15 (LB) to "watch out that no bitterness takes root" in our lives. Like the poison from a ruptured appendix, bitterness totally infiltrates our spiritual systems and causes a breakdown of our feelings of concern for others. Our vision becomes so narrowed that we can see only ourselves and our seemingly insolvable problems. As a result, we strike out nearsightedly at almost anyone who comes across our paths, just as Sarai did at Hagar.

Father, forgive me for resenting what You have allowed in my life. Help me to realize that through trials You are conforming me into Your image. Make me willing to be willing, whatever it takes.

HE WHO CANNOT FORGIVE OTHERS BREAKS THE BRIDGE OVER WHICH HE MUST SOMEDAY CROSS.

THE GOD OF A SLAVE

Love your enemies, do good to those who hate you, bless those who curse you, pray for those who mistreat you. If someone strikes you on one cheek, turn to him the other also (Luke 6:27-29, NIV). Read Genesis 16:7-16.

How could Sarai turn on me like that?
She brought her problem on herself;
She was the one who gave me to old Abram.
Old Abram! Does his God exist?

(Later)

I can't believe it! Abram's God
Has come to me, a mere Egyptian maid!
Ishmael, meaning "whom God hears,"
Will be my son, my strong young son.
Yes, thou God seest me!
The God of Abram sees—and loves—me too!
—Hagar

God is *not* a respecter of persons. Stop and think—who is the person that irritates you the most? Then realize that God loves that person as much as He loves you! Unlike our human friends, God does not take sides in our petty arguments. He looks down as a heavenly Father, being grieved and yet loving us still.

Let's face it—it's impossible for us to love the people around us in the way the Lord does. So we need to admit to Him our lack of love. . .confess that we're repulsed by certain people. . .and ask *Him* to love those people *through* us.

Father, thank You for Your love that keeps on loving me in spite of myself. You've known what I'm really like all along. I recognize that in myself I find it impossible to love _____

Make me a channel of Your love, Father; love that person through me.

SYMPATHY IS YOUR HURT IN MY HEART.

SARAH: LEARNING TO LEAN

By faith Abraham, even though he was past age—and Sarah herself was barren—was enabled to become a father because he considered him faithful who had made the promise. And so from this one man, and he as good as dead, came descendants as numerous as the stars in the sky and as countless as the sand on the seashore (Heb. 11:11-12, NIV).

We don't know what happened between Hagar and Sarai in the years between the time Hagar returned to her mistress in chapter 16 and the eventful birthday party mentioned in chapter 21 when Hagar was "evicted" for a second time. We do know that Sarai's lifelong prayer for a son was finally answered—and we can imagine that in this period of happiness, for a time at least, things went smoothly in the nomad settlement.

As you read these chapters, remember that these people did not have the Holy Spirit to bestow His gifts in their lives. We have far less reason to be impatient, unloving, and self-righteous than these women from a different culture and dispensation. "The fruit of the Spirit is love, joy, peace, patience, kindness, goodness, faithfulness, gentleness and self-control. . . . Those who belong to Christ Jesus have crucified the sinful nature with its passions and desires. Since we live by the Spirit, let us keep in step with the Spirit. Let us not become conceited, provoking and envying each other" (Gal. 5:22-26, NIV).

O. T. PASSAGE THIS WEEK: Genesis 17—21

SPECIAL PRAYER NEEDS THIS WEEK:

ANSWERS TO PRAYER THIS WEEK:

A LONG LAST LOOK

Remember Lot's wife (Luke 17:32, KJV). Read Genesis 19:1-29.

My heart aches for our nephew Lot
Who has lost his foolish, greedy wife.
She couldn't give up her earthly wealth;
She lingered for one long last look.
But as she lagged behind the group,
Her body caught the rain of fire.
A salty pillar stands there now,
A terrible symbol of her greed.

Jehovah, You are truly God!
Forgive my lack of faith in You.

—Sarai

Was God being vindictive and angry when Lot's wife became a pillar of salt? It's important to realize that she was not so much punished *for* her sin as punished *by* her sin. Against God's command, she lingered by the wayside and looked back. . .and the volcanic ashes embalmed her. The fire and brimstone mentioned here may have been an explosion of the chemicals collected at the south end of the Dead Sea, which could literally have covered her.

"One last look!" Are you postponing a decision that God is asking you to make? "No man, having put his hand to the plough, and looking back, is fit for the kingdom" (Luke 9:62, KJV).

Father, forgive my halfheartedness in serving You. Thank You for giving Your all for me. I present my body as a living sacrifice; purify it for Your use.
INDECISION ENDS IN DISASTER!

VISIT OF EL SHADDAI

Sing, O barren woman, you who never bore a child; burst into song, shout for joy, you who were never in labor (Isa. 54:1, NIV). Read Genesis 17:1-22.

> *In spite of all my doubts and fears,*
> *El Shaddai—"the Nourisher"—has come to me!*
> *He has touched my womb! I am with child!*
> *I'm eighty-nine, and yet I know*
> *I'll bear our long-awaited son.*
> *He has changed our names, this God of love:*
> *My husband's name is Abraham,*
> *A fruitful father of the nations.*
> *I, too, have changed. . .*
> *My name is "princess"—not "contentious"—now!*
> > *—Sarah*

The socialite-turned-tent-dweller has become a princess —perhaps not in the eyes of men, but certainly in God's eyes! This fact is accentuated in the third chapter of 1 Peter, where Sarah is called one of the "holy women" who adorned themselves with a gentle and a quiet spirit, "which is of great worth in God's sight" (1 Pet. 3:4-6). The contention, jealousy, and bitterness are in the past, and Sarah has become the woman God intended her to be all along.

What's even more exciting is that God is working right now in *your* life to make YOU into a beautiful woman—not the "you've-come-a-long-way-baby" woman we see all around us—but the woman who possesses God's unfading beauty.

Thank You, Father, for Your plan for my life. Help me to be quiet so I'll be able to hear Your voice. Help me to be gentle so that others will be able to share their burdens with me. **PLEASE BE PATIENT; GOD'S NOT FINISHED WITH ME YET!**

LAUGHTER

You are now her [Sarah's] true daughters if you do right and let nothing terrify you—not giving way to hysterical fears or letting anxieties unnerve you (1 Pet. 3:6, Amplified). Read Genesis 18:1-15; 21:1-7.

I laughed at first when, as the custom is,
Our visitor repaid our hospitality
With promise of a son.
My laugh was silent, deep inside—and full of doubt.
But, being God, He heard. . .
And asked why Sarah laughed.

"Is anything too hard for God?" He asked.
I was afraid. . .but then I knew
He understood, forgave my fears.
He turned my laugh of unbelief to joyous laughter.
And when our son is born,
Isaac—meaning "laughter"—will be his name.
—Sarah

Why pray when you can worry? Oops, I said that wrong—or *did* I? It seems most people find it a lot easier to worry than they do to pray. Anxiety turns into worry, and worry becomes fear, sometimes even hysterical fear.

We need to remember that *nothing*—"our fears for today, our worries about tomorrow, or where we are. . .—nothing will ever be able to separate us from the love of God demonstrated by our Lord Jesus Christ when he died for us" (Rom. 8:38-39, LB). When you begin to worry, try praise as an alternative mind set!

Thank You, Father, for reminding me that fear and anxiety are not a necessary part of my life. Remind me, when I indulge in those emotions, that they are actually an insult to You.

GOD IS STILL IN CONTROL!

SARAH STILL HAS PROBLEMS

I know that nothing good lives in me, that is, in my sinful nature. For I have the desire to do what is good, but I cannot carry it out (Rom. 7:18, NIV). Read Genesis 21:8-10.

> *And then the never-forgotten bitterness*
> *Toward my slave Hagar and her son*
> *Rose up again: "That Ishmael is a bully!*
> *I must protect my son—Abraham's true heir—*
> *From being cheated of his rights."*
> *And so I sent them back*
> *Into the desert, mother and son,*
> *A rerun of an earlier scene.*
> *I should have learned my lesson then.*
>
> *—Sarah*

Even at the age of ninety, Sarah had not learned how to appropriate God's power to control her contradictory personality. It seems as though Sarah should have learned to trust God after the miracle of Isaac—but how quickly we forget! Unfortunately, because of this last Old Testament incident in Sarah's life, we tend to remember Sarah as contentious, even though God had changed her name.

What do people associate with our names? How will they remember us? Do we return to old problems from our past which the Lord has covered with His blood? Or are we maturing spiritually, so that each day we are being conformed more and more into His image?

Father, I thank You that You have delivered me from my old sinful nature. Help me to "die daily" to my selfish desires. Help me especially with this problem: _____ .
TO KNOW IS ONE THING. . .TO DO IS ANOTHER.

BACK IN THE DESERT!

For it is written that Abraham had two sons, one by the slave woman and the other by the free woman. His son by the slave woman was born in the ordinary way; but his son by the free woman was born as the result of a promise (Gal. 4:22-23, NIV). Read Genesis 21:11-21; Galatians 4:22-31.

So here I am again, back in the desert!
This time I'm not alone;
My promised son is here with me.
At first I doubted that You cared
When Ishmael almost died of thirst.
But when You heard his feeble cries,
You came and rescued us from death.
Not only did You save our helpless lives,
You gave me a new will to live.
You promised me a nation great
Would spring from my son Ishmael.

—Hagar

The Apostle Paul uses the story of Sarah and Hagar to illustrate God's old and new covenants with His children. Hagar, the slave wife, is symbolic of the law or present-day Jerusalem and Judaism, which is still in bondage to Jewish law. (The Arabic name for Mt. Sinai, where the Ten Commandments were given, is Mt. Hagar). But Sarah, the free-born wife, is representative of the "new Jerusalem," the mother-city of Christians. We are not in bondage to Jewish law; we, as Isaac, are the children of promise. . .and we are saved by grace, God's undeserved favor.[1]

"But because of his great love for us, God, who is rich in mercy, made us alive with Christ even when we were dead in transgressions" (Eph. 2:4-5, NIV).

Thank You, Father, for Your love, Your mercy, Your grace. I do not deserve any of it, but because you love me, You have made it all available, free of charge. Thank You, Father.
RELIGION: WHAT MAN *IS TRYING* TO DO FOR GOD;
SALVATION: WHAT GOD *HAS DONE* FOR MAN!

VERY HUMAN PEOPLE

As the heavens are higher than the earth, so are my ways higher than your ways and my thoughts than your thoughts (Isa. 55:9, NIV). Read Romans 4:1-25.

God speaks to Sarah and to Abraham—and to us:

Yes, Abraham, here you are,
Father of many nations.
You were a man of faith in many ways—
But human, then, as well.
I loved you as a friend;
I talked to you and told you all my plans;
I promised Isaac. . .but I knew of Ishmael too,
Because I knew you couldn't wait
To see my promises fulfilled.
What seemed to you a century
Was but a fleeting second in my view of time.
I blessed your promised Isaac
And, like you, I cared for Ishmael too
And made of him a nation.

But, Sarah, do you see
The problems that impatience caused?
The fight that started long ago
Between your husband's sons
Still flourishes today.
Ah, could My children learn to trust Me fully—
How different life on Planet Earth could be.

Father, thank You for this lesson in faith. Help me to take You at Your Word.
GOD SAID IT, I BELIEVE IT, AND THAT SETTLES IT!

REBEKAH: A BEAUTIFUL CONNIVER

Rebekah conceived ₍two sons under exactly the same circumstances₎ by our forefather Isaac. And the children were yet unborn and had so far done nothing either good or evil. Even so, in order further to carry out God's purpose of selection ₍election, choice₎, which depends not on works or what men can do, but on Him Who calls ₍them₎, It was said to her that the elder ₍son₎ should serve the younger ₍son₎. . . (Rom. 9:10-12, Amplified).

The once-beautiful and contentious Sarah was dead, and the cave of Machpelah had been bought (at great expense) for Abraham's "princess." His great sorrow was shared by Isaac, but eventually the grieving father realized that he had too long neglected the matter of finding a wife for his son—but certainly not a heathen girl! Abraham entrusted his faithful senior servant, Eliezer, with the responsibility of making the long journey back to Mesopotamia to find a suitable bride from their own people.

Eliezer found the beautiful Rebekah, and all went well for a time. Although Rebekah was beautiful of countenance, however, we have no record that she ever learned the secret of beauty of spirit.

Rebekah did not understand that "God's gift is not a question of human will and human effort." Beautiful Rebekah felt compelled to maneuver and manipulate people in order to accomplish what she thought was supposed to happen. She seemed to think that God needed her help to fulfill His prophecy concerning her twin sons. Rebekah and Isaac's marriage, which appeared to be so ideal at first, seems to have degenerated into partiality and strife.

Rebekah's scheming had a great influence on the personality of her son Jacob. What "contagious" character traits are you passing on to other members of your family?

O. T. PASSAGE THIS WEEK: Genesis 24—28

SPECIAL PRAYER NEEDS THIS WEEK:

ANSWERS TO PRAYER THIS WEEK:

FIRST LOVE FORSAKEN

And Isaac brought her into his mother Sarah's tent, and took Rebekah, and she became his wife; and he loved her: and Isaac was comforted after his mother's death (Gen. 24:27, KJV). Read Genesis 24.

> *What has happened to us, Isaac?*
> *Where is that strong man I saw*
> *Striding toward me through the field,*
> *Hurrying to meet his bride?*
> *I loved you at first sight,*
> *Loved every line and limb of you.*
> *I knew the choice I'd made was right.*
>
> *I knew, too, you were twice my age—*
> *A contrast to the boys I'd known—*
> *I needed, welcomed your strong leadership.*
> *A rash, impetuous girl I was*
> *So far away from home.*
>
> *—Rebekah*

Remember those days when you wondered how you would get any sleep at night lying beside the one you loved? Your heart beat rapidly just thinking about it! Now you may wonder how you can sleep through the snoring! Things changed after marriage, didn't they—especially after the first baby, when you fell asleep as soon as your head touched the pillow!

Rebekah was young, beautiful, full of energy. There seemingly was no situation she could not handle. Isaac, still single at forty, was more than ready to welcome his bride... especially now that his beloved mother Sarah was dead. Their marriage seemed "made in heaven"!

Lord, I remember those first few days after You found me. Please restore that joy—"the joy of your salvation" (Ps. 51:12, NIV)—to my life. "Make me to hear joy and gladness, that the bones which thou hast broken may rejoice" (Ps. 51:8, KJV).

MARRIAGES THAT ARE MADE IN HEAVEN HAVE TO BE LIVED ON EARTH!

ANOTHER LESSON IN WAITING

Wait on the Lord: be of good courage, and he shall strengthen thine heart: wait, I say, on the Lord (Ps. 27:14, KJV). Read Genesis 25:19-26.

As the years went by I grew rebellious.
I heard your mother's—Sarah's—story
Time and time again.
Would I too wait 'til ninety for a child?
Your father's God—yes, your God, Isaac—
Seems so cruel
To lead us out into this land
Then seemingly forget the ones He's called.
I could not wait so long!
Please don't expect your wife
To be another Sarah.

—Rebekah

Have you ever felt overshadowed by an older sister or a mother-in-law—someone held up to you as an example of how you should live? You say to yourself, "But I can't be like her! I don't enjoy housecleaning (or cooking) the way she does. I'm me!"

Rebekah never had the opportunity to hear Sarah's story from her mother-in-law herself. She may not have known as much about Sarah's doubts and fears as we do. It may have seemed to young, impatient Rebekah that Sarah's story was an impossible act to follow. A kind, loving God allowed Rebekah to wait twenty years before her twins were born. Why? Perhaps to give her time to learn patience and trust. Did she learn her lesson? Sadly enough, no.

Lord, help me to keep my eyes on You instead of on people. Help me not to become disillusioned by human failures or discouraged by seemingly superhuman feats others have done. Thank You for loving me just as I am. **"MY SOUL, WAIT THOU ONLY UPON GOD; FOR MY EXPECTATION IS FROM HIM" (Ps. 62:5, KJV).**

TWIN TROUBLE

Love is patient, love is kind. . .it is not easily angered (1 Cor. 13:4-5, NIV). Read Genesis 25:27-34.

As rebellion flared within my heart
Toward this strange Jehovah,
The twins began to stir within me.
Your prayer for a child was answered, Isaac,
In double portion.

And God—your God—said elder would serve younger.
I knew it from the start.
My little Jacob was so loving, so endearing,
But hairy Esau wanted only to be fed.
There was no love, no family pride, in him. .
—Rebekah

Recently, I heard a Christian psychologist say that he is constantly amazed by the great number of Christian mothers who are frustrated and antagonized by a certain child in their family. Perhaps parent and child are too much alike, or perhaps the child reminds the mother of a childhood enemy or family member, or perhaps the parents take sides.

Rebekah favored Jacob right from the start. Perhaps she used God's prophecy to justify her adverse reactions to Esau, for it seems that she had no qualms whatsoever about planting the plot in Jacob's mind. Her attitudes gave impetus to Jacob's involvement in a pattern of deceit that would haunt him throughout his life.

Father, I confess my wrong attitudes in dealing with

_____ .

Help me to recognize the problem and to meet it head-on, or to seek help from a pastor or counselor. Thank You for caring.
A CHILD LEARNS BY EXAMPLE.

A DIVIDED HOUSE

If a house is divided against itself, that house cannot stand (Mark 3:25, NIV). Read Genesis 27:1-29.

But you loved Esau, Isaac—favored him, in fact—
Said Jacob's tricky ways disturbed you.
Esau, you said, was honest about his needs,
But Jacob always plotted, planned, and schemed.

Well, Isaac, I'm a schemer too!
And if your judgment dims along with sight,
I'll make a way for Jacob to achieve
The first place that his brilliant mind deserves.
Remember: your God said it would be so.
—Rebekah

Any governing body that cannot come to an agreement within itself is incapable of leadership. This is obvious in a nation, but, it seems not as easily recognizable within a home. Many marriages operate under the slogan: "You go your way and I'll go mine." Is it any wonder that young people are so rebellious?

"No man can serve two masters". . .and neither can children. They must be trained in the way they should go by parents who are united in their faith and impartial in their love for their children. "Children are an heritage of the Lord" (Ps. 127:3, KJV), and a great responsibility.

Thank You for Your beautiful plan of operation for the family. Help us to submit to each other within our home out of reverence for You (Eph. 5:21).

ARE YOU PREPARED TO SUBMIT TO GOD'S PLAN FOR YOUR FAMILY?

RECOMPENSE

The Lord. . .will punish Jacob according to his ways; according to his doings will he recompense him (Hos. 12:2, KJV). Read Genesis 27:30-45; 28:1-5.

What have I done? Esau and Isaac
Are furious at the trick we played,
And Esau hates me and his brother.
I must make sure my younger son survives.
I'll send him back to Haran—maybe there
He will find the good life
And return to me someday.
Oh, Jacob, how I will miss you!

—Rebekah

Rebekah had passed on her scheming nature to her son Jacob, whose name means "supplanter." Like his mother, Jacob did not care *how* he got what he wanted, as long as he got it. He was willing to take the chance of completely alienating himself from his father and his brother in order to grasp the blessing that belonged to Esau.

We can expect to receive what we give, and Jacob would experience later, in his relationship with Laban, the bitter pangs of being cheated by a family member. And Rebekah schemed herself right out of sharing her sons' lives—she lost them both.

Father, forgive me if I have been guilty of manipulating people. Help me to remember to go to You with my disappointments, my griefs, and my unsolvable problems, and to leave them in Your hands, knowing that You will work them out for Your glory if I just learn to wait.

FAITH THROUGH PRAYER AND PAIN CAN ACCOMPLISH ANYTHING.

HE'S IN CONTROL!

Therefore turn thou to thy God: keep mercy and judgment and wait on thy God continually (Hos. 12:6, KJV). Read Isaiah 12:1-6.

Did old Rebekah ever see her son again—
The son she craved, influenced, spoiled?
The Bible gives no record that she did. . .
And Jacob found his clever scheming met its match
In Laban's playing of the game of life.

Rebekah, did you ever realize
That Isaac's God was really your God too?
And being God, He didn't need your help
In carrying out His plan for you
And those you loved.

God is always in control—
Both then and now.

Remember all of Sarah's lessons in waiting? She finally learned that God would fulfill His promises in His own time, but her daughter-in-law Rebekah had a difficult time with that same lesson. So do I! How about you?

"So then [God's gift] is not a question of human will and human effort, but of God's mercy" (Rom. 9:16, *Amplified*). In spite of every incident that was outside of God's will, the Kingdom of God would continue to move forward toward the fuller realization of God's purpose. The divine plan would be realized in the entry of Jesus Christ into the world as God-man, even though His ancestors were scheming, quarreling, undeserving humans!

Father, I thank You for Your gracious gifts in my life. Remind me to count my blessings, to name them one by one. You have done so much for me, and I thank You and praise Your name.

GRACE: GOD GIVING US WHAT WE DO NOT DESERVE. MERCY: GOD WITHHOLDING THAT WHICH WE DO DESERVE.

DEBORAH: THE BEAUTY OF THE BURDEN-BEARER

There are some people whom God has given an extra measure of agape love—people who have the gift of "helps" (1 Cor. 12:28), people who are able to reach out in such a way that they seem to live their lives vicariously through other people. These "helpers" ask for few joys of their own, because they are content to share in the joys of others. Sorrows are shared just as intimately, and "helpers" walk through the valleys of life and death with many a friend.

Such a helper or burden-bearer was the nurse, Deborah, who left Haran with young Rebekah (Gen. 24:59), and lived to see Rachel and Leah's children. In Genesis 35:8 we read that the oak tree under which she was buried was named "The Oak of Weeping." Undoubtedly she was mourned greatly by all who had known and loved her.

"Let this same attitude and purpose *and* [humble] mind be in you which was in Christ Jesus.—Let Him be your example in humility—Who, although being essentially one with God *and* in the form of God [possessing the fullness of the attributes which make God God], did not think this equality with God was a thing to be eagerly grasped or retained; But stripped Himself [of all privileges and rightful dignity] so as to assume the guise of a servant (slave), in that He became like men *and* was born a human being. And after He had appeared in human form He abased and humbled Himself [still further] and carried His obedience to the extreme of death, even the death of [the] cross!" (Phil. 2:5-8, *Amplified*).

O. T. PASSAGE THIS WEEK: Genesis 24; 25; 35:8

SPECIAL PRAYER NEEDS THIS WEEK:

ANSWERS TO PRAYER THIS WEEK:

THE REWARDS OF SERVICE

For with the measure you use, it will be measured to you (Luke 6:38, NIV). Read Luke 6:27-38.

Jehovah, You have been good to me!
My life has been so full; my memories have been rich.
Although I have no family of my own,
There are so many whom I love as mine.
And they love me.
My first child was Rebekah, sweet of face
And lovely, too, of character.
I watched her grow
And dreamed for her great dreams.

—Deborah

Deborah's life, as a single woman, could have been very lonely, even in her place in the midst of the family by which she was employed. Having people around us does not guarantee freedom from loneliness—but loving the people around us does! And Deborah must have loved and been loved, because she gave of herself freely.

Do you measure what you give. . .put limits on your service? Or are you a Deborah, giving as Jesus gave—freely, without limits, exuberantly?

Father, I'm stingy. I realize that today. Help me not to hold back. Help me to give even my rights to You. Thank You for giving Your all for me.

HAVING **PEOPLE AROUND US DOES NOT GUARANTEE FREEDOM FROM LONELINESS—BUT** *LOVING* **THE PEOPLE AROUND US DOES!**

LABORERS TOGETHER WITH GOD

So they sent their sister Rebekah on her way, along with her nurse (Gen. 24:59, NIV).

In the church God has appointed. . .those able to help others (1 Cor. 12:28, NIV). Read Matthew 17:11-19.

The day that old man came
And asked for water and a place to stay
I knew that he was sent from God.
The old man liked Rebekah at first sight—
Her friendliness, her eagerness to please,
Her servant's spirit, and her vibrant strength.
These qualities combined to tell him this was she—
The woman God had picked for Isaac's wife.
Of course she wanted me to go with her;
In this new life she needed someone from the old.
*   —Deborah*

Probably young, impetuous Rebekah hadn't given second thought to the fact that her nurse Deborah had given up her lifelong home to accompany the bride-to-be on her adventurous journey. Rebekah probably just assumed that Deborah would go. After all, Deborah had always been within arm's reach or sound of her call ever since Rebekah could remember!

Are there people in your life whom you take for granted —your mother, your father, your parents-in-law, a special caring friend? Take time today to say a few words. . .make a phone call. . .write a note of appreciation. Express your gratitude to those who have helped you.

Thank You, Father, for the many people who have been instrumental in shaping my life and guiding me toward You. Help me to give as I have been given to. Thank You most of all for Your gift of love.

GOD OFTEN ENTRUSTS US WITH A LITTLE TO SEE WHAT WE WILL DO WITH A LOT.

WATCHING A LOVE STORY

When others are happy, be happy with them. If they are sad, share their sorrow (Rom. 12:15, LB). Read 1 John 2:1-11.

So I went happily, leaving all behind.
I had no other family but Rebekah's.
I would nurse Rebekah's children as my own,
Just as I had nursed my lady as a child.

I watched Rebekah when she first caught sight
Of Isaac meditating in the field,
Her lovely eyes aglow with warmth
And promise of the happy days to come.
She got down from her camel instantly
To meet one she already loved.

—Deborah

What was Deborah thinking on that long camel ride to Hebron where they would meet Isaac? Was she thinking of an earlier time in her own life when she too had anticipated a happy marriage? What did she think when she met the forty-year-old Isaac? Did she too love him—but always from a distance?

Have you learned to rejoice with those who rejoice as well as weep with those who weep? (Sometimes the former is more difficult!) Can you get excited about helping to make other people—perhaps your employer or your husband—successful? Or must the success be your own in order for you to rejoice?

Forgive me, Father, for the twinges of envy I've felt at my friends' good fortune. Help me to rejoice with those who rejoice. . .help me to learn to serve others.

"LOVE LOOKS THROUGH A TELESCOPE; ENVY, THROUGH A MICROSCOPE."

—Henry W.Shaw

THE WAITING TIME

Bear ye one another's burdens, and so fulfill the law of Christ (Gal. 6:2, KJV). Read 2 Corinthians 1:3-7; Psalm 62.

Who could have guessed that twenty years would pass
Before a child would come into the home?
I thought my nursing days were done and wondered if
I would ever get the chance to hold a son.
Rebekah's beauty seemed to fade before my eyes;
Anxiety replaced that loving warmth I'd known,
And Isaac waited, wondering
Why God's great promise was so long in coming.
I suffered for them both.
—Deborah

Deborah had rejoiced in Rebekah's joy, and now she was also able to weep with Rebekah in the realization of her barrenness. Probably Deborah was one of Rebekah's greatest sources of comfort during this time—the woman who had always been a haven in times of storm.

Are others able to turn to you in their times of need? Can they lean on your shoulder when they need reassurance and comfort? Or are they afraid or embarrassed to show you their hurts?

Thank You, Father, for sending Your Son to bear my burdens. Thank You, Jesus, for hurting for me. Teach me to share others' hurts as You have shared mine...and let me hurt with the things that wound Your heart.

THE JOB DESCRIPTION FOR "BURDEN-BEARER" REQUIRES UNSELFISHNESS.

CONFLICT!

Two nations are in your womb, and two peoples from within you will be separated; one people will be stronger than the other, and the older will serve the younger (Gen. 25:23, NIV). Read Ephesians 6:5-9.

> *And then God's answer came! Rebekah had conceived!*
> *But what a war went on within her womb!*
> *Two nations struggled there, just as they would*
> *In future days. Anticipation turned to fear;*
> *That pregnancy weighed heavy on Rebekah's heart,*
> *And I too wondered what would come of it. . .*
> *These warring children yet so young.*
> —*Deborah*

The times of rejoicing had come again. . .replaced again by feelings of fear. Rebekah had begged for one child; now she faced a dual responsibility, and already there was conflict. What did the strange prophecy mean? Again Rebekah probably turned to her lifelong friend for words of reassurance.

Have you ever felt conflicting feelings rising within you? Have you ever felt like a "split personality"? Jesus Christ can integrate the confusing discrepancies of your personality—if you will allow Him to.

Father, some days there are so many emotions tearing me apart: anger, resentment, frustration, worry, guilt. Help me to be still in the realization that You are in control. . .and therefore I don't need to be.

THE LORD MAY CALM YOUR STORM, BUT MORE OFTEN HE'LL CALM *YOU*.

BEAUTIFUL IN GOD'S EYES

Charm is deceptive, and beauty is fleeting; but a woman who fears the Lord is to be praised (Prov. 31:30, NIV). Read Hebrews 12:14-17.

> *Big, awkward, red-haired, teen-aged Esau!*
> *Oh, how he tried to win his mother's love,*
> *Gain her approval—but we all could see,*
> *Right from the start, that Jacob was her choice.*
> *I couldn't understand her preference,*
> *Her obvious partiality.*
> *They say a father's sins are visited on a child;*
> *The same is true of mothers too.*
> *Rebekah's lack of love inspired contempt*
> *Within young Esau's heart, and as he was despised,*
> *He too despised his birthright and his God.*
> *—Deborah*

Rebekah, who seemed to have everything, lost both her sons through her scheming ways—one physically, one emotionally. Deborah, who seemed to have nothing, may have had the love of everyone in the family. . .hence the name for her burial place—"The Oak of Weeping."

"But many who are first will be last, and many who are last will be first" (Matt. 19:30, NIV). A servant spirit is beautiful in God's eyes because its possession means conformity to the image of His Son.

Oh, Father, I *do* rebel so many times within my spirit. Humble me if that's what I need in order to serve You better. "Whatever it takes for my will to break, that's what I'll be willing to do."[1]

A HORSE MUST BE BROKEN BEFORE IT CAN BE TRAINED.

JUDITH AND BASHEMÀTH: REBEKAH'S THORNS IN THE FLESH

Do not be yoked together with unbelievers. For what do righteousness and wickedness have in common? Or what fellowship can light have with darkness?. . .What does a believer have in common with an unbeliever?. . . As God has said: 'I will live with them and walk among them, and I will be their God, and they will be my people. Therefore come out from among them and be separate,' says the Lord (2 Cor. 6:14-17, NIV).

The Bible tells us so little about Esau's two Hittite wives, Judith and Bashemath, that almost all of their story must be supposition. It is probable, as in the famous story of Rachel and Leah, that one of the two girls dominated the relationship. Let us suppose that hot-headed Esau was initially attracted to Judith, a totally uninhibited pagan girl who probably laughed at Esau's strict Jewish background.

Why had Abraham said to his servant years earlier: "Thou shalt not take a wife unto my son of the daughters of the Canaanites" (Gen. 24:3, KJV)? Why was intermarriage so frowned on? What were the results of mixed marriages? What are the effects of a divided home on the children in that home? How will a child react when one parent tries to teach scriptural principles while the other parent sits back and laughs? Imagine the heartbreak over the years.

O. T. PASSAGE THIS WEEK: Genesis 26:34-35; 27:46—28:9

SPECIAL PRAYER NEEDS THIS WEEK:

ANSWERS TO PRAYER THIS WEEK:

EAT, DRINK, AND BE MERRY

And I will say to my soul, Soul, that hast much goods laid up for many years; take thine ease, eat, drink, and be merry (Luke 12:19, KJV). Read Genesis 26:34-35; Ecclesiastes 2:1-11.

> *Esau the hunter—yes, I've heard of you!*
> *You're just as red and hairy as I've heard,*
> *But much more handsome than I had thought.*
> *You are like the big strong animals you pursue.*
> *They tell me that your Hebrew girls*
> *Are few and far between.*
> *My father Beeri can give you some advice:*
> *Enjoy life while you're young!*
> *Forget what Abraham said—he's dead and gone!*
> *—Judith*

The antagonism between Rebekah and her son Esau must have driven him away from home and everything his father had taught him—straight into the arms of the local girls Rebekah disliked so much! Esau, son of the wealthy Isaac, must have been considered quite a catch.

Rebekah had lost Esau's love years earlier (Esau was forty when he married) through her obvious preference for Jacob; she had no right to demand respect from him now. Is there a double standard in your home? Do you expect your children to adopt your moral standards and your belief in Jesus Christ without their being able to see evidence of His love in your life?

Father, forgive me for the inconsistencies in my life. Sometimes I say one thing and, just a short time later, I contradict my words by my unloving actions. Convict me through Your Spirit, Father, when I lash out at my family. Thank You for Your love that keeps on loving me in spite of myself.

"CHRISTIAN PARENTS NEED TO BE CERTAIN THAT WHAT THEY SAY AND WHAT THEY DO HARMONIZES."[1]

HER LIPS ARE SWEETER THAN HONEY

For the commandment is a lamp. . .to keep thee from the evil woman, from the flattery of the tongue of a strange woman (Prov. 6:23, 24, KJV). Read Proverbs 7:1-5.

> *See, Esau, life is much more fun*
> *With Hittites than your Hebrew God!*
> *He's always preaching sermons at you,*
> *Telling you to do the strangest things—*
> *Like Abraham sacrificing his own son!*
> *Now tell me, what good could that possibly do?*
> *Suppose he hadn't seen the ram, held back his knife?*
> *How can you* know *Jehovah spoke?*
> *—Judith*

A person starved for respect and love will listen eagerly to someone who shows interest in him, whether the advice he receives is good or bad. Esau was probably no exception to this. If he told Judith the stories that had been handed down to him from his father Isaac and grandfather Abraham, they must have sounded very strange to the Hittite girl, and perhaps Esau doubted their truth as she laughed.

Since adults like Esau can be influenced very easily by unbelief, make sure you don't underestimate the strength of peer pressure on a child's heart and emotions! Build a strong wall of loving security around your child as you help and teach the child to develop his/her own personal relationship with God.

Father, I hear myself being so critical of my children (or other family members) some days. Please curb that in me. Remind me of how longsuffering Your Spirit has been in my life, and how loving when I was so unlovely. Help me to view my "little priorities" as promises, not problems.
"WE WANT OUR CHILDREN TO FOLLOW A PERSON, NOT A SET OF RULES."[2]

PREPARATION FOR BATTLE

Lust not after her beauty in thine heart; neither let her take thee with her eyelids (Prov. 6:25, KJV). Read Proverbs 4:1-27.

If I marry Esau, I can't stand alone
Against his Hebrew laws and tyrant God!
I need a friend, a fellow Hittite—
Bashemath! Together we could fight
Those phoneys in my Esau's family!
I'll talk him into marrying Bashemath as well. . .
Old Isaac and Rebekah
Will find their life has changed.

—Judith

The Bible doesn't tell us why Esau married two Canaanite girls when he knew that even one would be a grief to his parents—but perhaps it was for just that reason! Rebellion can do terrible things in people's hearts, and Esau probably felt he had good reason to be rebellious.

I have watched young people enter marriages that were destined for ruin right from the start; they almost seemed bent on choosing a life partner who was just the opposite of what their parents wanted for them. Why? Often because those "Christian" parents preached one message but lived another.

Help me, Father, in my position as parent or youth leader (or simply a member of the body of Christ) to be aware that my life is being watched.

"SARCASM OR EMBARRASSMENT ARE THE FASTEST WAYS TO DEMOLISH A RELATIONSHIP."[3]

WAR AT HOME

A wise son maketh a glad father: but a foolish son is the heaviness of his mother (Prov. 10:1, KVJ). Read Genesis 27:46; Proverbs 9:13-18.

Well, Bashemath, did you see
Rebekah watching as we danced?
She hates our customs and our gods
As much as I hate hers!
She has always hated Esau, too!
But that old woman will regret
The favor she's shown Jacob—
Till I get through with her!

—Judith

Rebekah was being repaid for her trickery, deceit, and lack of love. Certainly she showed no love to her "heathen" daughters-in-law, and certainly they felt no love for her. But how could they? Jesus Christ had not yet come to teach love for our neighbors, and neither side had the ability to understand anything but mistrust and bitterness.

Jesus Christ has come, and He has taught us to love one another. . .yet in many family situations there is still mistrust and bitterness. James asked the question: "What is causing the quarrels and fights among you?" Then he follows with another question that is also an answer: "Isn't it because there is a whole army of evil desires within you?" (James 4:1, LB).

Our family needs Your healing love, Father. So many petty grudges from the past still cloud our minds and obscure our thinking. Help us to put the past into the past and keep it there. Help me to allow each person some growing room. **"IF A CHILD LIVES WITH CRITICISM, HE LEARNS TO CONDEMN."**[4]

PATCH UPON PATCH

See that no one is sexually immoral, or is godless like Esau, who for a single meal sold his inheritance rights as the oldest son (Heb. 12:16, NIV). Read Genesis 28:6-9; Proverbs 10:1-11.

> *I can't believe it! After all I've done,*
> *It seems that Esau is as tricky as his brother!*
> *He told me he didn't care about the faith*
> *His father Isaac taught him as a child,*
> *But just to please old Isaac, he has gone*
> *To find another wife—a wife more fitting,*
> *Who will understand old Abraham's laws!*
> *He only wants his father's blessing, not my love.*
>   *—Judith*

Esau was still trying to regain his father's blessing, by whatever strategy was necessary. Perhaps a new wife, who was at least partly Hebrew, would soften old Isaac's heart! And so Esau went a-courtin' to the house of Ishmael, his uncle, and married his cousin, Ishmael's daughter.

Esau sounds like some halfhearted Christians who don't want to miss out on spiritual rewards, but don't want to forsake their old carnal habits either. So they try to add on a "good work" (like contributing to a religious organization) without changing their life style. Jesus told us, however, that to sew a patch of unshrunk cloth on an old garment will only make the patch tear away from the garment, "making the tear worse" (Matt. 9:16, NIV).

Only You, Father, can tear out sin by the roots. Dig deep into the flesh of my life and operate, amputate, wherever necessary. I know I can trust Your surgical skill.

PRUNING MAY BE PAINFUL, BUT IT HAS A PURPOSE.

A SAD ENDING

Afterward, as you know, when he wanted to inherit this blessing, he was rejected. He could bring about no change of mind, though he sought the blessing with tears (Heb. 12:17, NIV). Read Ephesians 4:17-32.

Oh, cursed is the day I first saw Esau!
Cursed is the day I married him!
What I would give to live among the Hittites,
To be my father's daughter once again!
Now all that faces me is bitter,
As bitter as my withered mother-in-law.
For Esau has brought a new wife back with him;
I have lost my home and Esau's love as well.
                                    —Judith

Judith's bold personality had lost its initial attraction for Esau. Perhaps he had tired of Judith and Bashemath's continual defiance of Isaac and Rebekah. It was no longer amusing to mock his parents' beliefs, but he would live his life with that mockery. Esau had been caught in his own trap.

Many of us, like Esau, have been trapped within walls of our own building, and we may be afraid to go out and face the outside world. Bitterness and guilt have poisoned our lives seemingly beyond repair. But there is a difference between our lives and Esau's—Esau and his wives did not have the Holy Spirit to bring His fruits into their lives (for the asking), and we do. WE DO!

Father, I need the fruits of Your Spirit: love, joy, peace, patience, kindness, goodness, faithfulness, gentleness, self-control (Gal. 5:22). Help me to die daily to my self-centeredness.

THE SECRET OF JOY: JESUS FIRST, OTHERS SECOND, YOU LAST.

Week 10

RACHEL: WAITING AND WEEPING

Then Herod, when he saw that he was mocked of the wise men, was exceeding wroth, and sent forth, and slew all the children that were in Bethlehem, and in all the coasts thereof, from two years old and under, according to the time which he had diligently inquired of the wise men. Then was fulfilled that which was spoken by Jeremy the prophet, saying, In Rama was there a voice heard, lamentation, and weeping, and great mourning, Rachel weeping for her children, and would not be comforted, because they are not (Matt. 2:16-18, KJV).

Because of these verses and the original prophecy in Jeremiah 31:15, we picture Rachel as the loving, concerned Jewish mother whose first priority is the welfare of her children. Did you realize that Rachel, like her forerunners Sarah and Rebekah, waited for many years before a child was given to her. . .and that she died in childbirth as her second son was being born?

The story of Jacob and Rachel has been handed down to us as one of the greatest love stories in history—but their story had many complications and problems, as we'll see during the next two weeks. Through it all Rachel matured from a self-centered beauty to a truly beautiful mother in Israel.

Are your problems helping you to grow spiritually?

O. T. PASSAGE THIS WEEK: Genesis 29:1—30:24; 31:17-35; 35:16-20

SPECIAL PRAYER NEEDS THIS WEEK:

ANSWERS TO PRAYER THIS WEEK:

COMPLETE SURRENDER

I plead with you to give your bodies to God. Let them be a living sacrifice, holy—the kind he can accept. When you think of what he has done for you, is this too much to ask? (Rom. 12:1, LB). Read Genesis 29:1-20.

The lessons that I've learned since I met Jacob!
My life, so simple as a shepherd girl,
Encountered many problems since the day
He saw me, kissed me, claimed me as his own.
Ah, Jacob—you met your match in father Laban;
You worked full seven years to earn my love,
Though it was yours already.
But what was seven years? We had each other.
Anticipation built through all that time.
—Rachel

"Some day my prince will come!" That line—or something similar—had rung through Rachel's mind over and over, like a refrain. . .and then he had come! Her very own prince! She'd been in the midst of performing her usual duties, watering her sheep at the well, when he had suddenly appeared, as though out of her dreams, just as Abraham's servant had found Rachel's aunt Rebekah. She loved him almost immediately, and his love for her is a matter of record.

Jacob had to buy Rachel's hand in marriage, although her love was given to him freely. Christ paid the price to redeem His bride at Calvary. After all He has done for us, can we give Him anything less than ourselves—spirit, soul, and body?

If I've been holding something back from You, Father, please show me what it is. I want to turn over every part of my life, to give it to You as a living sacrifice. Thank You for accepting me just as I am.

WHEN WE GIVE TO CHRIST *EVERYTHING WE ARE,* **WE RECEIVE IN RETURN** *EVERYTHING HE IS.*

PUNISHED BY HIS PAST

The days of punishment are coming, the days of reckoning are at hand (Hos. 9:7, NIV). Read Genesis 29:21-27.

I couldn't forgive my father for his trickery.
(I paid him back years later.)
He held me back—our promised wedding night
Was given to my older sister, not to me.
I feared for Laban's life: my Jacob
Was shattered by the cruel joke,
And yet his memory told him it was justice,
Repaying him for what he had done to Esau long ago.
                                        —Rachel

Did Rachel ever forget what her father had done? Probably not. Later in the story, when Jacob took his family and left Haran (Gen. 31:34), we find that Rachel stole Laban's household gods. C. I. Scofield points out that "the possession of the household gods of a father-in-law by a son-in-law was legally acceptable as proof of the designation of that son-in-law as principal heir."

Did Rachel risk incurring her father's fierce anger (and perhaps Jacob's disapproval) in order to get revenge? It seems very likely.

Thank You, Father, for showing me the effects of deceit through the stories of these very human people. Help me to resist the impulses for dishonesty in my own life, trivial as they may seem at the time.

TRICKERY HAS A WAY OF REPEATING ITSELF—IN REVERSE.

THE LOVE TRIANGLE

Love is strong as death and jealousy is as cruel as Sheol (Song of Sol. 8:6, LB). Read Genesis 29:28-30.

The wedding week was over, and at last I too was yours.
You worked another seven years to earn me as your own.
But Leah always seemed to come between us
Though I knew you loved me more
And thought of me the nights you had to spend with her.
But she was always there! So little time alone—
I felt it was her home I had entered, not my own.
I couldn't bear to watch her watching you,
Her weak eyes squinting wearily to watch us both.
                              —Rachel

Rachel must have understood the reasoning behind her father's trickery, as she certainly would have been familiar with the marriage customs of the times—the older sister in a family, according to law, was to be married before the younger sister—yet her understanding may not have made life any easier. It could not change the fact that Leah was always there!

Have you ever been involved in a "triangle" relationship? Triangles are very uncomfortable. . .unless the third person in the triangle is Jesus Christ! His presence enriches every horizontal relationship and deepens the participants' love— just the opposite of a human triangle.

I ask You, Lord, to become a part of each relationship in which I am involved. Open my eyes, Father, to see the greatness of Your love, and work through me to show others Your love.

WHATEVER FILLS YOU CONTROLS YOU!

CONFIDENCE CRUMBLES

Pride goeth before destruction, and an haughty spirit before a fall (Prov. 16:18, KJV). Read Genesis 30:1-8.

Then I found that I was barren.
Leah had beaten me in the game of life,
For she was pregnant—four times altogether,
Four sons—and I had none.
I felt I'd die of shame.
"Give me children, or I'll die!" I cried.

I gave you Bilhah as another wife
To bear me children in our sisters' fight.
And God gave "justice"—Dan—and Naphtali,
Which means: "I'm winning in this fierce contest."
                                        —Rachel

Beautiful Rachel's pride crumbled rapidly in the face of a problem that even her self-confident personality couldn't handle. Up to this point she had breezed through every obstacle, but now—perhaps for the first time in her life—she felt the need to turn to God.

"Destruction" can be good if its end result is a realization of our own helplessness and God's omnipotence. Are there traces of pride in your life? Do others sense a haughty spirit within you. . .even if you haven't admitted it yet?

Father, help me to always remember that I am nothing in myself. When pride raises its ugly head, remind me of the times I floundered helplessly. Help me to learn to abide in You. **WE CANNOT CONTROL OUR ACTIONS, BUT WE SHOW WHO CONTROLS US BY OUR *REACTIONS*.**

WIFE WAR

How good and how pleasant it is for brethren to dwell together in unity! (Ps. 133:1, KJV). Read Genesis 30:9-20.

My mixed emotions were so complicated!
I loved you, Jacob, much too much to share
Your soul and body with my older sister. . .
And yet I knew she loved you just as much as I.
It hurt me as I watched her suffer,
It hurt me when you spent a night with her.
Unlike the games we played in childhood combat,
There was no winning in this adult tug-of-war!
—Rachel

The sisters' fight over the mandrakes that young Reuben found (the mandrake was "a leafy plant eaten by peasant women in the belief that this would aid them in becoming pregnant") was probably only one of many cases of the never-ending friction within Jacob's growing family.

The dire results of polygamy were so evident in this family that the practice was only tolerated, never accepted, by the Hebrews in later days. Our nation, with its rapidly increasing divorce rate, should learn a lesson from this biblical account of a divided home.

Father, thank You for the precious little lives around me. Help me to lead them not only by my words but also by my walk. Give me the faith of a child, Father, when I doubt Your knowledge of what's best for me.

"IF A CHILD LIVES WITH HOSTILITY, HE LEARNS TO FIGHT."[1]

WAIT A WHILE

And we know that all things work together for good to them that love God (Rom. 8:28, KJV). Read Genesis 30:22-24; 35:16-20.

> *And as our life went on, I found my pride was gone.*
> *My beauty was no consolation when*
> *I couldn't give you a son.*
> *God taught us patience through those fourteen years—*
> *And more—of waiting for a child*
> *And gradually I learned to trust your God.*
> *And so when it was time for God to bless*
> *My body with a child, I could rejoice!*
> *He took away the curse of barrenness*
> *And gave us Joseph ("hoping for another");*
> *He also cured the blight of pride within my heart!*
> *—Rachel*

Another lady-in-waiting! Rachel's prayers for a son were finally answered in Joseph, and she had faith to believe that God would send her another son—Benjamin. God answered . . .in His own time. But in giving birth to Benjamin, Rachel took her final breath.

God gives us three kinds of answers to our prayers: YES, NO, and WAIT A WHILE. The first answer is the one we want to hear, but how we grow spiritually when God gives us the other answers! Right now might be a good time to analyze your current prayer list.

Father, teach me to pray according to Your will instead of mine. There's a certain problem I've been praying about selfishly; help me to be part of the answer to that problem. **BE ANXIOUS FOR NOTHING, PRAYERFUL FOR EVERYTHING, THANKFUL FOR ANYTHING.**

LEAH: LESSONS IN LOVE

Now Laban had two daughters; the name of the elder was Leah, and the name of the younger was Rachel. Leah's eyes were weak and dull looking, but Rachel was beautiful and attractive. . . . And when the Lord saw that Leah was despised, He made her able to bear children; but Rachel was barren (Gen. 29:16-17, 31, Amplified).

Leah's physical description is summarized quickly in the previous verses. The very expressive oriental eyes were an important part of a girl's "beauty pageant qualifications". . . and in this area Leah could not compete with her sister Rachel. Leah probably struggled with an inferiority complex for many years of her life; her attitude toward her Creator, however, was not one of bitterness, but one of praise. She loved Jacob faithfully despite his unmistakable love for Rachel, and I think she loved Rachel too.

Many women, placed in Leah's uneasy spot, would have felt cheated—cheated out of beauty, cheated out of love, cheated out of a happy marriage. Many women would have expressed resentment toward a beautiful sister, an unloving husband, an unfair God. Instead, Leah was thankful for the children God had given her, and in the years after Rachel died, we can imagine that her beauty in spirit was a real comfort to Jacob.

"Why art thou cast down, O my soul? and why art thou disquieted within me? hope thou in God: for I shall yet praise him, who is the health of my countenance, and my God" (Ps. 42:11, KJV).

O. T. PASSAGE THIS WEEK: Genesis 29:31—31:18

SPECIAL PRAYER NEEDS THIS WEEK:

ANSWERS TO PRAYER THIS WEEK:

REJECTED!

For we are God's workmanship, created in Christ Jesus to do good works, which God prepared in advance for us to do (Eph. 2:10, NIV). Read Isaiah 45:5-12.

> *My sister Rachel! Some days I almost hate her*
> *For having everything I want to have. . .*
> *For doing everything I want to do. . .*
> *For being everything I want to be.*
>
> *They say I'm shy—but why attempt to match*
> *Her beauty, poise, and confidence?*
> *She has always been ahead of me.*
> *I couldn't even find a husband on my own!*
> *My father had to trick poor Jacob into marrying me.*
> > *—Leah*

We've discussed Jacob and Rachel's reactions to his enforced marriage to Leah—but what about Leah's feelings? How humiliating that wedding night must have been for Leah, knowing that she was unwanted. The future, years full of insult heaped upon injury, must have seemed to stretch endlessly, wearily ahead for the girl whose name means "weary."

Satan loves to victimize us in depression through comparison. We need to fight back by letting him know that we are very special to God. As the clay mentioned in today's reading, we may not be able to understand the great Potter's design—but He has each intricate step perfectly planned.

Father, I've never really, completely accepted myself. I often feel that other people don't accept me. Many times I feel compelled to cover, to put on a front. . .or to hide. Help me, Father.

"IF WE REJECT GOD'S BASIC DESIGN IN MAKING US, IT MAY THEN ALSO BE DIFFICULT TO PUT CONFIDENCE IN THE DESIGNER FOR OTHER AREAS OF OUR LIFE."[1]

AN IMPOSSIBLE SITUATION

Love is patient, love is kind. . .it does not boast, it is not proud (1 Cor. 13:4, NIV). Read Genesis 29:31-35.

Yes, we both love him—Jacob!
I long to touch that thick black hair
That she caresses nightly.
Those strong, broad shoulders are her haven—
Seldom mine.

Except. . .except those nights he comes to me
In search of sons,
The one thing Rachel's beauty couldn't give.
Her barren womb drives him to me.
He is my husband too. . .
Yet he loves her.

—Leah

Leah had probably lived in her sister's shadow for a long time—but her problems must have multiplied in the unfortunate three-sided marriage! Life might have been tolerable for Leah had she remained emotionally uninvolved, had she not desired Jacob—but it seems obvious that she loved Jacob just as intensely as he loved Rachel.

In today's world it seems incredible that such a lopsided marriage could exist. . .yet other relationships call for the same kind of love that was asked of Leah—a patient, self-sacrificing, humble love, *agape* love. Are you reaching out with that kind of love?

Father, I realize that what I call love is so impatient, so self-seeking. I demand response and reaction from my family and my friends. Open my eyes, Father, to see the greatness of Your love.

REMEMBER: YOU CAN GIVE WITHOUT LOVING BUT YOU CANNOT LOVE WITHOUT GIVING.

PTL ANYHOW!

Love. . .does not envy. . .it keeps no record of wrongs (1 Cor. 13:4-5, NIV). Read Psalm 103.

Even knowing he was only there with me
To carry on his name,
I loved him fiercely, tenderly,
Hoping my very strength of passion
Would bring him back again.
He couldn't compare my eyes with hers
Or see my lack of beauty in the welcome night.

Did he return?
Oh, yes, but only for more sons. . .
Not for my love.

—Leah

The names Leah gave to her sons tell us a lot about her feelings. Reuben, the name of Leah's oldest son, means: "See, a son." Leah thought: "Jehovah has noticed my trouble—now my husband will love me." At Simeon's birth, Leah said: "Jehovah heard that I was unloved, and so he has given me another son." Levi means "attachment": "surely now my husband will feel affection for me, since I have given him three sons!" (Gen. 29:32-34, LB).

By this time Leah could have become very bitter because of Jacob's continued preference for the still childless Rachel, but Judah (the name of Leah's fourth son) simply means "praise." It seems Leah is growing in inner beauty with each year and each son!

Thank You, Father, for helping me to realize that inner beauty is much more important than outward beauty in Your eyes. Teach me to cultivate that inner beauty through praising You.

SMILE—IT WILL CHANGE YOUR FACE VALUE!

AGAPE LOVE

Love. . .is not rude, it is not self-seeking, it is not easily angered, it keeps no record of wrongs (1 Cor. 13:5, NIV). Read Matthew 5:43-48.

Yet, Jacob, I can feel no hate
For just as you once tricked your brother,
You in turn were taken in by Laban's scheme,
Enslaved by Rachel's love—
Demanding, spoiled. . .my little sister Rachel.
For even though she has your love,
And everything I've yearned for
(Except my sons), I love her too.
I have always loved her.

—Leah

At one time in the scriptural account (Gen. 30:14-15), we are told that Leah spoke angrily to Rachel, but somehow the story of these two sisters leaves us with the feeling that Leah loved Rachel deeply. Perhaps as children Leah had even helped to "spoil" Rachel by giving in to her pretty little sister's demands.

The Bible tells us that Rachel envied Leah her children, but we do not get the impression that Leah gloated over Rachel's barrenness although, from a human point of view, she would have had good reason to do so. Are you facing a situation in which you need to overlook a wrong done to you . . .to seek to fulfill someone else's needs rather than your own?

Father, You're pointing out to me a situation where I've "forgiven but not forgotten." I guess that's not really forgiveness, is it? Help me, Father, to learn to show Your kind of love. **LOVE BEGINS WHEN ANOTHER'S NEEDS BECOME MORE IMPORTANT THAN MY OWN.**

REACH OUT AND TOUCH SOMEONE

Love does not delight in evil but rejoices with the truth. It always protects, always trusts, always hopes, always perseveres (1 Cor. 13:6-7, NIV). Read Genesis 31:1-18.

> *So why hate Rachel?*
> *It is God who made her*
> *Beautiful and vibrant, with a kind of magic glow*
> *That draws men's glances everywhere she walks.*
>
> *And yet my sister has suffered too*
> *For want of children.*
> *How she aches to hold a little one within her arms!*
> *God gives, and takes away,*
> *And blessed is His name!*
>
> *—Leah*

By the time we reach Genesis 31:14, it is obvious that Rachel and Leah are in unity. The years seem to have drawn them together, and they are solid in their stand against Laban's continued trickery. (It is possible, however, that this was only a temporary alliance, that the sisters were drawn together by their common desire for an estate for their own sons.)

It's very important to be aware of the hurts in others' lives and to realize that everyone faces his or her own set of problems. Have you been too immersed in your own personal crises to reach out to someone who needs your understanding and concern?

Father, I guess I *have* been self-centered. Perhaps some of my problems are here so that I'll be able to understand and sympathize with others. You've said in Your Word, Father, that all things work together for good to those who love You . . .and I do love You. Thank You for loving me.
SYMPATHY IS YOUR HURT IN MY HEART.

YOU ARE LOVED!

Now I know in part; then I shall know fully, even as I am fully known (1 Cor. 13:12, NIV). Read Job 38:1-7; 42:1-3.

And though I'm plain, God gave me sons,
Fulfilled the promise that He made
To our great father Abraham.
"God noticed me". . ."Jehovah heard!"
My sons will carry on the name!
I am a part of God's great plan;
He loves me just the way I am.

—Leah

Isn't it reassuring to realize that Bible characters were human too—with the same hang-ups, complexes, and personality problems that we keep uncovering in our own lives? It certainly must have been difficult being Leah, the unwanted third person in a lopsided marriage, just as it's very difficult to accept ourselves when we are rejected by others. Our rejection may have begun early in life. . .and we feel it will never end.

But God has a unique plan for my life and your life, "prepared in advance" (Eph. 2:10, NIV), and, as Job finally realized, "no plan of Yours [God's] can be thwarted" (Job 42:2, NIV). In the words of the song, "I am loved, you are loved; I can risk loving you, for the One who knows me best loves me most."

Father, thank You for Your love that accepts me with no strings attached. If You accept me, Father, then I can accept myself, and reach out to others who need acceptance too. Thank You for making us "accepted in the beloved" (Eph. 1:6, KJV).

LITTLE IS MUCH WHEN GOD USES IT.

DISOBEDIENT DINAH

After Jacob came from Paddan Aram, he arrived safely at the city of Shechem in Canaan and camped within sight of the city (Gen. 33:18, NIV).

Dinah's story is shocking, and we turn away from its violence, even in this day and age. What can we possibly learn from Genesis 34?

Many fathers have quoted Ephesians 6:1—or the fifth commandment—to their sons and daughters, but at the same time have completely ignored the fourth verse of the above passage: "Fathers, do not exasperate your children" (NIV). Jacob, of course, did not have the benefit of Paul's advice in Ephesians, nor did he have the guidance of the Holy Spirit in raising his children. We also need to realize that this was a time of backsliding in Jacob's life and understand its effect on his children's lives. Until the move to Bethel following this story, Jacob's family had foreign idols (see Gen. 35).

The surprising part of Genesis 34 is not its violence or its sexual overtones, although they both come through loud and clear. We cannot even be too surprised by the fact that the "heathen" Canaanites seemed to be much more honorable than some of God's "chosen" people. (Isn't that still true today?) "The heart is deceitful. . .and desperately wicked: who can know it?" (Jer. 17:9, KJV). What *is* surprising—yes, amazing—is that a merciful God loves us in spite of the sin He hates!

Keep those thoughts in mind as you read the story of Jacob and Leah's daughter, Dinah, a troubled, lonely teen-ager whose story, in some ways, sounds very much like a modern teen-ager's dilemma.

O. T. PASSAGE THIS WEEK: Genesis 33:18—35:7

SPECIAL PRAYER NEEDS THIS WEEK:

ANSWERS TO PRAYER THIS WEEK:

PROBLEMS AT HOME

But if anyone causes one of these little ones who believe in me to sin, it would be better for him to have a large millstone hung around his neck and to be drowned in the depths of the sea (Matt. 18:6, NIV). Read Genesis 33:18—34:1.

You would have left home, too,
If you'd been in my shoes!
I didn't know one girl my age,
One friend who'd understand. . .
Just men—my brothers, all of them!
And then, of course, my father's pet—
Spoiled Joseph! He's the only one
My father loves of all of us.
It's common knowledge that
My father never loved my mother. . .
But Joseph is aunt Rachel's son.

—Dinah

Loneliness can strike in a crowd—or in a big family! Loneliness can strike anytime you feel unloved, and it's very possible that's how Dinah felt. As the only girl in the family, she may have spent most of her time in the "kitchen," helping her mother Leah. Perhaps she had only one thing in common with her older brothers—their common hatred of Joseph, the one child in the family who, it seems, was loved by their father Jacob.

It is also possible that Dinah, being an only daughter (and obviously attractive), may have been pampered and spoiled by her brothers. In either case, she was bored with her home life and ready for adventure—and Jacob had camped within sight of the city of Shechem!

Help me to be aware of others' needs, Father. Help me especially to reach out to that lonely, dissatisfied teen-ager in my family, church, or neighborhood.

TO BE A LISTENER YOU MUST FIRST STOP TALKING.

HYPOCRISY AT HOME

Woe to you. . .you hypocrites! You clean the outside of the cup and dish, but inside they are full of greed and self-indulgence (Matt. 23:25, NIV). Read Matthew 23:13-32.

So I left home—I couldn't take
The constant family feuds.
They preached at me to trust in God,
Stay separate from the heathen nations,
And yet I saw hypocrisy
Within my family home.
I needed to get out and find
A life style of my own.

—Dinah

Fight, fight, fight! Dinah was sick and tired of fighting: fighting between her mother Leah and her aunt Rachel, fighting between her brothers, fighting between Joseph and herself. What was the point of being different from the outside world when the "world" seemed so much happier than her own family?

Family life must be warm, loving, wholesome, full of fun . . .if Christian parents hope to compete with the strength of attractions outside the home. And parents' lives must be consistent with what they teach! How does your home rate? Be objective; look at it from a child's point of view, or a teenager's.

Thank You, Father, for the home in which You've placed me. Help me to work at making it a place where Your children will enjoy living together.

TAKE TIME OUT TO LAUGH—IT HELPS CARRY LIFE'S LOAD.

DINAH DISAPPEARS!

Above all else, guard your affections. For they influence everything else in your life (Prov. 4:23, LB). Read Genesis 34:1-4.

I left in search of greener pastures.
I found them soon—in Shechem's fields.
I found my heart's desire in Shechem town.
I had wandered through the streets and shops,
Enjoying glances from the men,
Wondering where to find a friend,
When suddenly he was there,
His intense passion changing me
From girl to woman in one day.

—Dinah

Nothing makes a teen-ager more vulnerable than combined feelings of rejection and rebellion. In her haste to get away from the hypocrisy at home, Dinah fell into Satan's trap on her first day out. Remember: Satan comes as an angel of light!

You may know a teen-ager who needs someone to talk to . . .a teen-ager who has no one. Maybe you feel you just don't have time to get involved—but maybe you're that teen-ager's last chance. If you don't listen, where will that girl go next? Or that boy?

Father, teach me to listen. Help me to recognize Your priorities for my life when they come my way, whether I'm ready for them or not. Help me to be ready, Father.

AGE IS A MATTER OF MIND; IF YOU DON'T MIND, IT DOESN'T MATTER.

LOVE AT FIRST SIGHT

Let him kiss me with the kisses of his mouth—for your love is more delightful than wine (Song of Sol. 1:2, NIV). Read Genesis 34:5-12.

At first I fought back angrily.
I thought I hated men;
I vowed I'd never be enslaved,
My mother's life relive.
But soon I realized that this prince,
Although he raped me, cared for me.
He showed more love in those brief days
Than I had known in years.
His father said he would talk to mine.
I would be Shechem's wife!

—Dinah

It's obvious that Dinah's prince developed a real affection for her; how lasting that affection would have been is questionable, since a royal harem was quite customary in those days. Of course Dinah was too young and too gullible to think about such a possibility.

Dinah desperately needed a father's loving guidance at this point in her life. Yet when Jacob found out where Dinah was, he did nothing. Obviously the lines of communication were in sad need of repair. Or had there ever been any communication?

Have I failed, Father, in my lack of sensitivity to members of my family? Do I have time for outsiders, but not enough time for my children, my own brothers and sisters, my own parents? Forgive me, Father.

HAVE YOU LISTENED FOR THE PITTER-PATTER OF LITTLE PRIORITIES?

LACK OF CONCERN

You are like whitewashed tombs, which look beautiful on the outside but on the inside are full of dead men's bones and everything unclean (Matt. 23:27, NIV). Read Genesis 34:13-29; Proverbs 3:29-35.

Savagery—that was all it was,
Enacted in the name of God!
My father sat back motionless,
Did nothing while my brothers spoke,
Deceived my prince with promises.
They're hypocrites, each one of them!
Oh, Simeon, Levi, I would to God
He would take your lives—you have ruined mine!
—Dinah

Jacob's lack of leadership (and his lack of concern for Dinah) becomes more and more evident in this scene. He did not attempt to find his missing daughter; he allowed his sons to handle all negotiations; and he did nothing to intervene in his sons' dastardly plans for revenge. Obviously Dinah's brothers had no concern for her well-being either, but only for the family reputation (which suffered more from their lack of control than from Dinah's).

What a terrible example this whole situation was to the neighboring Canaanites! And how often we bring shame on the cause of Christ by the way *we* live! Examine your life to see what kind of a testimony you are leaving in your business dealings. . .your social contacts. . .the people whose lives you touch each day.

Father, help me to be worthy of Your Son's name. Make my life as a Christian so salty that others become thirsty for Your living water.

ARE YOU MAKING A MARK ON THE WORLD, OR IS THE WORLD MAKING A MARK ON YOU?

A SELF-CENTERED FATHER

Fathers, do not embitter your children, or they will become discouraged (Col. 3:21, NIV). Read Genesis 34:30—35:7; 28:10-22.

I wonder if he will ever know
The pain he has caused by lack of love.
My mother has always felt that pain;
My brothers always tried to gain
My father's love in varied ways.
Perhaps their savage deeds were done
To make my father notice them. . .
And all he does is sit and moan.
His reputation is ruined now!

—Dinah

Jacob finally reacted to the problem Dinah had "caused." He recognized his backslidden condition and obeyed God's command to move to Bethel ("house of God") to erect the altar he had promised God to build there many years earlier (on his way to Haran).

Just think of the problems that could have been avoided had Jacob observed his vow to the Lord much earlier, instead of looking to the city of Shechem for protection! Where do I look for protection?

Thank You, Father, for this story that shows the danger of "camping too close" to temptation. Please keep nudging me until I move unto holy ground.

THE CROSS IS GOD'S COMPASS POINTING THE LOST TO HEAVEN.

UNDERSTANDING TRICKY TAMAR

For God so loved the world, that he gave his only begotten Son, that whosoever *believeth in him should not perish, but have everlasting life (John 3:16, KJV).*

On the significance of the story of Tamar, Eugenia Price writes: "We err when we try to find 'lessons' in all these Old Testament accounts. They are not little 'morality plays.' They are records, historical records, however sketchy at times, of the lives of some of the people of Israel and their friends and enemies. We are not to try to be like them or not to be like them. *We are to look for what God did in all they did.* We are to look for what God did directly, at the time of their behavior or misbehavior, and in this story we are to look also for what He dared to do later. All through the twilight era of the Old Testament, God was planning, moving toward the day when He would send His Son, Jesus, to redeem His people from their sins. To give them a way to live fully, abundantly without tricks and devices such as Tamar used.

"This is the exciting, overwhelming, humbling message of the somewhat risque' story of the beautiful Tamar: God sent His Son through her!

"One author said it shocked his 'inner, finer feelings to see Christ's lineage interwoven with such abhorrent degradation. . . .' It definitely does *not* shock mine. It relieves me all the way to the depths of my soul to see that the Holy God of Israel loved enough to make use of ordinary people. . . .

"This is the Most High God striding across the earth shouting, 'I love! I love! You cannot achieve holiness. Nothing you can do by way of morality can bring us together. By *grace* are you saved.'"[1]

O. T. PASSAGE THIS WEEK: Genesis 38

SPECIAL PRAYER NEEDS THIS WEEK:

ANSWERS TO PRAYER THIS WEEK:

HUSBAND #1

Be careful, and watch yourselves closely so that you do not forget the things your eyes have seen or let them slip from your heart as long as you live. Teach them to your children and to their children after them (Deut. 4:9, NIV).

For rebellion is as the sin of witchcraft (1 Sam. 15:23, KJV). Read Genesis 38:1-7.

> *I thought our marriage would be wonderful—*
> *Great Jacob's grandson's wife, indeed!*
> *But life turned out quite differently*
> *From what I had dreamed and planned. . .*
> *And soon I found that even though*
> *My husband came from righteous stock,*
> *There was rebellion in his heart.*
> *His thoughts were centered on himself—*
> *His own desires, his wants, his lusts. . . .*
> *And finally God snuffed out his life.*
>
> *—Tamar*

Er and Tamar—it may have seemed like a good match at first. Jacob's entire family had become well-known in Canaan, and they were very prosperous. The scandal around Dinah and Shechem had died down, and Tamar probably had no idea that her father-in-law, Judah, was the man who had suggested selling Joseph to the "gypsies" (see Gen. 37:26-27).

Perhaps Tamar was shocked when she discovered the hypocrisy within this "religious" family. Perhaps because of it she was turned off on the worship of Jehovah, at least for a time.

Father, does my life point others to You? Or are they turned off by my many inconsistencies? Help me, Father, to live on an even keel. . .not to be double-minded.

GOD HAS NO GRANDCHILDREN!

HUSBAND #2

You, my brothers, were called to be free. But do not use your freedom to indulge the sinful nature; rather, serve one another in love (Gal. 5:13, NIV). Read Genesis 38:8; Deuteronomy 25:5-10.

> *According to the custom of the time,*
> *Er's brother was to carry on his line;*
> *And though I didn't love Onan,*
> *I hoped at least to gain a child*
> *Through my relationship with him.*
> *My life was lonely without love—*
> *A child would brighten up my days*
> *And give me someone who would care.*
> *—Tamar*

What seems to us to be very strange was the accepted custom of the day. If a man died without leaving an heir, any brothers were obligated to marry the widow; the first son from that marriage was to carry on the dead brother's name, and receive the inheritance and blessing, thus the rights of the firstborn did not pass on to his brother, but to the child.

God made very clear His concern for loyalty within the family. Any uncooperative brother could be taken to court by the widow, where his sandal could be removed by the widow. She was also allowed to spit in his face as a sign of contempt, and his line would be known as "The Family of the Unsandaled" (Deut. 25:10, NIV).

Thank You, Father, for my family. Thank You in spite of all the problems that exist. Please give me Your kind of love for the members of my family.

ONLY THE SON CAN PASS ON THE LIFE OF THE FATHER.

SELF-CENTEREDNESS

So I say, live by the Spirit, and you will not gratify the desires of the sinful nature (Gal. 5:16, NIV). Read Genesis 38:9-10.

> But Onan didn't want to raise
> A child who wouldn't belong to him.
> He didn't want his brother's wife;
> He too cared only for himself.
> But God was angered by his act,
> Done in contempt of family,
> And so God took away his life
> As Onan kept new life from me.
> —Tamar

Onan was a selfish person who had no desire to give a child to his brother's widow—a child who would be his responsibility and yet would legally belong to his dead brother. Such refusal was considered to be disrespect for one's family responsibilities.

The fifth chapter of Ephesians shows a clear connection between being continually filled with the Spirit and having a happy, fulfilling family life. Being filled with the Spirit means learning to submit to each other within the home, learning to say "I'm wrong" and "I'm sorry."

Father, I realize my need to be continually filled with Your Spirit. Empty me completely of "self-sins"—self-pity, self-confidence to the point of pride, self-centeredness—so that there is room for Your Spirit. I'm sick of ME, Lord. . .I need YOU!

BEING FILLED WITH THE SPIRIT MEANS LEARNING TO SUBMIT TO EACH OTHER WITHIN THE HOME.

A JINX?

Any why beholdest thou the mote that is in thy brother's eye, but considerest not the beam that is in thine own eye? (Matt. 7:3, KJV). Read Genesis 38:11; 2 Corinthians 5:10-21.

> So only Shelah now was left—
> My brother-in-law, still just a boy—
> And father Judah sent me home
> In fear I had jinxed his family.
> He promised that young Shelah would
> Support me and take care of me—
> "But give him first a chance to grow!"
> So I went home to await his word.
>
> —Tamar

Judah couldn't face the wickedness of his own sons—or possibly his share of responsibility for their life style. (He couldn't see the "beam" in his own eye.) It was much easier to blame the problems on Tamar, to call her the "jinx."

We're doing the same thing that Judah did when we blame our problems on our environment or people around us. We're simply shifting the burden of guilt. Like a child we say, "But it wasn't my fault! He made me do it!" Spiritual maturity means taking responsibility for wrongdoing, confessing it, and leaving the burden of guilt at the foot of the cross.

Father, help me to recognize sin in my life. Help me to do something about it as soon as I recognize it. Thank You for Your readiness to forgive when I humble myself and "turn from (my) wicked ways."

DID THE DEVIL *REALLY* MAKE YOU DO IT?

DOUBLE STANDARD

Thou hypocrite, first cast out the beam out of thine own eye; and then shalt thou see clearly to cast out the mote out of thy brother's eye (Matt. 7:5, KJV). Read Genesis 38:12-26.

> *But as the years went on I knew*
> *That Judah would not keep his word.*
> *He too withheld new life from me*
> *And I was growing old.*
> *So as he had tricked me through the years,*
> *I played a trick on him.*
> *His double standard I would expose*
> *For all his friends to see;*
> *Self-righteous Judah would be caught,*
> *Bound by his lies and his deceit.*
> —Tamar

Tamar's trick was scandalous. . .but had Jesus been present at the assembly called to burn her as a punishment for her prostitution, He might have said: "Let him who is without sin light the first torch." The very man who was ordering Tamar's death was the man who was the father of her child!

Hypocrisy in Jacob's family again! Does it run in the family? It almost seems as though hypocrisy is hereditary! But then, hypocrisy is just. . .sin. What characteristics are associated with your family? What do people think when they hear *your* name?

Father, I thought I left my past behind me, but when I listen to myself talking to my children, I hear some of those same things that hurt me as a child. Help me, Father, to practice what I preach. Help me to radiate Your love to my own family before I go out to evangelize the world.

DON'T LET YOUR TALK GET AHEAD OF YOUR WALK.

LOOKING AHEAD

For there is no respect of persons with God (Rom. 2:11, KJV). Read Genesis 38:27-30; Matthew 1:1-3.

Somehow the God of Israel understood
My loneliness, my hurts, and fears.
He took away the shame of barrenness
And gave me sons to dry my tears.
Though there are many who look down on me,
I find such comfort in the thought
The God of Israel cares for me,
And thought me worthy of His love.

—Tamar

As we discussed in the introduction to this week, Jesus was of the lineage of Tamar. He was a direct descendant of this woman of questionable morals. Does this mean that Jesus Christ approved of Tamar's scheme to become a mother and, in the same breath, teach her hypocritical father-in-law a lesson?

In a similar New Testament situation Christ said: "Go, and sin no more." And all through this period of Old Testament history, when people had neither the Bible nor the Holy Spirit to guide them, God's intricate plan was moving toward that momentous day when His sinless Son would take the form of a man to redeem man from his sin. As a part of that plan, a holy and righteous God could—and did—work through another impatient, hurting, anxious woman.

Father, thank You for accepting me just the way I am. Thank You that You've promised to make the changes that are needed when I'm ready for them. Thank You for loving me. . .no strings attached.

"IT IS IMPOSSIBLE TO PRAY FOR AND GOSSIP ABOUT A PERSON AT THE SAME TIME."[1]

POTIPHAR'S LONELY WIFE

Now Joseph had been taken down to Egypt. Potiphar, an Egyptian who was one of Pharaoh's officials, the captain of the guard, bought him from the Ishmaelites who had taken him there (Gen. 39:1, NIV).

Potiphar's wife—how do we feel about her? Do we sort of look down our Christian noses at this licentious, evil-minded woman, piously thanking the Lord that *we're* not like her? Surely there can be no similarities between our lives and *hers!*

Dinah, Tamar, now Potiphar's wife—

" 'Well,' you may be saying, 'what terrible people you have been talking about!' But wait a minute! You are just as bad. When you say they are wicked and should be punished, you are talking about yourselves, for you do these very same things. And we know that God, in justice, will punish anyone who does such things as these. Do you think that God will judge and condemn others for doing them and overlook you when you do them, too? Don't you realize how patient He is being with you? Or don't you care? Can't you see that He has been waiting all this time without punishing you, to give you time to turn from your sin? His kindness is meant to lead you to repentance" (Rom. 2:1-4, LB).

As you read Genesis 39, keep this thought in mind: my potential for wrong thoughts and wrong actions is staggering—unless I am continually indwelt, filled, and guided by the Holy Spirit.

O. T. PASSAGE THIS WEEK: Genesis 37; 39

SPECIAL PRAYER NEEDS THIS WEEK:

ANSWERS TO PRAYER THIS WEEK:

MARRIED TO A WORKAHOLIC

Let your manhood be a blessing; rejoice in the wife of your youth (Prov. 5:18, LB). Read Proverbs 2:1-22.

Work, work, work! My husband's god is work!
Not Isis or the other deities—but work!
He has no time for me.
I wait in vain to hear his knock upon my door.
Great Potiphar! I thought my life would be
Full of excitement, fame, and love.
Instead it's empty.
He's too busy, too important
To have time for me.
There is no love between us—yet I stay.
There is no other place to go.

—Potiphar's wife

Potiphar was a very important man, a member of the Pharaoh's personal staff and captain of his bodyguard (Gen. 39:1). (The Living Bible also refers to him as Pharaoh's chief executioner.) It's very likely that the demands of Potiphar's job kept him away from home most of the time.

So it's very possible that Potiphar's wife was desperately lonely. It's also possible that she was merely bored, looking for new excitement in her life. Egyptian religion did not major in morals,. and our lady of luxury had little sense of right or wrong. Obviously this woman's life was totally empty of meaning.

Thank You, Father, for sending Your Son that I might have life. . .abundant life. Teach me to appropriate *Your* abundance in my everyday life by emptying my life of self-sins and opening myself to the filling of Your Spirit. As I speak to You now, Father, I confess those sins—I breathe them out— and I breathe in Your loving Spirit.

AS LONG AS WE ARE FRUSTRATED AND DISCON-TENTED, WE ARE CONCENTRATED ON OURSELVES.

THE STAGE IS SET!

A worthy wife is her husband's joy and crown; the other kind corrodes his strength and tears down everything he does (Prov. 12:4, LB). Read Genesis 37.

> A new slave has arrived,
> A slave whose well-built body could contain a god.
> I've heard he is the son of Jacob,
> Wealthy nomad of the north.
> He's much too handsome to be wasted as a slave!
> I'll recommend he works inside the house
> Where I can see him as I wish.
>
> —Potiphar's wife

Joseph's strange story interrupted his mistress' lonely boredom and appealed to her longing for excitement. His sun-bronzed Hebrew features were a welcome change from the black Nubian slaves. And Potiphar "did not concern himself with anything except the food he ate" (Gen. 39:6).

If ever the stage was set for possible adultery, certainly here! Have you ever sensed a similar situation? Did you pause to luxuriate in the pleasurable attraction, or did you flee from it (2 Tim. 2:22)?

Thank You, Father, for this story that warns me of the danger of staying too close to temptation. Thank You for Your Word that enables me to discern and to resist Satan's attacks.

"MANY OF US SUFFER FROM TEMPTATIONS FROM WHICH WE HAVE NO BUSINESS TO SUFFER, SIMPLY BECAUSE WE HAVE REFUSED TO LET GOD LIFT US TO A HIGHER PLANE WHERE WE WOULD FACE TEMPTATIONS OF ANOTHER ORDER."[1]

RESULTS OF INSECURITY

Submit yourselves, then, to God. Resist the devil, and he will flee from you. Come near to God and he will come near to you (James 4:7-8, NIV). Read Genesis 39:1-7; Proverbs 5:1-23.

Young Joseph brings out feelings that
I thought I buried long ago.
I cannot let him see!
He's but a slave
And I'm his mistress.
Yet I long to breathe his name,
To feel his touch.
Could it be possible?
Could Joseph love me?
Or will I always be unloved?

—Potiphar's wife

Did Potiphar's wife experience feelings of insecurity? It's very possible. Bill Gothard, in his outline on the "Development of an Immoral Woman," points out that rejection by an unloving father is often the first step on the downward trail, followed by other real or imagined rejections. The feeling of rejection eventually develops into a hatred toward men and a desire for revenge through sexual exploitation.

That downward trend can be arrested and reversed by the realization that "nothing will ever be able to separate us from the love of God" (Rom. 8:38, LB).

Father, Thank You for Your long-suffering love that found me even before I looked to You for help in my need. Let me never forget that without You I am nothing. . .and yet, Father, thank You for the knowledge that in Your strength I can do anything You ask me to do.

"GRADUALLY I LEARNED THAT THERE IS MORE POWER IN PRAYING FOR PEOPLE THAN IN PREACHING AT PEOPLE, ESPECIALLY WHEN I HAVE RELEASED THEM FOR GOD TO ANSWER MY PRAYERS IN ANY WAY HE DESIRES."[2]

THE LUST OF THE EYE

Look straight ahead; don't even turn your head to look (Prov. 4:25, LB). Read Genesis 39:8-10; Proverbs 6:20-35.

The arrogance of that slave,
Refusing my advances!
I'm told I'm beautiful,
Yet he despises me.
He mumbles words like wickedness and sin
And goes his way about this house
Ignoring me.
What does he mean by sin?

—Potiphar's wife

Potiphar's sensuous wife was infuriated by Joseph's calm responses to her advances. She probably took his lack of interest as a personal insult and perhaps one more rejection in a long series of rejections. And remember: she was probably acting very normally for a woman of her time and culture, so don't judge her too harshly! She had never been taught God's Word.

Pehaps there's a relationship you've been secretly treasuring—an unhealthy admiration you've been allowing to take hold in your life. "Watch your step!" Proverbs 4:26 warns us quite clearly. Another wise proverb (6:32) tells us that the man or woman who commits adultery is an "utter fool," because adultery destroys the soul. And Jesus equates lust with adultery (Matt. 5:28).

Father, I thank You for Your cleansing power that can wash me "whiter than snow." I confess to You right now any wrong thoughts or actions that have been polluting my soul. I condemn them as sin and I ask Your forgiveness and Your total cleansing.

THE FOUR R'S TO RESIST THE DEVIL: RESIST, REFUSE, REJECT, REBUKE!

DECISIONS DETERMINE DESTINIES

She does not know the path to life. She staggers down a crooked trail, and doesn't even realize where it leads (Prov. 5:6, LB). Read Genesis 39:11-19; Proverbs 7:6-26.

I won't give up! I'll wear him down
Day after day; he can't withstand
My charms for long.
Perhaps he waits because
He fears we'll be found out.
There'll come a time when we are all alone.
I'll play his game. . . .
I can wait too.

—Potiphar's wife

Once a woman has made up her mind to achieve a certain goal, a setback in her path may only make her more determined. This seemed to be true of Potiphar's wife—the more the handsome Hebrew avoided her, the greater her desire for him increased.

If only Potiphar's wife had been a believer in the one true God, what feats her determination might have accomplished! She might have been another Rahab, or another Deborah! Are you as determined to serve God as you are to achieve certain goals on which you've set your heart? Which is more important to you: the appearance of your home or the state of your heart?

Father, I want only what You want for my life. I know that Your will for me is best. I submit myself to Your leadership and I move out of the driver's seat once and for all. Help me to set my priorities in order.

CHECK: WILL MY DOING THIS BRING HONOR AND GLORY TO GOD?

THE WAGES OF SIN

But afterwards only a bitter conscience is left to you, sharp as a double-edged sword (Prov. 5:4, LB). Read Genesis 39:20-23; Proverbs 9:1-12.

> Joseph is gone. . .and I'm alone again.
> Revenge is mine,
> But there's no sweetness in it.
> The servants laugh at me behind my back
> (They *know the truth, if Potiphar is blind!)*
> And I am miserable because I lied.
> That's strange. . . .
> I never cared before about the truth.
> Is Joseph's God tormenting me?
> —Potiphar's wife

Potiphar's wife must have felt like a fool! She had "won the victory" by showing Joseph who was boss, but her victory was empty. Life was back to the same old lonely, monotonous routine again. . .except now she was talked about, laughed at, mocked behind her back. Surely the servants must have known what really happened!

"Why was I so stupid?" the writer of Proverbs asks in 5:13-14. "For now I must face public disgrace" (LB). And then he warns in verse 21: "For God is closely watching you, and he weighs carefully everything you do." He sees our thoughts as well as our actions, and His holiness cannot tolerate sin.

Father, I thank You for the atonement through Your Son's death in my place that provided for my *justification,* so that by accepting Your forgiveness I can have eternal life *just-as-if-I-never-sinned.* Forgive me for the way in which I have judged others when I too have sinned in thought if not in action. Thank You, Jesus, for the cleansing power of Your blood.

"GOD WILL NEVER REVEAL MORE TRUTH ABOUT HIMSELF UNTIL YOU HAVE OBEYED WHAT YOU KNOW ALREADY."[3]

Week 15

SHIPHRAH AND PUAH:
THE AGE-OLD ISSUE OF CHILD MURDER

Then a new king, who did not know about Joseph, came to power in Egypt. 'Look,' he said to his people, 'the Israelites have become much too numerous for us' (Exod. 1:8-9, NIV).

You've probably never heard of Shiphrah and Puah. Strange names, aren't they? In Exodus 1:15, you'll find that Shiphrah and Puah were the Hebrew midwives who held in their hands the destinies of all the Hebrew boy babies.

Shiphrah and Puah were the first courageous fighters against something Jehovah despised then and still despises today—the murder of innocent children! God has no mercy on those who offend a child in any way: "It would be better for him to be thrown into the sea with a millstone tied around his neck" (Luke 17:2, NIV). How much more terrible will God's judgment be on those who take the lives of little ones!

Child murder has persisted through the ages. In 2 Kings 16:3 we read that Ahaz, king of Judah, "sacrificed his son in the fire, following the detestable ways of the nations the Lord had driven out before the Israelites" (NIV). This same kind of sacrifice is also mentioned in 2 Kings 17; Jeremiah 32:35; and Ezekiel 16:20-21.

As a result of this offense and others, "the Lord was very angry with Israel and removed them from his presence...." In contrast to His treatment of Israel, we will see in this week's study that God blessed Shiphrah and Puah for their courageous stand.

As you read Exodus 1, think about how a loving God must feel about the many lives that are being taken through the widespread practice of abortion. How will God judge America?

O. T. PASSAGE THIS WEEK: Exodus 1

SPECIAL PRAYER NEEDS THIS WEEK:

ANSWERS TO PRAYER THIS WEEK:

AVAILABILITY

The name of the one ₁midwife₁ was Shiphrah, and the name of the other Puah (Exod. 1:15, KJV). Read Exodus 1.

Babies—how I love them!
Each new life is a thrill to me
As though it were my very own.
Each mother is my sister.
I live vicariously
Through each young mother's life.
I never will give birth
But I can help give life.

—Shiphrah

Midwifery, as the forerunner of the modern nursing profession, was a demanding occupation. Shiphrah and Puah, the Hebrew midwives mentioned in Exodus 1, probably had to be available to their "clientele" at any hour of the day or night. They may have worked with the Egyptian women as well as the Hebrew women, and the new generation of Egypt passed through their hands!

Verse 21 implies that Shiphrah and Puah were childless or perhaps unmarried. Like the nurse Deborah whose life we studied earlier, these two women exhibited a spirit of genuine concern for other people's children. They could have spent their lives feeling cheated (that feeling is one of Satan's favorite traps), but instead they gave of their lives freely.

Teach me to really give, Father.
"BUT MUST I KEEP GIVING AND GIVING AGAIN?"
"AH, NO," SAID THE ANGEL—HIS EYES PIERCED ME THROUGH—
"JUST GIVE 'TIL THE MASTER QUITS GIVING TO YOU!"

—Unknown

SIMPLY TRUSTING EVERY DAY

And the Egyptians made the children of Israel to serve with rigour (Exod. 1:13, KJV). Read Psalm 128.

Today I'll hear from Jochebed, I'm sure.
Her time is coming soon
And Miriam waits impatiently
To see her little brother.
(She's so determined it's a he!)
Her father Amram works so hard;
I know it tears his heart apart
To see his children suffer now
For want of food and clothes.
He loves his family so!

—Shiphrah

Among those anxiously awaiting the arrival of a child were Amram and Jochebed (see Exod. 2:1; 6:20). (We will study the lives of Jochebed, Moses' mother, and Miriam, Moses' sister, in weeks 16 and 18.)

To the new king in Egypt, the Hebrews were like pests in need of extermination, and the visitors-turned-slaves were being used ruthlessly. (Does that remind you of a later era in history?) The Hebrews' resentment of the rough treatment must have been intensified by the knowledge that their children would face an equally desperate existence.

Current problems facing our children tear our hearts apart as we see them involved in situations that were unheard of when we were their age. We want to protect them, shelter them as much as possible—yet we must entrust their lives to the safekeeping of their heavenly Father.

Sometimes, Father, it seems like it's easier to worry than to trust You. I guess it's because I'm in the habit of worrying. Help me to learn to present my requests to You, Father, with thanksgiving instead of negative thoughts.

GOD LOVED ME SO MUCH THAT HE GAVE ME HIS SON—CAN I DO LESS IN RETURN?

UNCERTAINTY

And the king of Egypt spake to the Hebrew midwives (Exod. 1:15, KJV). Read Matthew 10:28-32, 42.

> *The Pharoah's called me—Puah too!*
> *Have we displeased him with our work?*
> *Perhaps he has a plan in mind. . .*
> *The Hebrews multiply each day.*
> *There are so many Hebrew boys;*
> *Their life of bondage is resolved*
> *Before they see the light of day.*
> *I wonder if Jehovah cares*
> *That these His children live as slaves.*
> *—Shiphrah*

It must have been very unusual for a humble Hebrew midwife to be called into the presence of the Pharaoh. Imagine their anxiety and uncertainty! What could he want of them? Had an Egyptian mother reported them for some unknown mishap? Did one of the royal household carry a grudge against them?

I imagine Shiphrah and Puah called out to Jehovah before they entered the royal grounds. That's certainly the best way to prepare our spirits for an unexpected, highly unpredictable encounter. Do you make a practice of preparatory prayer?

Father, I can't face this day alone. I have no way of knowing what even this hour will hold, and I need Your Spirit's guidance and wisdom. Thank You for teaching me to lean on You and to depend on Your Word.

PRAYER IS AS VITAL AS THE BREATH IN OUR LUNGS.

CHILD MURDER!

When you help the Hebrew women in childbirth and observe them on the delivery stool, if it is a boy, kill him; but if it is a girl, let her live (Exod. 1:16, NIV). Read Ezekiel 20:27-32; 23:36-39.

> *It's dastardly! Inhuman man*
> *To even think vile thoughts like these—*
> *And then to voice his evil plan,*
> *Commanding us to carry out*
> *His murderous schemes.*
> *Although he is my king,*
> *There is no doubt within my mind*
> *Which Lord I should obey.*
>
> *—Shiphrah*

This was the final straw! The midwives were responsible to obey their king up to a certain point, but they knew that this order could not be obeyed. Jehovah, the Giver of life, could not and would not condone the taking of life. (This is made very clear in the Ezekiel passage—the Israelites later chose to "sacrifice" their own children to heathen gods, making them as guilty as a Pharaoh.)

It's almost unbelievable that modern nurses are often asked to participate in basically the same kind of murder. Some of them have left the nursing profession rather than become an "accessory to the crime." As Christians we need to take a strong stand against the age-old crime of child murder that today is called abortion!

Father, we are so influenced by the world's thought patterns. Please give us Your gifts of discernment and wisdom as we face Satan's constant onslaught. Help me to find a firm foundation in Your Word.

THE GIVER OF LIFE CANNOT CONDONE THE TAKING OF LIFE.

TRUST AND OBEY

The midwives, however, feared God and did not do what the king of Egypt had told them to do; they let the boys live (Exod. 1:17, NIV). Read Daniel 6:1-28.

Ah, Jochebed, your son is born!
I have never seen a child like this!
Jehovah's blessing on his birth
Has touched your lives and ours as well.
We need not fear the Pharaoh's words.
The God who breathes new life within
Will save our lives from Pharaoh's hand,
And keep His hand upon your child.
                                        —Shiphrah

Like Daniel, who continued to pray against the king's orders, the midwives were courageous because they knew they were in the right! So often our minds are clouded with fear of the future because of underlying guilt concerning sin in our lives, but Shiphrah and Puah were confident that they were acting in obedience to God's rules of life and that He would protect them from Pharaoh's wrath.

"Perfect love casts out fear". . .and God is love personified! I need not fear the future for myself or my children if I have permanently given God the "driver's seat" of my life. As long as He's in control, I can even take a nap in the back seat!

Father, forgive me for taking over the driving time and again. I've messed up the trip so badly, Father, as I've weaved in and out of traffic and caused some accidents by my reckless driving. Help me to obey the STOP signs in Your Word and to understand when the light turns green.

WHO'S IN THE DRIVER'S SEAT OF YOUR LIFE?

THE BLESSINGS OF OBEDIENCE

And because the midwives feared God, he gave them families of their own (Exod. 1:21, NIV). Read 1 John 2:1-11.

> *God has rewarded faithfulness*
> *To His commandments and His Word!*
> *Because we have refused to kill,*
> *He gave new life to each of us.*
> *We now have families of our own*
> *Whom even Pharaoh cannot touch.*
> *God has proved that we can trust in Him;*
> *I'll never doubt His love again!*
>
> *—Shiphrah*

After all those years of delivering babies, perhaps Shiphrah and Puah had the happy privilege of delivering each other's children. What a truly blessed event it must have been as, for the first time in their lives, the sweet babies they held were their own!

What beautiful ways God has of rewarding His children for "services rendered"! "If anyone obeys his word, God's love is truly made complete in him" (1 John 2:5, NIV). Certainly no other blessing could have been as precious to Shiphrah and Puah. How has God blessed in your life? Do you keep a record of the answers God gives to your prayers? Think back over the years, and you'll be amazed. (Try keeping an "ASKS AND ANSWERS" notebook—start today!)

Father, I just don't praise You enough. Forgive me for taking so many blessings for granted. Teach me to be appreciative to You and to the people in my life. Thank You especially for _____ .

"COUNT YOUR BLESSINGS, NAME THEM ONE BY ONE."[1]

JOCHEBED: THE POWER OF PRAISE

Now a man of the house of Levi married a Levite woman and she became pregnant and gave birth to a son (Exod. 2:1, NIV).

Jochebed, the mother of Moses, would have had good reason to give up. She could have said, "I might as well let my son die; he'd be better off dead than living a life of slavery. There's no hope for us in Egypt. . .and Pharaoh will never let us leave."

But the meaning of Jochebed's name holds the clue to her attitude toward life: "Jehovah is glorious!" The meaning of a child's name, if explained to him and firmly impressed on his mind, can have a great effect on his life. It certainly seems as though this may have been true in Jochebed's case, for her attitude was not one of fear or resignation.

David said in Psalm 50:23, "God says. . .true praise is a worthy sacrifice; this really honors me. Those who walk my paths will receive salvation from the Lord" (LB) or, "to him that ordereth his conversation aright will I shew the salvation of God" (KJV).

What does that tell us about our walk and our talk?

Praise the Lord in all things,
Whether good or bad.
If you don't learn to be content,
You'll someday wish you had.
Problems show the person.
For all the world to see.
Is the Lord in full control
In each catastrophe?

O. T. PASSAGE THIS WEEK: Exodus 2:1-10

SPECIAL PRAYER NEEDS THIS WEEK:

ANSWERS TO PRAYER THIS WEEK:

IN EVERYTHING GIVE THANKS

Do not be anxious about anything, but in everything, by prayer and petition, with thanksgiving, present your requests to God (Phil. 4:6, NIV). Read Exodus 2:1-10 for background story.

They ask me how I can rejoice
When everything is going wrong.
The land of Goshen is filled with strife;
There's hardly room for all of us.
The kings no longer recognize
Our freedom, rights, or daily needs. . .
But yet I trust my God who works
In many strange, mysterious ways.
"Jehovah's glorious!" is my name,
And I will never doubt its truth.

—Jochebed

As we saw last week in Exodus 1, the time in which Jochebed was born was a very difficult time in the nation's history. The Pharaoh felt no obligation to Joseph's descendants, and he feared the potential of their rapidly increasing population. Brutal taskmasters mistreated and oppressed the Hebrew slaves, forcing them to work long, hard days, carrying heavy loads of mortar and brick to their neverending building projects.

It's easy to praise the Lord and to trust Him when things are going smoothly—but what about when things aren't going our way? Can we say with the Apostle Paul: "I have learned, in whatsoever state I am, therewith to be content" (Phil. 4:11, KJV)?

Father, as I pray for the problems within my family and other relationships and the larger problems within this troubled world, I thank You for the knowledge that You are in control. As I lay each burden at Your feet, enable me, Father, to leave it there.

HAPPINESS IS IN WANTING WHAT YOU HAVE, NOT HAVING WHAT YOU WANT.

EXALTED PEOPLE

Thou wilt keep him in perfect peace, whose mind is stayed on thee: because he trusteth in thee (Isa. 26:3, KJV). Read Acts 7:2-19.

Amram! What a man he is!
I feel so proud to be his wife.
Although he works as a poor slave,
He always holds his head so high.
His mother named him perfectly—
"Exalted people" we'll become.
I know that somehow God will guide
His people Israel from this land.

—Jochebed

Despite the troubled times, some of Jacob's descendants still clung tenaciously to the belief that Jehovah would deliver them from their oppressors. . .that the slave-race would once more become an "exalted people." Such was the family of Amram and Jochebed (their marriage and lineage is recorded in Exod. 2:1; 6:20; Num. 26:59). Amram's mother must have believed God's promises and taught Moses' father to pass on the heritage of his name.

God had promised Abraham that his descendants would possess the land of Canaan, even though old Abraham and Sarah had no child. That promise was eventually fulfilled. God promised to punish the nation that would enslave His people for four hundred years—and He did! God's promises can be trusted!

Thank You, Father, for reminding me that, in this world of changing values, You can be trusted. Forgive me for my tendency to waver. Thank You for Your perfect peace.

IF YOU WERE ARRESTED AND ACCUSED OF BEING A CHRISTIAN, WOULD THERE BE ENOUGH EVIDENCE TO CONVICT YOU?

PERFECT PEACE

For you created my inmost being; you knit me together in my mother's womb. I praise you because I am fearfully and wonderfully made (Ps. 139:13-14, NIV). Read Isaiah 26:3-21.

The midwives have been ordered to
Destroy the Hebrew baby boys.
And now I bear another life.
If it's a boy, will they obey
The Pharaoh's cruel command to kill?
Jehovah God, I trust You now;
I put this life into Your hands.

—Jochebed

No doubt word of Pharaoh's command to the midwives (recorded in Exod. 1:15-16) soon spread among the Israelites. Women soon to give birth must especially have reacted to the horror of such a command. Pharaoh's cruel order must have struck fear to Jochebed's heart, but she learned to trust God with her son Moses' life very early in his life. . .even before he was born! Learning to trust—what a difficult lesson it is for all of us!

Dedicating a child to the Lord in a worship service may be easier than letting him follow the call of God at a later point in his life. . .especially if you don't agree with his understanding of God's will. Or perhaps he is breaking your heart in totally ignoring God's will for his life—can you trust God in that situation?

Thank You, Father, for the way in which You've planned my life and the lives of my family even before we were born. Thank You for Your watch-care over us. Help me to relax in Your perfect peace of mind and heart.

"WORRY IS A RESPONSIBILITY GOD NEVER INTENDED US TO HAVE."[1]

PERFECT PLAN

All the days ordained for me were written in your book before one of them came to be (Ps. 139:16, NIV). Read Psalm 125.

Our beautiful boy-child has been saved!
The midwives serve a greater Lord
Than kings of Egypt—praise to God!
And you, my child, you will surely live
To praise the Lord with your own lips.
I have a feeling that your name
Will ring down corridors of time.

—Jochebed

Perhaps Jochebed had wondered what the midwives' reaction to Pharaoh's order would be. After all, their lives were at stake! Or perhaps Moses' mother knew Shiphrah and Puah well enough to know that they would obey God no matter what! Perhaps, when they saved her baby, she took courage from their courage and disobeyed Pharaoh's new order—to throw the baby into the river (Exod. 1:17—2:2).

Is my life as a Christian consistent enough that people have no doubt about the stand I will take on controversial issues? Is my knowledge of God's Word extensive enough to give me a firm foundation? Or am I like the double-minded person spoken about in the first chapter of James, who tosses back and forth like a wave of the sea? Am I "strong and very courageous" (Josh. 1:7, NIV), as Joshua was commanded to be?

Father, I thank You for the stability You have given to my life. Thank You for Your precious Word and the principles that lay a firm foundation for my life. Help me to search out those principles and to apply them courageously on a daily basis.

"GOD EXPECTS HIS CHILDREN TO BE SO CONFIDENT IN HIM THAT IN ANY CRISIS THEY ARE THE RELIABLE ONES."[2]

FAITH REWARDED

If I rise on the wings of the dawn, if I settle on the far side of the sea, even there your hand will guide me, your right hand will hold me fast (Ps. 139:9-10, NIV). Read Psalm 135.

> *Our plan worked just as we had hoped!*
> *The princess saw the baby's bed*
> *And wanted my son as her own.*
> *She pays me well to nurse my son,*
> *And he is mine to hold again.*
> *My heart cries out in praise to You*
> *For giving back my son to me.*
> *Jehovah, You are glorious!*
>
> *—Jochebed*

Here again we see evidenced Jochebed's trust in God (see Exod. 2:3-9; Acts 7:20-21). Jochebed remained calm enough to impart her own peace of mind to her daughter Miriam, who played her well-rehearsed part perfectly. Perhaps Jochebed was resourceful enough to realize that since the Egyptians had a special reverence for the life-giving Nile, Moses would be safest there. (Ironically, she was still obeying the Pharaoh's command to throw the boy-children into the river!)

What kind of spirit do my children reflect? When Mom hits a bad day for one reason or another, does the whole house know it—and suffer because of it? Or is everyone in the family aware that in crisis situations Mom turns to the heavenly Father for wisdom and assurance?

Forgive me, Father, for the many times in which I certainly have not evidenced a quiet spirit. Calm the tensions within me, Father; help me to remember to pray—with thanksgiving—about everything. Thank You for always being ready to listen.

"THERE IS A QUIET PLACE. . .WHERE GOD CAN SOOTHE MY TROUBLED MIND."[3]

A SPECIAL PLAN

Train up a child in the way he should go: and when he is old, he will not depart from it (Prov. 22:6, KJV). Read Psalm 136.

The time has come to give him up!
Although the mother in me fears,
I know the Lord who has kept him safe
Will keep him through these dangerous years.
To Pharaoh's daughter he returns. . . .
She has named him Moses—he's "saved from"
A certain death to serve You, Lord.
You have a special plan for him;
He's saved to save his people.

—Jochebed

Verse 10 of the second chapter of Exodus simply tells us that when the child grew older, Jochebed took him to Pharaoh's daughter and he became her son. There is no note of panic here—simply the continued calm assurance that God would take care of Moses. We can be sure that Jochebed's prayers followed Moses through the years in Pharaoh's palace, to the land of Midian, and back to Egypt once again. . . yet she made no attempt to hold him back from the course God had charted for his life.

Trusting in time of trouble—it certainly seems that Jochebed had mastered that lesson. Have I?

Thank You, Father, for this lesson in trust that I've learned through the story of Jochebed. Help me to remember what I've learned when I tend to be fearful, overprotective, possessive. Thank You that You care more about my family than I do.

I'D RATHER WALK IN THE DARK WITH GOD THAN WALK ALONE IN THE LIGHT.

ZIPPORAH: A GLIMPSE OF MOSES' WIFE

Now a priest of Midian had seven daughters. . . .Moses agreed to stay with the man, who gave his daughter Zipporah to Moses in marriage (Exod. 2:21, NIV).

We've all heard so much about Moses, but most people probably couldn't even say who his wife was. Though he was one of the greatest leaders of all time, his wife is called by name in only three passages.

Her name was Zipporah, and the Bible tells us very little about her—just enough to give us a few clues about her personality. She did not seem to play a part in either his lofty plans or his tremendous hardships.

Zipporah disappeared from Moses' life for some time; there is no mention of her from Exodus 4 through Exodus 18. Then we hear her name again, but with no accompanying details. What do we learn from this lengthy "silent period" in Zipporah's life? Did Moses neglect his family, was he afraid for their safety, or was Zipporah such a liability to Moses that God had to put her aside so that her husband could accomplish his God-given task? We'll never know the answer to that question here on earth.

Let's take time to reflect on Christ's words: "Anyone who loves his father or mother more than me is not worthy of me; and anyone who does not take his cross and follow me is not worthy of me. Whoever finds his life will lose it, and whoever loses his life for my sake will find it" (Matt. 10:37-39, NIV).

What does that mean in my life. . .and yours? Does my life center around *my* goals—or God's plan for my life?

O. T. PASSAGE THIS WEEK: Exodus 2:11—4:31; 18:1-27

SPECIAL PRAYER NEEDS THIS WEEK:

ANSWERS TO PRAYER THIS WEEK:

RUNNING

But Moses ran away into the land of Midian (Exod. 2:15, LB). Read
Exodus 2:11-22.

> The tall, young, strong Egyptian—Moses!
> (He tells me that he's really Hebrew,
> But what's the difference? I don't know.)
> I only know that he attracts me.
> His regal bearing and his poise
> Are such a contrast to the shepherds
> Who fight with us for pasture.
> His courtesy makes me feel like Pharaoh's daughter.
> —Zipporah

Zipporah—another shepherdess with stars in her eyes!
Perhaps Zipporah was the oldest of Jethro's (also called Reuel
in chapter 2) seven daughters. Certainly she must have been
attractive for Moses to have chosen her, for he had been surrounded by beautiful women in Pharaoh's court. But had he
been taught by Pharaoh's daughter to look for beauty of
spirit?

Chapter 2 of Exodus shows us the differing backgrounds
and differing beliefs of Moses and Zipporah. Those differ-
ences would complicate a rather hurried marriage. Moses had
run away from a problem situation, but as is so often true
when we run away, his temporary "haven" would soon sprout
its own areas of conflict.

I remember, Father, different times in my life when I ran
away—only to encounter even greater problems. Teach me,
Father, to deal with the situations that come my way with
wisdom from Your Word.
**IN JESUS' LIFE EVERY PROJECT WAS DISCIPLINED TO
THE WILL OF HIS FATHER.**

THE NEED TO UNDERSTAND

Now I am going to send you to Pharaoh, to demand that he let you lead my people out of Egypt (Exod. 3:10, LB). Read Exodus 3.

> *I cannot understand his dreams—*
> *Strange dreams they are to me.*
> *He speaks of rescuing his people*
> *From the Egyptian Pharaoh.*
> *Why can't he just be happy here with me?*
> *Why can't he just forget the past*
> *And be content to live a normal life?*
>
> *—Zipporah*

Zipporah didn't understand Moses, and she didn't understand his dreams. She didn't understand his loyalty to his people Israel or to the God of his fathers. Did she even try to understand? It seems Zipporah was totally unable to give her husband the help and loyalty he needed at this crisis point in his life.

Am I capable of caring enough for someone—my husband, my neighbor, my child—to forget my prejudices and presuppositions and attempt to see things from their perspective? Can I forget my list of impossibilities long enough to believe that "I can do all things through Christ" (Phil. 4:13)?

Thank You, Father, for bringing me out of myself, for leading me beyond myself in a new understanding of other people and of You.

IF HUMAN LOVE DOES NOT CARRY A MAN BEYOND HIMSELF, IT IS NOT LOVE.

YOUR FATHER THE FANATIC

When you have led the people out of Egypt, you shall worship God here upon this mountain (Exod. 3:12, LB). Read Exodus 4:1-17.

I understand my husband less and less.
I thought our Gershom's birth—a son!—
Would turn his thoughts away from his strange dreams,
Would make this man content to stay at home.
But even Gershom's name reflects his thoughts:
"I am a wanderer in a foreign land."
Why is this land still foreign, Moses?
Is Midian never to become your home?
                                        —Zipporah

Zipporah probably became more and more discontented as she realized that the man who had seemed so much more attractive than the "local yokels" now seemed unable to give her the normal, happy life that the other shepherd families enjoyed. Moses was always off dreaming somewhere, talking to bushes, or playing with snakes. . .sometimes Zipporah wondered if her husband were completely sane.

We often find it difficult to understand someone whose life is totally dedicated to God, because we do not realize the inner struggles that have taken place before anyone becomes completely submissive to God's will. It is easier to call someone a "fanatic" than to share his total involvement in spiritual things.

I must admit, Father, that I've always been a bit afraid of being called a fanatic. I just don't want people to think I'm peculiar. . .but help me, Father, to be most concerned about what *You* think of me.

"TELL GOD YOU ARE READY TO BE OFFERED, AND GOD WILL PROVE HIMSELF TO BE ALL YOU EVER DREAMED HE WOULD BE."[1]

THERE'S JUST NO RESPECT AROUND HERE

Tell them, 'Jehovah, the God of your ancestors Abraham, Isaac, and Jacob, has sent me to you' (Exod. 3:15, LB). Read Exodus 4:18-19.

> *Another child has come into our home.*
> *Now surely Moses will be more content*
> *To stay at home and raise his family.*
> *And yet the past still haunts his mind*
> *And Eliezer's name—"God is my help"—*
> *Reminds his father of another time*
> *When his strange God delivered him*
> *From Pharaoh's hand. But I realize*
> *That neither God nor Pharaoh ever let him go.*
> *—Zipporah*

Many wives have used the legitimate concerns of finances, upkeep and care of the home, or the children's upbringing and education as a means of detouring their husbands from God's calling for his life. The meaning of Eliezer's name—"God is my help"—shows, however, that no matter how Zipporah felt, Moses' mind set had not changed.

It is obvious, however, in Exodus 3 and 4 that Moses was lacking in self-confidence. Did this have something to do with his marriage relationship? Zipporah did not have the advantage of Paul's advice in Ephesians 5:33 (as we do!): "And let the wife see that she respects and reverences her husband—that she notices him, regards him, honors him, prefers him, venerates and esteems him; and that she defers to him, praises him, and loves and admires him exceedingly" (*Amplified*).

Father. . .I've got a lot to learn.

"THE STAMP OF A SAINT IS THAT HE CAN WAIVE HIS OWN RIGHTS."²

BATTLE OVER CIRCUMCISION

You will clothe your sons and daughters with the best of Egypt (Exod. 3:22, LB). Read Exodus 4:20-31.

So here we are—the time has come
Just as I felt for years it would.
We're on our way to Egypt. How I fear
What will become of us!

Jehovah—great Jehovah!—has reminded Moses
That Gershom was not circumcised,
That bloody custom I could never understand.
I would rather be a widow than go on like this.
—Zipporah

Circumcision was instituted by God as a part of the covenant between God and Abraham. It was a sign of Abraham's faith that God would carry out His promise to bless the Hebrew nation. Omission of the circumcision was much more than forgetting an ancient ritual; it was a direct disobedience to God's Word and a definite lack of faith.

Zipporah simply did not understand her husband's God. She had had little or no teaching of His faithfulness in the past, and she could not trust Him with her family's present or future. How could she accept that her husband had been called of God to save an entire nation when she didn't respect his leadership within their own family?

Father, I often have problems trusting You with *all* areas of my life and my family's lives. It seems easier to trust You in some areas than in others. Help me especially to trust You in this area: _____ .

SUBMISSION MEANS THAT A WIFE TRUSTS GOD TO LEAD HER AND HER FAMILY THROUGH HER HUSBAND.

SEPARATION AND REUNION

A worthy wife is her husband's joy and crown; the other kind corrodes his strength and tears down everything he does (Prov. 12:4, LB). Read Exodus 18:1-27.

Sometimes I felt a twinge of guilt
At letting him go on alone.
My father says I never tried
To understand this man of God,
That Moses too feared the unknown,
Needed my loyalty and love.
I thought he needed only God.

Perhaps someday, when Moses has fulfilled
His crazy dreams—or tired of them—
We'll have a chance to try again.

—Zipporah

"Word soon reached. . .Midian about all the wonderful things God had done for his people and for Moses" (Exod. 18:1, LB). At that point it seems that Zipporah was proud to be recognized as Moses' wife once again—now that he had proved himself! Moses had sent Zipporah back home to Midian, possibly for a variety of reasons. Perhaps he felt he just couldn't handle her problems and Israel's too.

The Bible tells us nothing whatever about Moses' reaction to his reunion with Zipporah in chapter 18, although it's obvious he was happy to see his father-in-law and to obtain his wise advice. Moses could have rejected Zipporah just as she had rejected his beliefs, but I rather think that he profited from his experiences as leader of a nation and became a patient husband and a wise father.

Father, thank You for helping me see that the people in Your Word were just as fallible and human as I am. Thank You for letting me know that there's hope for my personality to change as I become conformed to the image of Your Son. **"TRIBULATION WORKETH PATIENCE" (Rom. 5:3, KJV).**

MIRIAM: THE UNWITTING MUTINEER

Then Miriam the prophetess, Aaron's sister, took a tambourine in her hand, and all the women followed her, with tambourines and dancing. Miriam sang to them. . . (Exod. 15:20-21, NIV).

Sing unto the Lord, sing praise unto the Lord,
For He has triumphed gloriously!
Sing unto the Lord, sing praise unto the Lord,
The horse and rider He has thrown into the sea.
Sing unto the Lord, sing praise unto the Lord,
Sing a joyous song of victory.

Adapted from Exodus 15:21

We can visualize Miriam's face lifted to the skies as she leads Israel in her song of praise. In her face there is strength of character, perseverance, determination—characteristics cultivated by a life dedicated to the struggle of the young nation of Israel. Miriam was a prophetess—a woman inspired to teach the will of God.

Yet in such a strong personality it is almost inevitable that the meaning of her name should be fulfilled—"rebellion"! A self-sufficient person like Miriam may see dependence on others as a weakness. . .and Miriam may have viewed Moses' family responsibilities (Num. 12:1) as a hindrance to his leadership of her "one true love," the nation of Israel.

Even though it seems she repented of her criticism against Moses, the seeds of rebellion had been sown.

As we study this strong personality, we need to realize the need to set the right example for others through our actions and *reactions*. Someone is always watching!

O. T. PASSAGE THIS WEEK: Exodus 15—17; Numbers 12:1-6; 20:1-13

SPECIAL PRAYER NEEDS THIS WEEK:

ANSWERS TO PRAYER THIS WEEK:

SATISFIED TO BE SINGLE

The Lord hath appeared of old unto me, saying, Yea, I have loved thee
with an everlasting love: therefore with lovingkindness have I drawn thee.
Again I will build thee, and thou shalt be built, O virgin of Israel (Jer.
31:3-4, KJV). Read Exodus 15:1-26.

> *I have always known, since I was just a girl,*
> *That God would lead His people out.*
> *"Jehovah's glorious!" I was taught;*
> *"Exalted people" we were called.*
> *My parents' faith was deep and strong:*
> *God would fulfill His covenant,*
> *Fulfill the meanings of their names.*
> *I feel God's love upon my life.*
>
> *—Miriam*

The meaning of a name, if properly impressed upon a child's mind, can have a great influence on his life. Small wonder that the home of Amram and Jochebed (parents of Moses, Aaron, and Miriam) produced such a leadership trio! Mom and Dad had undoubtedly passed on their heritage to their children. . .and Israel had become the focal point of Miriam's life.

Miriam the prophetess—alone but not lonely! She had found fulfillment in the spiritual leadership of her people. Is God calling you to a similar leadership role, and asking you to devote *all* your energies and abilities to Him?

Father, I know that You want what is best for me. There are so many other things vying for my attention in this noisy, seductive world. Help me to be still so that I can hear Your voice.

"IF YOU GIVE GOD YOUR RIGHT TO YOURSELF, HE WILL MAKE A HOLY EXPERIMENT OUT OF YOU. GOD'S EXPERIMENTS ALWAYS SUCCEED!"[1]

GRUMBLE, GRUMBLE

Now the man Moses was very meek, above all the men which were upon the face of the earth (Num. 12:3, KJV). Read Exodus 16; 17:1-7.

> It's unbelievable to me
> How quickly people can forget!
> Already they neglect to praise. . .
> Instead, complaints and murmurs rise.
> They murmur against Moses too—
> My brother has a thankless task.
> He takes it humbly, but I know
> His heart is sorely grieved.
>
> —Miriam

"Moses was the humblest man on earth" (LB). How else could he have put up with the ungrateful spirits of the people whom he had led out of bondage! It seems they never thought about the fact that Moses had given up life in the palace for a life of itinerant, thankless leadership.

Am I a "grumbler"? Do I immediately latch on to any problem? What is my attitude toward those in authority over me? Do I recognize that they have needs too? Or do I expect perfection of them. . .and react with scathing criticism when they trip on the pedestal I've built for them?

Father, help me to remember that my expectations are from You, and You alone. Help me not to expect so much of other people, or to feel so disillusioned when they disappoint me. Help me to be as concerned about meeting the needs of others as I am about their meeting my needs.

"GOD ASSURES US THAT THE HEART OF ONE WHO IS IN AUTHORITY IS IN HIS HAND, AND THAT HE TURNS IT IN THE SAME WAY HE DOES A MEANDERING RIVER BY USING THE PRESSURE OF THE CURRENT AND TIME."[2]

DISCORD IN THE CAMP

Let the elders that rule well be counted worthy of double honour, especially they who labour in the word and doctrine. . . . The labourer is worthy of his reward (1 Tim. 5:17-18, KJV). Read Numbers 12:1-16.

Why did she come into our lives?
Why does he need a woman? Why?
Did marriage work for him before?
Can't God fulfill his every need?
My love is for Israel and our God
Who has chosen Moses. . .Aaron. . .me.
Our unity of spirit is gone;
She has torn apart our family.

—Miriam

We cannot be sure if Moses' wife (spoken of in Numbers 12:1) is Zipporah or a second wife. This footnote taken from The Living Bible is helpful: "Apparently they (Miriam and Aaron) were referring to his wife Zipporah, the Midianite daughter of Reuel; for the land of Midian from which she came was sometimes called Cush. But areas of Ethiopia and Babylon were also known as Cush, so it is possible that the reference is to a second wife of Moses. It is indeterminate from the text as to whether the criticism was because she was a Gentile or (if she was a Cushite from Ethiopia) because of her color."

In either case, Miriam and Aaron were unhappy with Moses' choice of a wife—and God was unhappy with their critical spirits. What kind of spirit does God see in me?

I realize, Father, that some days my spirit is very critical. Forgive me for taking out my frustrations on my family and those around me. Help me to be forgiving to others as You have forgiven me.

CRITICISM BRINGS ABOUT NERVOUSNESS, WORRY, AND DEPRESSION!

18 — Thursday

THEY GET ALL THE CREDIT

Now we ask you, brothers, to respect those who work hard among you, who are over you in the Lord and who admonish you. Hold them in the highest regard in love because of their work. Live in peace with each other (1 Thess. 5:12-13, NIV). Read Philippians 2:5-8.

> If Moses needs a woman, then____
> He's not dependent on our God,
> And God can speak through each of us
> As well as through this man of clay.
> Why, had it not been for my words,
> My brother would not live today.
> I spoke to Pharaoh's daughter—now
> Perhaps I too will lead Israel!
>
> —Miriam

Miriam may have looked back across the years and said to herself: "Moses and Aaron get all the credit, just because they're men—but if it hadn't been for me, Moses would not even have survived! I'm tired of living in their shadow! It's about time I get some recognition! The great woman behind the great man is about to step out!"

The big I! What havoc it can wreak in our lives! "I did this or I could do that. . .if someone would only recognize me!" And, in bitterness and rebellion, we step out to show the world—and sooner or later, fall flat on our faces!

Father, I know that true joy comes in fulfilling the role in which You have placed me. Help me to have a servant's spirit, to find happiness in making others successful. I need to learn to wash others' feet, Father, and to admit mine are dirty too. **"IF YOU HAVE BEEN SHREWD IN FINDING OUT THE DEFECTS OF OTHERS, REMEMBER THAT WILL BE EXACTLY THE MEASURE GIVEN TO YOU!"**[3]

RESULTS OF SLANDER

Obey your leaders and submit to their authority. They keep watch over you as men who must give an account. Obey them so that their work will be a joy, not a burden, for that would be of no advantage to you (Heb. 13:17, NIV). Read James 3:1-18.

What have I done? My body's white—
The dreaded white of leprosy!
My sin of arrogance and pride
Has brought Jehovah's wrath on me!
Rebellion flared within my heart
Once bitterness had taken root.
I slandered my own brother's name. . .
And now my sin has found me out.

—Miriam

James pulls no punches in chapter 3 in discussing the terrors of the tongue: "What enormous damage it can do. . . The tongue is a flame of fire. It is full of wickedness, and poisons every part of the body. And the tongue is set on fire by hell itself, and can turn our whole lives into a blazing flame of destruction and disaster" (James 3:5-6, LB).

When we bought our home, a plaque was left hanging in the bathroom (of all places!) that gave us this little gem of wisdom every time we meditated in that room: "Even a fish wouldn't get caught if it kept its mouth shut!" Good advice, huh?

I know I talk too much, Father. Help me to think before I talk and while I'm talking. Help me to always speak in kindness and in truth. Deliver me from gossip.

"THE REASON WE SEE HYPOCRISY AND FRAUD AND UNREALITY IN OTHERS IS BECAUSE THEY ARE ALL IN OUR OWN HEARTS."[4]

TIME FOR REFLECTION

Remember what the Lord thy God did unto Miriam by the way (Deut. 24:9, KJV). But he that regardeth reproof is prudent (Prov. 15:5, KJV). Read Numbers 20:1-13; Deuteronomy 7:12-19.

> *My brother is so quick to forgive. . . .*
> *He begged the Lord to heal me of*
> *The dread disease I had brought about*
> *Through hatred, anger, bitterness.*
> *I have so much to think about*
> *These seven days outside the camp.*
> *My body is healing, and I feel*
> *My mind and heart are healing too.*
>
> *—Miriam*

The Lord did strike Miriam with leprosy—and yet she brought it on herself through rebellion and disobedience. Later, in Deuteronomy 7:15, the Lord promised to take away all Israel's sickness—especially the diseases of Egypt they remembered so well—if they would simply obey His commandments.

The tragedy is that they did not obey. When Miriam died, her body was scarcely in the grave before the people, perhaps frustrated by the loss of a valued friend, held an angry, rebellious protest meeting. . .and repeated Miriam's mistake. Our example lives on even after we die!

Father, help me not to hem others in with my expectations of them. Please bridge the gaps that I have created between myself and others with Your love. Thank You even for the painful reproofs that have proved Your love through Your chastening.

"LIFE SERVES BACK IN THE COIN YOU PAY."[5]

DAUGHTERS OF ZELOPHEHAD: FIVE SISTERS WHO WORKED AND BELIEVED TOGETHER

The story of the daughters of Zelophehad is a welcome contrast to the jealousy and mutual antagonism of Leah and Rachel. It was during one of many long days spent in compiling a census (in preparation for the entering and dividing of the Promised Land) that the incident told in Numbers 27:1-4 took place.

We can imagine Moses hard at work in the tabernacle when the sun's rays were blocked by the figures of five sisters standing in the doorway. They had come with a petition; before the princes and leaders of the nation they told how their father, a descendant of Joseph, had died in the wilderness—without a male heir. The five sisters boldly requested a possession along with their father's brothers.

The story of the daughters of Zelophehad is a landmark in the history of women's rights. God was very fair in His answer to those five courageous women who knew what they needed.

When the land was actually divided, the women again presented their claim, this time to the new leader, Joshua: "The Lord commanded Moses to give us an inheritance among our brothers" (Josh. 17:4). And Joshua followed through! This time there was no question about God's will.

"How ironic that God is blamed when it is He who is hurt most by male-female tugs-of-war. He is the only one who can see what might have been."[1]

O. T. PASSAGE THIS WEEK: Numbers 27:1-11; 36:1-12; Joshua 17:3-4

SPECIAL PRAYER NEEDS THIS WEEK:

ANSWERS TO PRAYER THIS WEEK:

THE NEED FOR SECURITY

But seek ye first the kingdom of God, and his righteousness; and all these things shall be added unto you (Matt. 6:33, KJV). Read Numbers 27:1-11.

> *Our father is dead and we have nothing to look forward*
> *to:*
> *No home to call our own,*
> *No land to make our dwelling place,*
> *To plant a garden, flowers, and shrubs.*
> *And what is worse,*
> *Our father's name will disappear.*
> *We must protest!*
> *Our father's land should be ours too.*
>
> *—Noah ("rest")*

Security is a major need in humans—especially in us women—and "a place of our own" seems essential to fulfillment of that need. As teen-agers we clamor for a room that will insure our privacy; later, we take delight in personalizing our own apartment or home. Living out of a suitcase on a regular basis is usually much more difficult for a woman than a man. It's very important to most of us to have a "nest."

Zelophehad's daughter Noah had good reason to want a place to "rest" (the meaning of her name). We can sympathize with her in feeling that a property settlement was very important, that security was necessary. . .but on days when our building-blocks of security come toppling down around us, remember to "consider the lilies of the field" (Matt. 6:28, KJV).

Thank You, Father, for the knowledge that our stay here—and everything we own—is only temporary and therefore not really a priority. Help me to remember that on days when inflation appears to be an unbeatable enemy and I'm ready to throw in the towel.

"IT IS THE THINGS THAT ARE RIGHT AND NOBLE AND GOOD FROM THE NATURAL STANDPOINT THAT [CAN] KEEP US BACK FROM GOD'S BEST."[2]

THE NEED FOR ENCOURAGEMENT

Praise be to the God and Father of our Lord Jesus Christ, the Father of compassion and the God of all comfort, who comforts us in all our troubles, so that we can comfort those in any trouble with the comfort we ourselves have received from God (2 Cor. 1:3-4, NIV). Read Philippians 4:4-8.

The men will say the fact our father died without a son
Is proof God didn't see fit
To give our family a possession in the land.
They will say His will is clear. . .
And we should stand back and give way
To those who have a legal claim.
> *—Mahlah ("sickness, disease")*

Mahlah, probably the oldest sister, may have been afflicted with sickness early in her life. Perhaps it struck again and again, causing days of depression and a negative attitude toward life in general. It would have been easy to just give up without trying—after all, what "women's rights" had ever been taken into consideration up to this point? But, encouraging each other, the sisters allowed no arguments to suppress the conviction of the justice of their cause.

There are times to stand in the wings and pray—and there are times to jump into the ring! (It's safe to say, however, that time in the ring should always be preceded by prayer in the wings!) Ask God for wisdom. . .and then stand your ground!

Help me, Father, to encourage others as I have been encouraged, to comfort as You have comforted me. Help me to supply that needed bit of strength at just the right time to someone in need.

TIME IN THE RING SHOULD ALWAYS BE PRECEDED BY PRAYER IN THE WINGS!

BUCKING THE CURRENT

And we desire that every one of you do shew the same diligence to the full assurance of hope unto the end: that ye be not slothful, but followers of them who through faith and patience inherit the promises (Heb. 6:11-12, KJV). Read Hebrews 11:32-40.

> *The customs of our day forbid our freedom*
> *To possess the land. . .*
> *But do we have the courage*
> *To protest those laws?*
> *And more important—*
> *Are those laws of God*
> *Or just of men?*
>
> —Hoglah ("a hunted bird")

Hoglah's name has a significant meaning: the partridge was known for sitting on eggs it had not laid, and gathering young that were not its own. Hoglah may have been accused of trying to claim land that—according to, perhaps, some of the men—was not legally hers. But the sisters' faith reached out to apprehend all that God was ready to give.

Any time we protest the status quo we can expect to have some unfair statements made about us. The test of our standing with God is whether we can evaluate those statements for any fragments of helpful truth. . .and then forget about them. To continue to fret and stew about injustice reflects self-centeredness.

Thank You, Father, for the inspiration of many who "against hope believed in hope" (Rom. 4:18, KJV). Thank You for the "hope of glory"—Christ in me.

"SELF-CONSCIOUSNESS IS THE FIRST THING THAT WILL UPSET THE COMPLETENESS OF THE LIFE IN GOD."[3]

AT PEACE WITH OURSELVES

I press toward the mark for the prize of the high calling of God in Christ Jesus (Phil. 3:14, KJV). Read Philippians 4:9-13.

There is room enough for us and all the rest!
God would not have us go without our rightful share
Because we are not men!
This land that flows with milk and honey
Flows for our needs too. . . .
God loves us just as much
As He loves each of them!

—Tirzah ("pleasantness")

With a name symbolic of pleasantness, we can picture Tirzah, the youngest daughter, as a girl at peace with herself, confident that the Lord was concerned about her needs and the needs of her sisters—and that He would provide.

We often base our judgments of God and the people around us by our own self-image. If we are unhappy with ourselves and our achievements (or lack of them), we tend to judge others harshly as well. If, on the other hand, we are content and fulfilled, we are able to believe in other people and to be an encouragement to them.

Help me, Father, to be content in whatever state or situation I am—whether I have much or little. Help me to remember that true significance and security are not a result of my finding myself—or my "place in the sun"—but of finding Your will for my life.

IF WE ARE UNHAPPY WITH OURSELVES, WE TEND TO JUDGE OTHERS HARSHLY AS WELL.

THE STRENGTH OF UNITY

Till we all come in the unity of the faith (Eph. 4:13, KJV). Read Ephesians 4:11-16.

Moses, we need to talk to you. . .
To plead our case, present our views.
Please listen as we speak!
We have respect for laws that are of God,
But should our father's name be lost
Because he has no son?
We need a place to live, to make our home.
Please intercede for us as you would men.
—Milcah ("counsel")

The story of the daughters of Zelophehad teaches us the value and strength of corporate faith. When one might have faltered, five stood together to claim and to possess. There is not only strength in real spiritual unity, but also the enjoyment of the fullest privilege and blessings.

Many Bible stories emphasize the effect of one individual's faith on the history of a nation and the unfolding of God's purposes. But God does not expect us to be isolated warriors in the battle; if one may chase a thousand, two can put ten thousand to flight (Deut. 32:30).

Help me, Father, to explore the practical implications of Your promise: "Where two or three are gathered together in my name, there am I in the midst" (Matt. 18:20, KJV). Show me the someone with whom I can share prayer power.

GOD DOES NOT EXPECT US TO BE ISOLATED WARRIORS IN THE BATTLE.

FAITH REWARDED

That I may apprehend ₍take hold of₎ that for which also I am apprehended of Christ Jesus (Phil. 3:12, KJV). Read Numbers 27:7-8; 36:1-12; Joshua 17:3-4.

> God is on our side!
> He heard our pleas;
> He is concerned about our needs!
> A mighty God who lives on high—
> His ears were open to our cry!
> He too will find us husbands now
> Within our tribe, within His will.
>   —The daughters of Zelophehad

Moses recognized the reasonable nature of the sisters' request, but perhaps he did not know how to handle the situation, for up to that point *only* male heirs had inherited positions and possessions. So Moses submitted the problem to the Lord—how, we are not told—and the divine reply was emphatic: "The daughters of Zelophehad speak right: thou shalt surely give them a possession."

So early in the history of Israel—before Jordan was crossed—these women trusted God to fulfill His promise once the Promised Land was actually under their feet. They claimed and obtained the promises by faith; when the answer from the Lord came, they still had to wait for many years (and remind Joshua of the promise) before they could actually claim their possession. But their faith was richly rewarded.

Help me, Father, to hang in there. . .help me not to be "double-minded". . .not to waver (James 1:6, 8).

WE LIMIT THE LORD BY REMEMBERING WHAT WE HAVE ALLOWED HIM TO DO FOR US IN THE PAST.

RAHAB: THE SCARLET CORD— HER SYMBOL OF FAITH

Then Joshua son of Nun secretly sent two spies from Shittim. 'Go, look over the land,' he said, 'especially Jericho.' So they went and entered the house of a prostitute named Rahab and stayed there (Josh. 2:1, NIV).

Do you realize that a former prostitute was one of the only two women named in the Hall of Faith (Heb. 11)? Many times throughout the Scriptures God used people from outside the nation of Israel to be a part of His great redemptive plan. Rahab was not only an outsider to the "chosen people"— she was (as the Apostle Paul said of himself) one of the worst of sinners.

And yet Jesus put wrong thoughts in the same category as adultery and fornication (Matt. 15:19). Lying and slander (or gossip?) are just as sinful as theft and murder.

Jesus said in John 8:7, "He that is without sin among you, let him first cast a stone" (KJV). He was referring to a woman who was taken in adultery in His own day, but He could have been speaking of Rahab. Perhaps Israelites looked at Rahab askance, but she probably had more faith in their God than they did.

"By faith—because she believed in God and his power— Rahab the harlot did not die with all the others in her city when they refused to obey God" (Heb. 11:31, LB).

So who among us can condemn Rahab, who grew up in the pagan city of Jericho with no teaching of sin and no exposure to God's Word? What does that say about our relationships to people "on the other side of the tracks"?

Are we condemning. . .or concerned?

O. T. PASSAGE THIS WEEK: Joshua 2:1-24; 6:1-25

SPECIAL PRAYER NEEDS THIS WEEK:

ANSWERS TO PRAYER THIS WEEK:

IS THAT ALL THERE IS?

Don't let the excitement of being young cause you to forget about your Creator. . . . Remember your Creator now while you are young, before the silver cord of life snaps (Eccles. 12:1, 6, LB). Read Joshua 2:1-24.

> *Can this be all there is to life?*
> *I've certainly had my fill*
> *Of stupid, leering, drunken men*
> *Who pay to have me for a night—*
> *I cannot bear another one!*
> *Though all the town knows who I am,*
> *Behind this front lives someone else*
> *Who seeks for more—much more—in life.*
> *—Rahab*

Rahab, the well-known "hostess" of Jericho! On the surface she may have appeared prosperous and satisfied with her life; business was good at the town's "Dew-Drop-Inn." That just the opposite was true is proved by her readiness to give up everything she once valued in hopes of a better life beyond the walls of Jericho.

Many people whom we think we know well are walking around behind a "front." The real person is yearning to come out from behind that facade. . .but doesn't know how. It's easy to "judge a book by its cover"—but be careful. Take time to find out what is hidden beneath the surface. You may be very surprised!

I need to learn to discern, Father, rather than judge. Help me to be sensitive to others' needs and yearnings. Help me to listen and to hear the unspoken words that someone is afraid to speak.

"DISCERNMENT IS GOD'S CALL TO INTERCESSION."[1]

A HOLY GOD

The Lord also told Moses to tell the people of Israel, 'You must be holy because I, the Lord your God, am holy' (Lev. 19:1, LB). Read Exodus 15:11-19.

I've heard some stories of a God
Whose ways are different from our gods.
He led His people out of bondage,
Held back the sea, then drowned their foes.
I would know more of such a God
Whose power is great, whose arm is strong.
But He demands great holiness. . . .
Would He despise the likes of me?

—Rahab

Tales of the great Jehovah of Israel had swept through Canaan like a brush fire after a summer drought, leaving most of the natives terrified, as Moses had prophesied in his song. Rahab's searching spirit, however, reached out for greater knowledge of this God, and her faith grew in direct proportion to her knowledge.

Rahab did not hold back from belief in God because of her way of life. Perhaps she felt little guilt and was unaware of sin until she heard of the holiness of Jehovah. The Canaanites had long since hardened their consciences and become reprobate (rejectors of God).

Make me aware of sin in my life, Father. Open my eyes to the "blind spots." Point out the secret sins that no one sees—except You.

"SEARCH ME, O GOD, AND KNOW MY HEART, I PRAY."

A PENITENT PROSTITUTE

Do not violate your daughter's sanctity by making her a prostitute, lest the land become full of enormous wickedness (Lev. 19:29, LB). Read Proverbs 4:1-27.

> *I rue the day I first was given*
> *The name of harlot—prostitute!*
> *I was not taught of good or bad;*
> *I was not taught belief in God.*
> *It simply seemed an easy way*
> *To help support my family.*
> *I was too young to realize*
> *The life I'd lead from that day on.*
> *—Rahab*

The Bible does not tell us when or why Rahab became a prostitute. Perhaps in Jericho it was considered an honorable occupation. (Later on in history, the Greek culture encouraged prostitution.) Rahab may have used her popularity to support the family about whom she was so concerned.

I wonder. . .are we encouraging sexual promiscuity in our sons and daughters by being too permissive, by giving them too much freedom in their dress, habits, activities? Analyze the current TV programs and their influence on your family. Are we allowing in our homes more temptation than our young people (and older people) can bear?

Forgive me, Father, for the way in which I have played a part in subjecting my children and others around me to temptation. Help me to "avoid all appearance of evil" for their sake. May I never be a stumbling-block to someone who is watching my life.

"WHAT PARENTS ALLOW IN MODERATION, CHILDREN EXCUSE IN EXCESS."[2]

COINCIDENCE OR PROVIDENCE?

Was not even Rahab the prostitute considered righteous for what she did when she gave lodging to the spies and sent them off in a different direction? (James 2:25, NIV). Read James 2:12-26.

*Can it be mere coincidence
That brought these men into my home?
No, their God has led them here—
He will lead me out of Jericho!
They have promised they will not forget
My kindness to them when they go.
But I can't leave my family here. . . .
My father, mother, brothers must go too.*
—Rahab

Rahab must have been a fast thinker! By the time the police squadron arrived at her home to pick up the spies (who had been reported), she had made the decision to protect them and had already hidden them. She must have been a good actress as well, for the police went as far as the Jordan River looking for the Israelites.

What about the lie Rahab told? We must realize that— totally without teaching of right and wrong, and without thought for her own life—Rahab was simply doing her utmost to please the God of Israel. She was saved through her trust in God and her willingness to serve Him.

Help me, Father, not to judge others by my own background and the light I have been given. Help me to see Your children through Your eyes; help me to love the unlovely as You loved me.

"A WRONG TEMPER OF MIND ABOUT ANOTHER SOUL WILL END IN THE SPIRIT OF THE DEVIL, NO MATTER HOW SAINTLY YOU ARE."[3]

THE HYPNOSIS OF FEAR

By faith—because she believed in God and his power—Rahab the harlot did not die with all the others in her city when they refused to obey God (Heb. 11:31, LB). Read Joshua 6:1-25.

The city has gone hysterical,
Half crazed with insane fear!
The daily marches around the walls
Have thrown a magic spell, and now
We wait to see what happens next.
The men come here and drink, but they
Avoid me like the plague.
The word has spread I helped the spies.
                                        —Rahab

Rahab's words to the spies were very true: "We are all afraid of you; everyone is terrified if the word *Israel* is even mentioned" (Josh. 2:9, LB). Added to this fear, six days of marching and trumpet-blowing must have practically hypnotized the city—but Rahab did not fear, because she believed in God and His power and had acted on her faith.

An experiment I call "My Worry Book" has proved to be one of my greatest experiences. I mentioned earlier that I keep a record of "Asks and Answers" in a little 49¢ spiral notebook (anyone can afford one of them!); the "asks" go on one page with the date I first started praying, and the page facing is reserved for the answers (with their accompanying dates). I've trained myself to write down every problem I find myself worrying about. As I write, the burden is transferred from my shoulders to His, and I'm free!

Thank You, Father, for being *Jehovah-nissi* (the Lord my banner or defender) and *Jehovah-shalom* (the Lord my peace). Thank You for the knowledge that You will fight my battles for me and bring Your people peace.

WHEN FEAR KNOCKS AT YOUR DOOR, SEND FAITH TO ANSWER IT AND YOU WILL FIND THERE'S NO ONE THERE.
                                        —Unknown

JUST AS I AM

As far as the east is from the west, so far hath he removed our transgressions from us (Ps. 103:12, KJV). Read Deuteronomy 21:10-14.

Ah, little Boaz, if you knew
The sinful life your mother led,
You would shrink from me—but praise His name,
God has sealed the lips of those who know!
Because I trusted in His name,
Forsook the past and all its sin,
Jehovah has turned my life around,
Included me among His own.

—Rahab

Did you realize that Rahab married Salmon, one of the spies she had protected, and came to be in the direct family line of King David? Of course, an even greater king than David also descended from that line—Jesus Christ! (See Matt. 1:5.) Again we see the loving grace of a mighty God who cared enough to reach out and save a prostitute from Jericho.

No matter what your background, God cares about *you* as well. Confession of your sin, turning your back on sin, and trusting in Him can begin a new life for you. If you have never made that decision, why not do it today?

Lord Jesus, I need You. Thank You for dying on the cross for my sins. I repent of my sin, and I open the door of my life and receive You as my Savior and Lord. Thank You for forgiving my sins and giving me eternal life. Take control of the throne of my life. Make me the kind of person You want me to be (from *Four Spiritual Laws*).

"GOD'S GRACE TURNS OUT MEN AND WOMEN WITH A STRONG FAMILY LIKENESS TO JESUS CHRIST."[4]

DEBORAH: A WOMAN WHO COULD HANDLE ANYTHING

The people had remained true to the Lord throughout Joshua's lifetime. . . . But finally all that generation died; and the next generation did not worship Jehovah as their God. . . . Instead, they were worshiping and bowing low before the idols of the neighboring nations. So the anger of the Lord flamed out against all Israel. . . . When the nation of Israel went out to battle against its enemies, the Lord blocked their path. . . . But when the people were in this terrible plight, the Lord raised up judges to save them from their enemies (Judg. 2:7-16, LB).

Deborah was the first woman judge and a prophetess as well; she called herself a "mother in Israel" or (in some translations) a "mother *to* Israel." Her gifts of discernment and wise leadership endeared her to the frustrated people of Israel, who were being oppressed by King Jabin with his nine hundred iron chariots.

Deborah's "mother's heart" must have yearned over rebellious Israel as Christ later yearned over Jerusalem: "O Jerusalem, Jerusalem. . .how often would I have gathered thy children together, even as a hen gathereth her chickens under his wings, and ye would not!" (Matt. 23:37, KJV).

As I studied this story, I wondered: Why did two women fight the major battles of the war against King Jabin? When does God allow women to become leaders? What lessons can we learn for today from this story?

Perhaps you're asking these questions too. . . .

O. T. PASSAGE THIS WEEK: Judges 2—5

SPECIAL PRAYER NEEDS THIS WEEK:

ANSWERS TO PRAYER THIS WEEK:

TRUE WISDOM

If any of you lacks wisdom, he should ask God, who gives generously to all without finding fault, and it will be given to him (James 1:5, NIV). Read 1 Kings 3:5-15.

> *I'm thankful for the wisdom God has given,*
> *And I am very much aware it is of Him.*
> *I can remember earlier days when my impulses*
> *Were just as foolish as the ones I judge.*
> *But since I have given my life fully*
> *To God—to use however He may choose—*
> *He has given my life back to use in service,*
> *To guide and lead His people Israel.*
>
> *—Deborah*

The mark of a truly wise person is humility—the realization that wisdom is from God. (Solomon asked God for wisdom, but in his later days he seemed to forget the source.) Deborah's humility is evident in her song in the fifth chapter of Judges, where she gives God praise for the deliverance of Israel. She calls herself merely a "mother in Israel."

It would have been easy for Deborah to become impatient with her rebellious "children" as she listened to their problems day after day. It's easy for us to become impatient with the foolish mistakes of others when we have reached a "higher spiritual level." It's very important at times like these to remember the mistakes *we* made (that we'd like to forget) that were just as bad—or worse!

Father, I recognize that "holier-than-thou" tendency in myself at times. Please point it out to me each time it raises its ugly, pious head. Help me to see myself as You see me.

"IF YOU REALIZE YOU ARE LACKING [IN WISDOM], IT IS BECAUSE YOU HAVE COME IN CONTACT WITH SPIRITUAL REALITY; DO NOT PUT YOUR REASONABLE BLINDERS ON AGAIN."[1]

FICKLE LOVERS

The Israelites once again did evil in the eyes of the Lord. So the Lord sold them into the hands of Jabin (Judg. 4:1-2, NIV). Read Judges 2:1-23.

If my people Israel could only realize
The sadness they have brought upon themselves!
Their constant sinning and their idol worship
Create a stench that God won't tolerate.
King Jabin is but a tool Jehovah uses
To turn His people Israel back to Him.
They finally seek His face in desperation. . . .
These foolish people never seem to understand.
—Deborah

Over and over again in their history the Israelites proved their fickleness. When they had a strong leader—and if they were happy with him—they followed the Lord Jehovah, but as soon as they lost their leader or became disillusioned with him, they turned their backs on God and began to worship the pagan idols of the land.

The pagan gods of today are different, but just as tempting to God's "chosen people": love of money, search for pleasure, materialism. How many times have I turned my back on God to embrace one of these "gods"?

Forgive me, Father, for my self-centeredness. Forgive me for the many times I have grieved You by my fickle and rebellious spirit. Thank You for the faithfulness of Your love to me.

"GREAT IS THY FAITHFULNESS, O GOD MY FATHER; THERE IS NO SHADOW OF TURNING WITH THEE."

LACK OF LEADERSHIP

He saw that there was no one, and he was appalled that there was no one to intercede (Isa. 59:16, NIV). Read Judges 3:1-31.

Lord, how this once great nation needs a leader
To follow Moses, Joshua, Ehud, Othniel.
These people need a man to lead in battle,
To rouse the troops of Israel from their sleep.

But everywhere I look, the men are frightened!
There's not a man among them who will lead.
Am I the one whom God has chosen?
How can a woman lead the men of Israel?
*   —Deborah*

Deborah probably left her palm tree courthouse burdened with the weight of the problems that were brought to her daily. Her mother's heart must have been broken by the oppression of Israel. . .and the knowledge that there was no one to lead her people but herself, even though personally she may have preferred to be a homemaker. We can visualize this wise, strong woman going home to weep and pray.

Does the weight of the burdens you carry seem to almost crush your spirit at times? Do you feel unable to face another day of problems without answers, of responsibilities without respite? Are you frustrated by your husband's inability—or lack of desire—to lead your family spiritually? Do you feel all alone?

Thank You, Father, that You care for me, that You care about all my problems. Help me to "cast my cares" upon You. Help me to remember that Your yoke is easy and Your burden is light.

LEADERS FIND IT MOST DIFFICULT TO ADMIT THAT THEY TOO HAVE NEEDS.

WAKE UP, BARAK!

If you do away with the yoke of oppression. . .then your light will rise in the darkness, and your night will become like the noonday (Isa. 58:9-10, NIV). Read Judges 4:1-7.

The Lord has told me: "Summon Barak!
Speak to him, rouse him from his sleep!
Tell him the time has come to mobilize,
That Israel's waited long for leadership."

So Barak, you—yes, you!—must lead our people!
The men of Zebulun and Naphtali
Are ready now to serve God and to follow.
God will deliver Sisera into your hands.
                                          —Deborah

Deborah must have spent much time praying about the problem of leadership. . .and then she had a very frank talk with the man God had impressed on her mind. It's obvious Barak never would have acted without Deborah's "pep talk." Perhaps he was so discouraged he "couldn't see the forest for the trees."

Sometimes husbands do not understand what God expects of them in terms of spiritual leadership, or they may not know how to go about assuming the leadership role. Perhaps your husband has never seen a spiritual leader in action within a home, and he may not be aware of your family's needs or your feelings. If there is a problem, talk to God about it first and then, in an honest, respectful way, talk to your husband.

Please heal my resentments, Father, and help me to cope with this problem area in a constructive manner. Help me to nudge without nagging, to suggest without criticizing, to accept others as You have accepted me.
"THE MOST DIFFICULT TRUTH TO ACCEPT IS THAT YOUR HUSBAND'S ACTIONS ARE ALMOST ALWAYS THE RESULT OF YOUR ATTITUDES TOWARD HIM."[2]

GOD WORKS THROUGH WOMEN!

Because of the way you are going about this, the honor will not be yours, for the Lord will hand Sisera over to a woman (Judg. 4:9, NIV). Read Judges 4:8-16.

Who would believe this man whom God has chosen
Won't go to battle unless I will go along!
Alright then, Barak, I'll go with you,
But honor for the victory won't be yours!
If you can't trust your God to lead in battle,
Then God will have to speak through me instead.
When men refuse to be the nation's leaders,
God chooses women who will put their trust in Him.
—Deborah

Deborah's message to Barak—"GO AND FIGHT!"—was not her own; it was straight from the Lord. Obviously a woman's heart was more open to God's leading than any man's heart at that point in history. . .and after Deborah had summoned Barak and talked him into fighting King Jabin, he still refused to go into battle unless she promised to accompany him.

Although Deborah did go with Barak to battle, she did not usurp his authority in this situation; he was still the official leader of the Israelite army. She was generous in her encouragement during the battle; without that encouragement Barak may have turned back just short of victory.

Thank You, Father, for the ways in which You show me Your concern for me. Help me to be an encouragement rather than a negative influence on my family. Thank You for Your patience during my slow periods of spiritual growth.

"IN THESE DAYS WHEN SO MUCH PRESSURE IS BEING EXERTED TO 'EQUALIZE' MEN AND WOMEN, LET EVERY CHRISTIAN BE DILIGENT IN STUDYING GOD'S WORD TO DISCERN *HIS* WILL."[3]

OBEDIENCE BRINGS VICTORY

Surely the arm of the Lord is not too short to save, nor his ear too dull to hear (Isa. 59:1, NIV). Read Judges 5:1-23.

I hear the sounds of music in the village;
Musicians gather at the village well,
Repeating over and over the victory ballad:
A peasant army fought a holy war!
Because the Lord Jehovah led His people,
Nine hundred charioteers have been destroyed,
And Sisera, mighty Sisera, lies in splendor
Within a tent, a tent pin through his head.
—Deborah

Although Deborah was very outright in her condemnation of those who did not help to defend Israel, the overall spirit of her song in Judges 5 is one of thanksgiving and true joy. The final stanza repeats the theme of thanksgiving:
"So may all your enemies perish, O Lord!
But may they who love you be like the sun
when it rises in its strength" (Judg. 5:31, NIV).
No mention is made of Barak's hesitancy to go into battle, only praise for his willingness to serve Jehovah and Israel. Does this tell us something about the tendency most women have to remind men of their past failures?
Thank You, Father, for this song of thanksgiving that teaches me to praise You for each victory. Thank You for the example of this great woman who was obedient to Your orders in spite of what people may have said about her.
"THE WIFE WHO PLAYS 'HOLY SPIRIT' IN HER HUSBAND'S LIFE DOESN'T REALIZE THIS IS THE MOST EFFECTIVE WAY TO GET HIM TO REBEL AND *NEVER* CHANGE."[4]

JAEL AND THE NAIL

And the children of Israel again did evil in the sight of the Lord. . .and the Lord sold them into the hand of Jabin king of Canaan, that reigned in Hazor; the captain of whose host was Sisera. . .and the children of Israel cried unto the Lord: for he had nine hundred chariots of iron; and twenty years he mightily oppressed the children of Israel (Judg. 4:1-3, KJV).

We've studied Deborah, a woman of many abilities who held an unusual position for a woman in Israelite society. There must have been other women, however, who at times looked with envy on Deborah's leadership. Perhaps Jael was one of these.

If the meaning of her name—"wild she-goat"—gives us a clue to Jael's personality, she must have been a daring, impetuous woman. Her fearless murder of Sisera would certainly seem to support this theory.

Very little is told us about Jael, and some questions will remain unanswered. Where was Jael's husband when she was pounding the tent pin through Sisera's forehead? What was his reaction to his wife's action? We can't answer these questions definitely, but we can find out a little more about Jael's husband, Heber the Kenite, which may give us some clues about their relationship.

Jael's husband, Heber, was a Kenite, a descendant of Moses' in-laws. Judges 4:11 tells us, however, that Heber had severed relations with the other Kenites and had made peace with Israel's oppressor, King Jabin. In other words, Heber was probably considered to be a traitor to Israel.

Put that information together with Jael's murder of Sisera. . .and the plot thickens! What kind of marriage do you suppose they had?

O. T. PASSAGE THIS WEEK: Judges 4:17-24; 5:24-31

SPECIAL PRAYER NEEDS THIS WEEK:

ANSWERS TO PRAYER THIS WEEK:

DIFFERENCE OF OPINIONS

If a house be divided against itself, that house cannot stand (Mark 3:25, KJV). Read 1 Corinthians 11:3-12.

> *If I could only be in Deborah's place!*
> *The people come from miles around*
> *To hear her wise advice, to seek her aid.*
> *She is a vital force in Israel,*
> *But I am trapped here in my husband's tent—*
> *My husband, Heber, friend to Sisera*
> *And ally to King Jabin!*
>
> *—Jael*

Obviously Jael did not agree with her husband's political alignments, but not every woman had the opportunity to express her ideas as forthrightly as Deborah did. Jael probably found it very difficult to live with Heber's betrayal of Israel; she may have despised what she considered cowardice in her husband.

Do you sometimes say to yourself, "Maybe I married the wrong one. . ."? Are you finding that your opinions and your husband's views often clash? Does a career seem much more appealing than being tied down at home?

Father, I don't have the answers to the questions in our marriage—but You do. I'm casting my cares on You, knowing that You care for both of us. Please bring us together in one spirit.

"FAMILIES WHO DISREGARD GOD'S LAW AND ORDER MAY FUNCTION, BUT THEY WON'T FUNCTION WELL."[1]

REBELLION AGAINST RESTRICTIONS

For where envying. . .is, there is confusion (James 3:16, KJV). Read Ephesians 5:21-30.

There's Deborah's husband, Lappidoth. . . .
He never puts restraints on her.
She has a gift from God, he says,
And who is he to interfere?
My husband wants me here at home,
Dependent on him totally!
I'd like to serve our nation too;
I envy Deborah her career!

—Jael

As we've pointed out, Heber (Jael's husband) had a friendly alliance with King Jabin, but Jael's heart was with Israel. Did she let Heber know how she felt? It seems that would have been in keeping with Jael's impetuous nature. Perhaps there were many arguments between them.

Howard Hendricks reports on a study by a Christian psychiatrist who found that 75 percent of the married people he surveyed considered their marriages to be a failure and felt their homes were unhappy. To quote Mr. Hendricks: "God often has to back us into a crisis corner where we can see only Him before we get ourselves into perspective. A discernment of roles is absolutely indispensable for purposeful living, for marital efficiency, and for family functioning."[2]

I admit, Father, that I've been rebelling against my "role." Somehow I've felt cheated and unfulfilled. I recognize that this feeling is one of Satan's favorite means of breaking up homes. Help me to find *Your* plan for my life.

"ROLES ALWAYS DETERMINE RELATIONSHIPS, AND RELATIONSHIPS CREATE RESPONSIBILITY."[3]

RESTLESSNESS AT HOME

Wives, fit in with your husbands' plans; for then if they refuse to listen when you talk to them about the Lord, they will be won by your respectful, pure behavior. Your godly lives will speak to them better than any words (1 Pet. 3:1-2, LB). Read 1 Peter 3:1-22.

> *She's gone to war! Oh, how I wish*
> *I could go too!*
> > *But Heber says*
> *I need to learn to be content at home.*
> *Sometimes I hate this tent of ours!*
> *I feel imprisoned here. . . .*
> *Time goes so slowly as I wait for news.*
> > > > *—Jael*

Undoubtedly Jael was a fighter! We can imagine this "wild she-goat" growing up as a tomboy who could beat up all the boys in Tent City! Her housework probably was forgotten as she dreamed of following Deborah to war—but to do so would have meant breaking the protective alliance that her husband valued so highly.

Women with personalities like Jael's have a hard time with the word "submission." "But I would have you know, that the head of every man is Christ; and the head of the woman is the man; and the head of Christ is God" (1 Cor. 11:3, KJV). Jesus Christ had a God-given function on earth, to be born of a woman, live, suffer, and die on the cross. In total submission to His Father's will, Jesus Christ followed the divine plan. Does that mean that He was or is inferior to God the Father? In no way! And in no way does submission to one's husband cast the wife into an inferior role.

Help me to function, Father, by Your specifications. Forgive my rebellion against my husband and against You. **"MEN AND WOMEN ARE EQUAL SPIRITUALLY BUT DIFFERENT FUNCTIONALLY."**[4]

MIXED MOTIVES

The heart is deceitful above all things (Jer. 17:9, KJV). Read James 4:1-12.

What is that noise I hear outside the tent?
There! Through the open tent flap I can see
A man approaching slowly, wearily. . . .
He looks familiar—yes, I think it is!
It's the proud Sisera, coming here to hide!
He does not know that I'm on Israel's side.
Perhaps I'll have the opportunity
To fight for freedom and for Israel!

—Jael

Whether she planned her strategy as she went out to meet Sisera or acted impulsively later, Jael seemed totally devoid of fear as she determined that this was her chance—the chance of a lifetime—to bring an end to Sisera's oppression of Israel. What drove Jael on? A desire for revenge? A hatred of evil? Honest patriotism? Or an intense need for significance? All are possibilities.

What forces impelled you to make the decisions that have shaped your life? Can you face your real motivations? Are they the right reasons?

Help me, Father, to understand myself. I realize that the big "I" too often dominates my motivations. Help me to keep my ego in its place.

"THE FIRST THING GOD DOES IS TO KNOCK PRETENSE AND THE PIOUS POSE RIGHT OUT OF ME."[5]

OPPORTUNITY FOR ACTION

A man tormented by the guilt of murder will be a fugitive till death (Prov. 28:17, NIV). Read Judges 4:17-24.

Come in, my lord, you're welcome here!
Come in and rest yourself from war.
No one will ever know you're here
For I will stand guard by the door.
There's no one here but you and me;
I'll make sure no one will disturb.
Just lay your body on this cot. . . .
Your sleep will be as sound as death.

—*Jael*

What Jael did, she did for Israel. We cannot judge her by our standards, for she had none of Christ's teachings, only the Old Testament code of law: "An eye for an eye, a tooth for a tooth." Sisera had mistreated the people of Israel, and now he would pay the price.

How differently God expects *us* to live! Jesus Christ taught us to show mercy to our enemies, to pray for those who despitefully use us. To get it down to the nitty-gritty. . . how do I react when an ex-friend "kills" my reputation by spreading malicious gossip about me—or by telling certain truths about me that I'd like to forget? Do I react in love?

Thank You, Father, that You loved me when I was so unlovely, and that You still love me in spite of myself. Help me to reach out to others with that same kind of love, especially _____.

"GOD HAS SEEN ME AT MY WORST AND STILL LOVED ME, TO THE POINT OF GIVING HIS LIFE FOR ME. . . THAT'S SECURITY!"[6]

SONG OF DEBORAH

Catch them in their own traps; let them fall beneath the weight of their own transgressions, for they rebel against you (Ps. 5:10, LB). Read Judges 5:24-31.

Blessed is Jael—yes, may she be blessed
Above all women who will live in tents!
For Sisera, mighty Sisera, asked for water;
Jael gave him milk and then a place to rest.
She took a tent pin and a workman's hammer
And pierced his forehead, opened up his skull.
She hit the tent pin through the general's temple,
And Sisera, mighty Sisera, lay there dead!
                                        —Deborah

Deborah was generous in her praise of Jael's deed. We have no way of knowing Heber's reaction when he found out what his wife had done. Probably, since Sisera was dead and King Jabin defeated, Heber returned to the "faith of his fathers". . .at least for a time. But we find in the next chapter of Judges that very soon the people of Israel began to worship other gods once again.

Heber is typical of many "second generation Christians" who are not really Christians at all. They have been brought up in the church, but have never made a personal commitment to Jesus Christ. Heber was concerned about saving his neck; "second generation Christians" are concerned about saving face, and will do anything to avoid being called a "fanatic."

Forgive me, Father, for the times when I've taken pride in my tactfulness, when all the time I was really avoiding a clear witness. Thank You for not being ashamed of me when I was ashamed of You.

REMEMBER: GOD HAS NO GRANDCHILDREN!

JEPHTHAH'S DAUGHTER: GRANDDAUGHTER OF A PROSTITUTE

Leontine R. Young writes: "The existence of unmarried mothers is not new in the world's history; nor is the problem of illegitimacy unique to the twentieth century. For ages past the girl who bore a child outside the limits of wedlock has been the target and frequently the victim of public attitudes and emotions. While these public attitudes have varied from one historical period to another, there is, taken as a whole, an amazing and rather appalling consistency in the way she and her child have been condemned by society. . . . There is indeed certain inevitability in the fact that the 'bastard' son should prove to be a villain."[1]

Yet, as in the story of Rahab, God's all-encompassing redemptive plan called for Jephthah, the son of a prostitute, to lead wandering Israel back to the worship of Jehovah. Perhaps Jephthah's mother was an orphan who had wandered into prostitution as a means of support, or perhaps her parents had urged their daughter into the service of Ashtaroth, the "goddess of love" (see Lev. 19:29).

The sins of the fathers *are* inherited by the children in illegitimacy (Deut. 5:9), but God also shows mercy to those who love Him and keep His commandments. We see this illustrated over and over again in the Old Testament as the "untouchables" are included in the history of salvation by an impartial God.

Yes, God shows mercy. . .unfortunately, God's people are often not as kind in their reactions.

O. T. PASSAGE THIS WEEK: Judges 10:6—11:40

SPECIAL PRAYER NEEDS THIS WEEK:

ANSWERS TO PRAYER THIS WEEK:

THE UNTOUCHABLES

Then the people of Israel turned away from the Lord again, and worshiped the heathen gods Baal and Ashtaroth, and the gods of Syria, Sidon, Moab, Ammon and Philistia. . . . They no longer worshiped Jehovah at all (Judg. 10:6, LB). Read Judges 10:6-18; 11:1.

> *I wish I could have met her—*
> *Gilead's mistress—my grandmother,*
> *A woman hated and alone.*
> *For some strange reason woman seems to bear the shame,*
> *The guilt, the tragedy of sin. . . .*
> *Men go scot-free.*
> *But no, that's not the truth of it. . . .*
> *My father suffered too.*
> *—Jephthah's daughter*

That Gilead was Jephthah's father was obviously common knowledge; this seems to indicate that the affair was a fairly permanent attachment. Perhaps Jephthah's mother even lived somewhere on Gilead's property, though certainly not in the home with Gilead's legitimate wife.

It's easy to imagine that Gilead tried to keep the relationship with the prostitute a secret, because each of us have experienced things in our own lives that we wanted to keep a secret. Perhaps you've also experienced the inner misery that results from unconfessed sin.

Thank You, Father, for the prodding of Your Holy Spirit that did not give up on me when I was so much in need of Your cleansing. I praise You, Father, for Your forgiveness—full and free.

"CONVICTION OF SIN BY THE HOLY GHOST BLOTS OUT EVERY RELATIONSHIP ON EARTH AND LEAVES ONE RELATIONSHIP ONLY—'AGAINST THEE, THEE ONLY, HAVE I SINNED!'"[2]

A THREAT

He is despised and rejected of men; a man of sorrows, and acquainted with grief: and we hid as it were our faces from him; he was despised, and we esteemed him not (Isa. 53:3, KJV). Read Judges 11:2-3; Matthew 22:37-40.

He only wanted them to call him brother. . . .
They hurt him deeply with their hate.
They saw him as a constant threat
And thrust him from the land he loved.
And many others left with him
Who were rejected, bitter, lone.
                                    —Jephthah's daughter

Jephthah probably fled because he was afraid for his life. The jealousy and cruelty of his brothers reminds us of the story of Joseph, whose brothers conspired against him to kill him. It becomes evident later from Jephthah's story that he had a good knowledge of and great faith in Jehovah; this could have heightened the intensity of his brothers' dislike.

The potential for spiritual greatness can also be a threat to others who feel inferior or are simply lazy, and the man or woman who is struggling to know and follow God's will for his/her life may find that even his closest friends discourage him in his search.

Thank You, Father, that Your Son, the "Suffering Servant," knew what it was like to be rejected. Thank You, too, that You have promised a way of escape from any temptation and that Your grace is sufficient.

"BEWARE LEST YOU THINK YOU ARE TEMPTED AS NO ONE ELSE IS TEMPTED."[3]

THE MIRACLE OF LOVE

Hatred stirreth up strifes: but love covereth all sins (Prov. 10:12, KJV). Read Isaiah 53:1-12.

My mother's love was his salvation. . . .
She planted confidence and love
Where hate and prejudice had been.
She believed in him, gave herself to him,
And he became a man again.
Out of their union I was born;
I was his chance to prove to all
The rejected son of a prostitute
Could leave a mark upon the world.
                                        —Jephthah's daughter

The Bible tells us nothing about Jephthah's wife (or even that he had one), but from the character of his daughter it seems very likely that he found a caring and understanding wife whose love broke the vicious patterns he had experienced up to that point. Perhaps when he fled to the land of Tob (east of the Jordan River) he found a new start and a love that changed his life.

Jesus was also "despised and rejected of men" (Isa. 53:3)—and, like Jephthah, through no fault of His own. When we experience unexplainable suffering, we need to remember that "just as the sufferings of Christ flow over into our lives, so also through Christ our comfort overflows" (2 Cor. 1:5, NIV).

Thank You, Lord Jesus, that You suffered in my place for my sin. Thank You, Father, for the comfort You administer through Your Son Jesus. Teach me to comfort others as You have comforted me.

"GOD RARELY ALLOWS A SOUL TO SEE HOW GREAT A BLESSING HE IS."[4]

THE TABLES TURNED

He was oppressed, and he was afflicted, yet he opened not his mouth (Isa. 53:7, KJV). Read Judges 11:4-10.

When Israel came to him, bowed down to him,
And begged my father for his aid,
It would have been so easy to say "No,"
Spit in their faces, kick them out,
And take revenge for what they'd done.
My mother lovingly gave advice:
"Give them a chance," she said to him;
"They cannot realize what they've done."
*   —Jephthah's daughter*

Jephthah's reputation as a great warrior finally brought to their knees the people who had treated him so roughly. Afraid for their lives because of the Ammonite threat, the leaders of Gilead begged Jephthah to come and lead their army. His reply, as could be expected, was bitter: "Why do you come to me when you hate me. . .? Why come now when you're in trouble?" (Judg. 11:7, LB). It's possible (although not stated) that a wife's loving persuasion could have softened Jephthah's angry reaction.

We can sympathize with Jephthah's reaction—and be amazed anew at the description of Christ's reaction to His accusers in Isaiah 53:7, "He opened not his mouth."

I realize more and more, Father, my need to be conformed to the image of Your Son. Forgive my impatience, my bitterness, my lack of love.

NEVER ALLOW ANYTHING TO COME BETWEEN YOURSELF AND JESUS CHRIST—NO EMOTION. . .NO EXPERIENCE. . .NO PERSON.

A LEADER UNDER AUTHORITY

Did ye never read in the scriptures, The stone which the builders rejected, the same is become the head of the corner: this is the Lord's doing, and it is marvellous in our eyes? (Matt. 21:42, KJV). Read Judges 11:11-33.

> *My father, captain of the troops!*
> *He was an outcast, now their head.*
> *They chose him as commander, chief—*
> *He's off to fight the Ammonites!*
> *He let them know God's in control*
> *And God will lead him in this war.*
> —*Jephthah's daughter*

Jephthah accepted his countrymen's promise to make him commander-in-chief if he would lead them to battle. He then demonstrated his true greatness by his message to the king of Ammon, explaining that the territory in question belonged to Israel simply because Jehovah had given it to them three hundred years before.

Jephthah was not afraid to speak out for God in the midst of idolatry. Because of this God honored him by anointing him with His Spirit and giving him victory in battle.

Thank You, Father, for this example of a man who gave You the praise that was due You when no one else recognized Your power. I need to learn to praise You in the midst of problems. Help me to learn to rejoice in *all* things.

"OUR LORD BEGINS TO BRING US INTO THE PLACE WHERE WE CAN HAVE COMMUNION WITH HIM, AND WE GROAN AND SAY—'O LORD, LET ME BE LIKE OTHER PEOPLE!'"[5]

A NATIONAL HEROINE

*I will pay my vows unto the Lord now in the presence of all his people
(Ps. 116:14, KJV). Read Judges 11:34-40.*

*I didn't know my father's oath. . . .
I went to meet him—dancing, proud;
But when his face came into sight,
I saw his eyes were full of tears.
He wants the best in life for me,
The happy home he never had. . .
But the faith my parents gave to me
Will keep me in this troubled hour.*
                              —Jephthah's daughter

Jephthah's vow to the Lord may have been satisfied by
consecrating his daughter to perpetual virginity (footnote,
Judges 11:39, LB). However we interpret the outcome of the
story, it is obvious that his daughter shared his feeling that he
could not take back his vow, and thereby demonstrated great
faith in her father and her God. She also became a national
heroine of Israel.

Difficult to understand—yes!—but perhaps a lesson in
the need to dedicate our children to God. Or does the story
simply warn us to be careful before, in the heat of battle, we
rashly make a vow? In either case, we see a very warm, human
man—and a daughter to whom he had imparted his faith—
whom God honored in spite of his background, his environment, and his mistakes!

Thank You, Father, that someday we will understand all
the problems that loom so large and unexplainable on our
horizons now. Thank You that You were able to use Jephthah
—that gives me hope for me!

**"THE BURDEN GOD PLACES SQUEEZES THE GRAPES
AND OUT COMES THE WINE; MOST OF US SEE THE
WINE ONLY."**[6]

SAMSON'S MOTHER:
LEGALISM vs. HOLINESS

This week we need to take a close look at Samson's background. What kind of parents did he have? Can we indict them for his unbridled sexual appetite?

We'll find that Samson's mother and father, Manoah, seem to be two people who are genuinely seeking God's will for their lives and for their son. We can imagine their heartbreak when young Samson, the hope of their old age and of the nation, asked them to arrange a marriage to a Philistine girl (Judg. 14).

What went wrong? God gave Samson's parents explicit directions in preparation for this child. Were these guidelines presented in the right way to their sensuous son? It seems very clear that Samson regarded his long hair merely as a magic formula by which he obtained power, rather than as the symbol of a separated life it was intended to be.

Dr. John White, in his book, *Eros Defiled: The Christian and Sexual Sin,* says we have "distorted the Scriptures by emphasizing externals more than Scripture does and by this presenting holiness in negative terms. *We have failed to stress the nature of and the reason for positive holiness of life.* Holiness itself has become either a form of legalism (by which we contribute to the cost of our salvation) or a sort of pseudo-psychological lift by which we will be more 'greatly used' or have a 'fuller life.'

"The principal reason for holiness as commanded in Scripture is 'You shall be holy; for I the Lord your God am holy' (Lev. 19:2).

"Sensing the hollowness of our lopsided Bible preaching, young and old alike have been unprepared for the dual onslaught of increasing sexual stimulation and the subtleties of new sexual philosophies."[1]

O. T. PASSAGE THIS WEEK: Judges 13—14

SPECIAL PRAYER NEEDS THIS WEEK:

ANSWERS TO PRAYER THIS WEEK:

THE ANNUNCIATION

My soul doth magnify the Lord (Luke 1:46, KJV). Read Judges 13:1-7.

Manoah, you cannot imagine
How our life has changed today!
A man of God was in our home—
A man or angel, I don't know—
He told me I will bear a son!
I, who was cursed with barrenness,
I have been told I'll bear a son!

—Manoah's wife

The parallels between this story and the angel's announcement to Mary are very noticeable: the circumstances surrounding the annunciation are similar (an angel and a woman talking alone); neither woman had ever borne a child; and both sons were sent to deliver Israel (in Samson's case, from Israel's oppressors the Philistines; in Jesus' case, from the oppression of sin).

But what a tremendous difference as well! Mary was a virgin who conceived by the Holy Spirit, while Samson had an earthly father. Jesus was sinless, while Samson succumbed to the lusts of the flesh again and again. Samson began the deliverance of Israel (Judg. 13:5); Jesus ended the oppression of evil over the world.

Father, I too have problems with "the lust of the flesh, and the lust of the eyes, and the pride of life" (1 John 2:16, KJV). I know these things are of the world, not of You, and that my emphasis on the things of this world hurts You deeply. Forgive me for my divided heart.

THE "LUST OF THE FLESH, AND THE LUST OF THE EYES, AND THE PRIDE OF LIFE" CAN ALSO BE INTERPRETED AS THE "CRAZE FOR SEX, THE AMBITION TO BUY EVERYTHING THAT APPEALS TO YOU, AND THE PRIDE THAT COMES FROM WEALTH AND IMPORTANCE" (LB).

ONE SEPARATED UNTO THE LORD

Don't copy the behavior and customs of this world, but be a new and different person (Rom. 12:2, LB). Read Numbers 6:1-21.

Our son will be a Nazirite.
He will eat nothing from the vine—
No raisins, grapes—or drink its wine,
Nor will he cut his hair or shave his beard.
And I too must observe these rules
While he is in my womb and when
I hold him nursing at my breast.
——Manoah's wife

The Nazirite (also Nazarite) was a person who was separated unto the Lord. "Abstention from wine, the symbol of natural joy, was the expression of a devotedness which found all its joy in the Lord. The long hair, naturally a reproach to man, was at once the visible sign of the Nazirite's separation and willingness to bear reproach for the Lord's sake."[2] As God's promise tried Samson's mother's faith, so these requirements tried her obedience; God requires both.

Conformity to peer pressure is a formidable enemy to parents who are trying to teach their children God's rules for life. Separation is so very difficult—the pull of the world is exceedingly strong. Total surrender to God on the part of the parents is a prerequisite to training a child "in the way he should go."

Forgive me, Father, for the many times that I've allowed the world to squeeze me into its mold. Help me not to compare myself with others but rather look to Jesus, who was completely separated from the world and yet loved it enough to die for it.

TOTAL SURRENDER TO GOD ON THE PART OF THE PARENTS IS A PREREQUISITE TO TRAINING A CHILD IN THE WAY HE SHOULD GO.

PREPARATION FOR PARENTHOOD

For if a man know not how to rule his own house, how shall he take care of the church of God? (1 Tim. 3:5, KJV). Read 1 Timothy 3:1-12.

Dear God, my husband so desires
To speak with that man whom You sent. . . .
He is concerned how we will train
This son that You have promised us.
If it is possible, O Lord,
Please rest his mind, grant his request.
*   —Manoah's wife*

The angel had already given Manoah's wife the needed instructions concerning Samson's training as a Nazirite, but Manoah was so deeply impressed with the responsibility of their calling as parents of this child that he asked for the angel to come again and teach them more. His sense of need at once found expression in prayer—a prayer for guidance as spiritual leader in his growing family.

Quite a contrast to the thoughtless self-confidence with which many Christian parents undertake the training of their children! How little time the average parent spends in prayer for the preparation and leadership of the Spirit to fit them for this spiritual priority—the shaping and molding of young lives!

It's so easy in today's world, Father, to allow nonessentials to crowd out the time I need to spend with my children and in prayer for them. Forgive me for my lack of concern for intercessory prayer.

"A GODLY PARENT HAS POWER WITH GOD TO INTERCEDE (FOR HIS CHILDREN)."[3]

SACRIFICES OF PARENTHOOD

For God will bring every deed into judgment, including every hidden thing, whether it is good or evil (Eccles. 12:14, NIV). Read Judges 13:8-23.

I thank You, Lord, for answered prayer,
For speaking to my husband too. . .
For emphasizing what was said
Of purity in life and mind.
We have witnessed Your great power, Lord,
Your wondrous love revealed to us.
My soul does magnify You, Lord,
My spirit will rejoice in You.
— Manoah's wife

The angel had nothing new to say to Manoah, nothing different from what he had previously said to the woman, and yet God was too concerned about Manoah to leave him in the dark. (Unlike his wife, however, Manoah did recognize the identity of the angel.) It's worth mentioning that the angel of the Lord also appeared to Joseph after He had talked to Mary. God *is* concerned with the problems of parenthood!

The angel reemphasized the secret of parental duty: the giving up of the fruit of the vine meant sacrificing the stimulus and excitement and enjoyment of the world and of the flesh. . .a separation to special purity and holiness. Godly parents are just as needed today!

Sometimes I rebel, Father, against the sacrifices I have had to make for my family. . .yet have I realized the true nature of the sacrifices You are asking of me? Please make of me the shining example You want me to be.

GOD'S SECRET OF PARENTAL DUTY: SACRIFICING THE STIMULUS AND EXCITEMENT AND ENJOYMENT OF THE WORLD AND OF THE FLESH.

I AM A PROMISE, I AM A POSSIBILITY[4]

For when he punishes you, it proves that he loves you (Heb. 12:6, LB).
Read Judges 13:24-25; 14:1-20.

> *Our son is born, and what a child!*
> *He is beautiful in every way—*
> *His features are perfect and his strength*
> *Amazes me at his young age!*
> *Will we be able to control*
> *This baby. . .boy. . .and then young man?*
> > *—Manoah's wife*

Sadly enough, this child of great potential went wrong. It seems obvious from his reaction to his parents in Judges 14 that Samson was accustomed to getting his own way. To the strenuous objections of his parents concerning his intended marriage to a Philistine girl, he replied: "She is the one I want. Get her for me!"

After all the instructions that had been given concerning separation from the world and unto the Lord, Manoah gave in to his headstrong son and meekly went ahead with making arrangements for an unequally yoked marriage! Perhaps the fear he expressed in Judges 13:22 was indicative of his personality. . .how much we need *strong* spiritual leaders in our homes!

Help me, Father, to stand firmly for the right in these days of compromise and uncertainty. Help me to administer discipline where it is needed in a loving way. Thank You for the way You have lovingly disciplined me when I have needed it.

TEACHING DEALS WITH A CHILD'S MIND; TRAINING, WITH HIS WILL.

WHAT MIGHT HAVE BEEN

Let God train you, for he is doing what any loving father does for his children (Heb. 12:7, LB). Read Hebrews 12:1-11; Judges 16:21.

I have been heartsick for my son. . . .
He was a captive of his lust.
Had I been able to foresee
The life our son chose to pursue
Perhaps I couldn't have kept on going.
He had such promise—look at him now!
But still I trust my God to honor
Our faith that He will save our son.
                                        —Manoah's wife

We can imagine Samson's mother visiting him in the prison after the Philistines had put out his eyes, looking at him with the agony only a mother can experience. . .looking back to those early years for reassurance that she had done all she could. "But if I had spent more hours praying—and less working and worrying—would things have turned out differently?"

That question echoes down the halls of time to present-day mothers grieving over backslidden children. How difficult it is to see our children in the cages they have built of their own choosing. . .and yet we must entrust our children to the Lord, realizing that, as in the story of Samson, they may have to experience severe chastisement before they turn to Him for help.

Help me, Father, to substitute trust for worry and praise for fear. Help me to remember that You love my children even more than I do.

"AS OFTEN AS THE WORK OF INSTRUCTING THE CHILDREN UPON EARTH THREATENS TO BECOME A BURDEN OR A WEARINESS, YOU MAY BE SURE IT IS A TOKEN OF SOMETHING WRONG WITHIN: THE LOVE TO GOD IN HEAVEN OR THE DELIGHT IN HIS WORD HAS BEEN FADING."[5]

DELILAH THE DELICATE?

Listen, my son, to your father's instruction and do not forsake your mother's teaching. They will be a garland to grace your head and a chain to adorn your neck. My son, if sinners entice you, do not give in to them (Prov. 1:8-10, NIV).

Delilah's name does mean "delicate," but it seems very obvious that if she was delicate, it was only in appearance. Her personality seems to have been as "hard as nails," but her physical beauty attracted Samson, enticed him, and ensnared him.

Samson, the miraculously given son of Manoah, was a judge of Israel whose awe-inspiring strength became a legend among the surrounding nations. Sadly enough, Samson was physically strong but morally weak; he was spirit-anointed but carnally minded. Samson was tremendously courageous in battle, but abominably weak in trial. A Nazirite whose life had been dedicated to the Lord, he was extremely legalistic in some areas, but totally irresponsible in others.

So much for this man of contradictions. What about Delilah? Why wasn't she thrilled that the famous Samson had fallen head over heels in love with her? Why didn't she think in terms of capture by marriage instead of capture by betrayal of her lover? Why was she so anxious for the Philistines' money?

Is there a "Delilah" in your neighborhood? If so, what is your attitude toward her? Is there room for change?

You may want to review Judges 13—15 as a background to this story. As you read, reflect on the way God could have used Samson to lead His people had Samson been *totally* submitted to God's will for his life.

O. T. PASSAGE THIS WEEK: Judges 16:4-21

SPECIAL PRAYER NEEDS THIS WEEK:

ANSWERS TO PRAYER THIS WEEK:

GROWING PAINS THAT REALLY HURT

The Lord supports the humble. . .his joy is in those who reverence him, those who expect him to be loving and kind (Ps. 147:6, 11, LB). Read Judges 16:1-12.

> *I never had a father like the other girls,*
> *I never felt the warmth and love they knew.*
> *I bounced, unwanted, from one home to yet another*
> *Like a reject or a beat-up, worn-out shoe.*
> *I was spit upon and laughed at and derided*
> *And the neighbors told me not to ever play*
> *With their precious, innocent young children.*
> *But inside I always knew there'd come a day. . . .*
> *—Delilah*

Delilah's background can only be conjecture, but so often the development of an immoral woman begins with the absence of a father or rejection by a father. Whether real or imagined, the rejection is incredibly painful and long-lasting in its effects. Many women spend their lives looking for a "father image," often to be even more hurt by continued rejections from other sources.

Perhaps you've felt cheated as you've watched happy, healthy relationships within other families. Making us feel cheated is one of Satan's favorite traps. The heavenly Father's love can fill that yearning, that empty spot if you'll accept *His* plan for your life.

There *have* been times, Father, when I've felt very hurt, very much cheated. Thank You for showing me that You do have a plan for my life and that, through Your Son who gives me strength, I can do anything—anything!—that's in Your plan for me.

"THE MOST BASIC HUMAN NEED IS A SENSE OF PERSONAL WORTH, AN ACCEPTANCE OF ONESELF AS A WHOLE, REAL PERSON."[1]

RESULTS OF REJECTION

Looking diligently lest any man fail of the grace of God (Heb. 12:15, KJV). Read Judges 16:13-21.

Then the tables would be turned and I'd be laughing!
I'd have money then to buy whatever I pleased;
I would repay those people for their scorn and hatred;
I'd make sure their griefs and problems never ceased. . . .
But the key to all of this was money!
There was only one way I knew how to earn
All the money that I felt was coming to me—
There was one trade every girl could somehow learn.
—Delilah

Rejection breeds feelings of inferiority and insecurity. The resulting competition for admiration from someone— perhaps anyone!—leads to more complicated problems. A woman hurt by either real or imagined offenses often attempts to bolster up her feelings of insecurity with the accumulation of material things or attempts to gain power in some area. Delilah's bitterness against her own people (she lived in the valley of Judah) led her to barter her power over Samson for the Philistines' money.

What's really important in my life? Money. . .possessions . . .status. . .acceptance. . .recognition. . .love? "Surface needs" can be traced to the basic need for a sense of personal worth, which requires two inputs: significance and security.

It's so easy, Father, to get wrapped up in *things*, in the accumulation of possessions and the care of those possessions. Remind me that where my treasure is, my heart will follow. Thank You for the greatest treasure in my life—Your unconditional, never-ending love for me.

"THE TWO REQUIRED INPUTS FOR A SENSE OF PERSONAL WORTH ARE *SIGNIFICANCE* **AND** *SECURITY.*"[2]

HARD AS NAILS

Looking diligently. . .lest any root of bitterness springing up trouble you (Heb. 12:15, KJV). Read 1 Timothy 6:6-12.

To everyone's surprise I was a beauty;
Men gladly paid to spend a night with me.
I didn't care who paid to use my body
Because I felt in spirit I was free.
I believed I could trust no one, so I didn't!
Each man I met was just a dollar sign. . . .
But always there was that great hurt inside me;
Revenge and bitter hatred filled my mind.
                                                            —Delilah

Scripture does not label Delilah as a prostitute, and it's very possible that she was not; her easy familiarity with the five Philistine heads of state, however, and the hardened way in which she dealt with Samson leads me to believe that this was not her first sexual encounter.

Another woman's revenge-taking against society in general (or men in particular) may not be nearly as obvious as Delilah's was. Resentment against a father (or lack of one) may show up in unexplainable reactions toward an employer, a husband, or a teacher. Ask the Lord to show you the true source of the problem—and then let Him deal with it.

Father, there's someone I need to talk to, something I need to straighten out. You know all about it. I've had a wrong attitude for so long toward _____ , and yet I've excused it and rationalized it away so many times. Give me the courage and wisdom I need to handle this situation *Your* way instead of mine.

"PROBLEMS DEVELOP WHEN THE BASIC NEEDS FOR SIGNIFICANCE AND SECURITY ARE THREATENED."[3]

RATIONALIZATION OF GUILT

. . .*and thereby many be defiled (Heb. 12:15, KJV). Read 1 John 3:7-24.*

I found that I could use my new profession
To double earnings if I used my head!
The leaders of the Philistines didn't snub me;
They paid better than the farmers for my bed.
Now they've told me if I capture Samson's secret,
They'll pay me greater wages than before.
A thousand dollars each from five Philistines—
And if they like my work, there may be more!
                                        —Delilah

Delilah, a small-town girl, must have felt very important negotiating with the Philistine chiefs of state. They probably promised her everything she wanted to hear, and we can imagine her mental cartwheels as the men described the promised rewards. Riches and power at last!

The incredible urgency of the need for security in a woman's life makes it easy for her to rationalize impurity— she replies to her feelings of guilt by justifying her actions in the light of her past hurts (or a psychologist does it for her). Sin is not recognized as sin, but as an understandable reaction to what she has endured.

Father, I need discernment in recognizing sin when I tend to excuse it sympathetically in others or rationalize it away in my own life. Thank You, Father, that You forgive and forget my sins when I confess them to You and turn my back on them.

"WRONG PATTERNS OF LIVING DEVELOP FROM WRONG PHILOSOPHIES OF LIVING."[4]

LOVE OR PHYSICAL ATTRACTION

There is a way that seems right to a man but in the end it leads to death (Prov. 16:25, NIV). Read Proverbs 7:6-27.

You, Samson, you pretend you love me?
I know too much about you to believe
That you want more than rights to this warm body.
But you'll see that I too can deceive.
I'll wind you around my little finger
Until you tell Delilah all you know. . . .
When you're asleep, I'll use my new-found knowledge
And, power gone, you'll wake and try to go.
*   —Delilah*

Flirtation and seduction are often continued symptoms of adult insecurity. There was little, if any, love involved in Delilah's affair with Samson; in the early stages she may have been attracted by his famed brute strength, but her primary interest in Samson was the money the Philistines had promised her as a reward for her lover's capture.

Have you realized the responsibilities of love and friendship? Do you have a tendency to use people, then drop them, rather than being sensitive to *their* needs? How do you define a friend—someone who helps you or someone whom you can help? Friendship involves both areas.

Thank You, Father, for the friends You have brought into my life. Help me to remember that friendship involves responsibility as well as pleasure. Your love has always been on the giving end. . .thank You for that.

"AS LONG AS SOMEONE BELIEVES THAT HE MIGHT SACRIFICE OR AT LEAST RISK HIS SENSE OF WORTH BY LIVING RESPONSIBLY, HE WILL CHOOSE TO LIVE IRRESPONSIBLY."[5]

THE MIGHT HAVE BEEN

Whoever finds me ₍wisdom₎ *finds life. . .but whoever fails to find me harms himself; all who hate me love death (Prov. 8:35-36, NIV). Read Judges 16:22-31.*

> *I thought I would relish watching Samson—*
> *My hate of men had focused in on him—*
> *But as I watched, my hate turned inward. . . .*
> *His sightless eyes have haunted me since then.*
>
> *All around me I see families, everywhere those happy families,*
> *Each time I see them laughing, I think how it might have been.*
> *Samson's dead, with those who killed him—yet I am the one who killed him!*
> *And the pain is overwhelming. . .to think how it might have been.*
>
> *—Delilah*

Delilah's past experiences may well have inspired a hatred toward all men, yet she probably did not enjoy her conquest of Samson for long. The mental picture of sightless, powerless Samson must have been an empty victory as she realized the inability of the betrayal money to satisfy her needs. Perhaps, in shame and remorse, she stayed away from the Philistine celebration and heard the horrible story later. The rulers who had promised her so much were dead. . .the man who had said he loved her was dead. . .Delilah's life was dead.

Father, thank You that You have erased the past from my life. Thank You, Father, that You've seen me at my worst and still loved me, to the point of giving Your life for me. **"TRUE SIGNIFICANCE AND SECURITY ARE AVAILABLE ONLY TO THE CHRISTIAN, ONE WHO IS TRUSTING IN CHRIST'S PERFECT LIFE AND SUBSTITUTIONARY DEATH AS HIS SOLE BASIS OF ACCEPTABILITY BEFORE A HOLY GOD."[6]**

NAOMI—OR MARA?

The meaning of Naomi's name was "pleasant." She was married to Elimelech, whose name means "my God is king." When famine struck the land of Israel, Naomi and Elimelech moved to the heathen land of Moab to find food for themselves and their two sons, Mahlon and Chilion.

Let's get a little background on the land of Moab. The man Moab, founder of the Moabite nation, was the son of Lot through incest (Lot's daughters slept with him while he was drunk). Jeremiah tells us that Moab magnified himself against the Lord, and it seems that his descendants followed his example.

It also seems likely that Elimelech and Naomi may have been in a somewhat backslidden state when they moved into this godless area. Certainly their move reflects a lack of trust in Jehovah's ability to provide for their needs.

When Naomi returned to Israel, she returned without her family. Her husband and both sons had died in the land of Moab, and she said sadly to her friends in Israel: "Don't call me Naomi any more—call me Mara ('bitter')."

But God was good and sent Ruth into Naomi's life. In the next two weeks we will explore their relationship.

Are you a Naomi or a Mara? Was your life going along pleasantly until tragedy struck—a death in the family, unexpected illness, a child lost to drugs, loss of your job, bankruptcy? Has a life—or a marriage—that once was happy turned sour?

Sometimes, perhaps without realizing it, we too leave God's "land of promise," as Naomi did. As you read the Book of Ruth, ask yourself these questions: Have I moved out of God's will for my life? What is my Moab?

O. T. PASSAGE THIS WEEK: Ruth 1; 4

SPECIAL PRAYER NEEDS THIS WEEK:

ANSWERS TO PRAYER THIS WEEK:

LONELY HOURS

My kinsmen stand afar off (Ps. 38:11, KJV). Read Ruth 1:1-3; Psalm 38.

> *Alone. . .alone. . .I feel so all alone. . . .*
> *There's no one here to understand*
> *The way I feel.*
> *My heart cries out*
> *For someone who can fill the empty spot*
> *My husband's death has left. My sons are here*
> *But I can't talk to them*
> *About my deepest hurts and fears.*
> *Their life is full of fun and games*
> *And mine is full of tears.*
>
> *—Naomi*

As we discussed yesterday, Naomi and Elimelech had traveled to the land of Moab because of famine conditions in Israel. After living there for some time, Elimelech died and Naomi was left alone with two fatherless sons to raise in a foreign land. How she must have yearned for the familiar sights of Israel!

Loneliness is a specter that haunts the lives of millions of people. It's as likely to occur in a crowd as it is in a lonely room. It cuts across the boundaries of race and social levels, of the rich and the poor. It can become a source of continuing depression if we allow it to monopolize our thought patterns.

There have been times, Father, when my absorption with my own loneliness has kept me from realizing the needs of others who may have been even lonelier than I was. Help me to remember that You are always with me, no matter how temporarily alone I may feel.

"DEPRESSION TEARS AT ONE'S PERSONAL RELATIONSHIP WITH GOD."[1]

DEPRESSION STRIKES!

*My kinsfolk have failed, and my familiar friends have forgotten me
(Job 19:14, KJV). Read Ruth 1:4; Job 19.*

*Mahlon and Chilion have found wives
And now I'm even more alone.
Their wives, of course, are Moabites—
They won't associate with me.
They have their gods,
        and I have my God.
Oh, bitter is the day we left Israel
And left our faith behind!*

                             —Naomi

Naomi may have hoped that her sons would wait to marry until the family returned to Israel and they could find girls of their own nationality and faith, but this is not what happened. Perhaps Mahlon and Chilion married girls they grew up with. In any case, both Ruth and Orpah, Naomi's daughters-in-law, were Moabites and outside the "chosen people."

Naomi and Job both felt that their family and friends had forgotten them. There was probably also the heightening feeling of uselessness so commonly associated with lengthening years. Added to this may have been the regrets, the "should-haves" from the past years.

Forgive me, Father, for the times I've neglected older members of my family or once-valuable friends who have "aged out" of my life. Remind me to show my appreciation for their concern and counsel over the years.

**"THEY MIGHT NOT NEED ME, YET THEY MIGHT!
I'LL LET MY HEAD BE JUST IN SIGHT;
A SMILE AS SMALL AS MINE MIGHT BE
PRECISELY THEIR NECESSITY."**

                            —Emily Dickinson

DEPRESSION LINGERS

I sat alone because of thy hand (Jer. 15:17, KJV). Read Ruth 1:5; Psalm 91.

Mahlon and Chilion are gone,
Felled by a single stroke
Of God's almighty sword.
How much more can I bear?
My husband is gone, and now
I've lost my sons as well!
O, God, it's punishment enough!
I'll leave this godless country
While I still have life and breath.

—Naomi

Naomi regarded the deaths in her family as a personal punishment from God. In Ruth 1:13 she tells her daughters-in-law, "the Lord's hand has gone out against me" (NIV). Her grief and loneliness had clouded her vision. She didn't understand that not all tragedy is punishment; much of it comes from Satan (example: Job) or from being part of this evil world. Remember that God can turn a tragedy into a victory!

When we, as children of God, succumb to depression, it affects our personal life as well as our Christian testimony. Satan uses this disturbance to rob us of the peace and joy that are rightfully ours. With an attitude of defeat and a pessimistic outlook on life, we are actually negative witnesses for the cause of Christ.

Father, I know You have a plan for my life and for my family. Help me to be an example of faith for those who watch me each day, not a stumbling block.

"THE POTENTIAL BLESSINGS OF A CHRISTIAN HOME ARE DESTROYED BY THE UNHEALTHY ENVIRONMENT OF DEFEAT."[2]

A RAY OF LIGHT

A man that hath friends must shew himself friendly (Prov. 18:24, KJV). Read Ruth 1:6-18; Psalm 103.

Dear Ruth and Orpah!
They really love me—to the point
Of wanting to go with me!
I never dreamed they cared so much!
But I'm a jinx. . .I'll ruin life
For them as I have mine.
And they'll regret they ever came with me.
And yet. . .
　　　　　It seems Ruth really wants to come.
　　　　　　　　　—Naomi

According to the custom of the day, parents kept a widowed daughter-in-law in the family by "marrying her off" to a younger brother of her former husband. (Remember the story of Tamar, who was married to two brothers and promised a third brother when he became of age?) But Naomi, as a widow, had no potential husbands to offer her daughters-in-law, so it may have come as a surprise to her that they actually wanted to stay with her.

Naomi was measuring her self-worth, her usefulness by what she was able to give her daughters-in-law (in terms of husbands). She didn't seem to realize that they must have valued her as a friend, a mother, a confidant, perhaps a teacher. She had much to give!

Help me, Father, never to evaluate my worth in definable quantities. Thank You that You have promised to renew my youth (Ps. 103:5). Thank You for Your everlasting mercies, Your never-ending benefits.

SOMEBODY *NEEDS* MY FRIENDSHIP.

A NEW NAME

For we brought nothing into this world, and it is certain that we can carry nothing out (1 Tim. 6:7, KJV). Read Ruth 1:19-22.

Call me no longer by the name Naomi—
That name belonged to happier days than these—
But call me Mara now. . .my life is bitter.
Yes, God Almighty has dealt bitterly with me.
I went out from this country full;
My husband and my sons walked by my side,
But God has sent me back again, my quiver empty,
With none but Ruth to ease the pain inside.
                                        —Naomi

Naomi, like so many of us, had certain "expectations" of God. It seems she *expected* a long life for herself and her husband, undisturbed by calamity or suffering. She *expected* health and happiness for her sons, yet the meanings of their names—"sickly" and "pining"—seem to indicate her lack of faith. When God did not "come through" in accordance with her expectations, she became bitter. .

Perhaps part of Naomi's problem was that she may have compared her situation with that of other families who seemed unaffected by tragedy. The Bible warns us against this kind of comparison. We need to learn to thank God for His unique plan for our lives and for the blessings He has given us.

Help me, Father, to bloom where I'm planted instead of always trying to transplant myself. Help me to learn to be content "in whatsoever state I am". . .or town. . .or house. Help me to think positively, in terms of blessings rather than problems.

DEPRESSION RESULTS FROM SELF-PITY.

TRUE LOVE

A friend loveth at all times (Prov. 17:17, KJV). Read Ruth 4:9-10, 13-17; Romans 8:26-39.

Who could have known the Lord's intentions
When things seemed only to be going wrong?
Who could have known I would nurse a baby
And in my heart there'd ring a song?
Boaz and Ruth have been to me a family;
My daughter-in-law is better than ten sons!
Her love has taken me through sorrow
And proved to me once more that God is love.
—Naomi

What caused this incredible change in Naomi's outlook? She was still a widow—and several years older—but between chapter 1 of Ruth and chapter 4 her attitude has made a complete turnabout. The answer is obvious: the love of her daughter-in-law Ruth, the concern of her kinsman Boaz, and the delight of the new arrival in the family, little Obed. Naomi had become such a radiantly happy person that Ruth and Boaz felt safe in placing their newborn child in her care.

What a difference love can make in a life! Is there someone in your world who needs your love?

Thank You, Father, for the difference Your love has made in my life. I know that precious water of love will become stagnant if it's kept bottled up within myself. Help me to keep it flowing. . .each day of my life.

LOVE, LIKE WATER, WILL STAGNATE IF IT DOESN'T KEEP FLOWING.

RUTH: LOVE IN ACTION

Eugenia Price writes: "Love is not limited by the type of relationship between two people. Love is only limited by human self-concern. We are not surprised at a deep love between two friends, between a husband and wife, between parents and children—but a love relationship between a woman and her daughter-in-law is pathetically rare. . . .

"The entire story [of Ruth and Naomi] is a total victory for love. Ruth was loved eventually even by those who had despised her, because she remained so constantly lovable. The girl received love because she gave only love away.

"Surely she was confused and hurt by the gossip and extreme show of prejudice against her because of her pagan ancestry, but there is no indication that she nurtured resentment or even rebellion. She went out into the fields to glean, openly, alone, facing the gossip calmly. She gave only love, so in the long run love had to come back to her. When we send out love, even if it is thrown back in our faces, it is still love when it returns!"[1]

A passage from the fifth chapter of Romans ties in very well: "We also rejoice in our sufferings, because we know that suffering produces perseverance; perseverance, character; and character, hope. And hope does not disappoint us, because God has poured out his love into our hearts by the Holy Spirit, whom he has given us" (5:3-5, NIV).

Gentle, loving Ruth—although born a Gentile, she too was included in the messianic line. Boaz and Ruth's son, Obed, was the grandfather of King David, from whom Jesus Christ was descended.

O. T. PASSAGE THIS WEEK: Ruth 2; 3; 4

SPECIAL PRAYER NEEDS THIS WEEK:

ANSWERS TO PRAYER THIS WEEK:

A NEW CREATION

Praise be to. . .God. . .the Father of compassion and the God of all comfort, who comforts us in all our troubles, so that we can comfort those in any trouble with the comfort we ourselves have received from God (2 Cor. 1:3-4, NIV). Read 2 Corinthians 5:11—6:2.

> My mother-in-law is truly a good woman,
> But every day her sadness seems to grow.
> She needs to leave this land of Moab,
> Go back to people and the land she knows.
> Perhaps someday I'll get the chance to show her
> My love for her is real and strong and true.
> I've learned to trust in Israel's God
> And He has changed my life, made all things new.
> —Ruth

The Bible tells us of Naomi's bitterness, but nothing is said about Ruth's emotions or reactions to her husband's death. It seems that Ruth had learned to cope with tragedy. Perhaps at some point in her life she had come to trust in Jehovah and to draw strength from Him to face each day.

Ruth—and many other new believers—put us "older Christians" to shame. We've grown up with the concept of faith, but do we really know how to depend totally on God? Or do we panic when we come upon an uncertain situation?

Thank You, Father, for giving me the example of Ruth's life in learning how to trust You. She had so little knowledge of You, and yet she trusted You so completely. Make my life into that kind of a pattern for others.

A CRISIS WILL REVEAL WHETHER WE HAVE LEARNED TO WORSHIP GOD AND TO TRUST HIM.

COMMITMENT, THE BASIS OF LOVE

Forgetting those things which are behind, and reaching forth unto those things which are before, I press toward the mark for the prize of the high calling of God in Christ Jesus (Phil. 3:13-14, KJV). Read Ruth 1:16-18; Psalm 131.

> *We're actually on our way to Israel,*
> *The land I've heard so very much about.*
> *What lies before me in the distant future?*
> *That God will guide my way, I have no doubt.*
> *I've left behind the sin and idol worship,*
> *My life is committed to His plan for me.*
> *Through serving others I will serve Jehovah—*
> *Commitment to His will must be the key.*
> *   —Ruth*

Ruth's words to her mother-in-law are among the most beautiful ever spoken: "Intreat me not to leave thee, or to return from following after thee: for whither thou goest, I will go; and where thou lodgest, I will lodge: thy people shall be my people, and thy God my God" (Ruth 1:16).

A girl's thoughts of love are often giddy, romantic, and full of fantasies. Later experiences with dirty diapers and exhausting night feedings may quickly change her definition of that illusory word. True love involves service to the ones we love—and that means total commitment!

Thank You, Lord Jesus, for the many opportunities for service You place before me. When I resent their drudgery and wish for greater things, remind me of the time You washed Your disciples' dirty feet.

SERVICE IS A DELIBERATE LOVE-GIFT.

GOD'S PERFECT WILL

They that trust in the Lord shall be as mount Zion, which cannot be removed, but abideth for ever (Ps. 125:1, KJV). Read Ruth 2:1-17; Psalm 146.

Protect me as I venture out this morning
And guide my feet where You would have them go.
You know our needs—You know that we have nothing;
Now to Naomi and myself Your watch-care show.

Well, here's a field where many men are reaping.
The owner must be wealthy—it's so large.
I'll ask if I can glean the grains they're dropping. . . .
Yes, that's my move, Lord! Now, please, You take
*   charge!*

—Ruth

Ruth did not have to wait until the Lord sent a special messenger or vision to tell her in which field she should glean. She had put her all into the Lord's hands, and as she did her part, she was confident that He would complete His.

Oswald Chambers says: "At first we want the consciousness of being guided by God; then as we go on we live so much in the consciousness of God that we do not need to ask what His will is, because the thought of choosing any other will never occur to us."[2] What a statement! Is that true in my life?

Help me, Father, to live, moment by moment, in the consciousness of Your presence. Make Your will for me so perfectly clear that I will follow You as simply as a small child follows its mother, never questioning her right or ability to lead the way.

"IF WE ARE SAVED AND SANCTIFIED, GOD GUIDES US BY OUR ORDINARY CHOICES: IF WE ARE GOING TO CHOOSE WHAT HE DOES NOT WANT, HE WILL CHECK AND WE MUST HEED."[3]

A PURPOSE IN SUFFERING

For just as the sufferings of Christ flow over into our lives, so also through Christ our comfort overflows (2 Cor. 1:5, NIV). Read Ruth 2:17-23; Psalm 25:1-12.

> *I thank You, Lord, for going out before me*
> *And touching hearts with Your great power and love.*
> *Thanks for Naomi and the way her spirit is changing—*
> *She's counting all her blessings from above.*
> *And thank You, Lord, for this man I've met—Boaz—*
> *Who has taken special interest in my life.*
> *Perhaps he fits into the plan You've mapped out for me. . .*
> *Naomi thinks some day I'll be his wife.*
>
> *—Ruth*

The spirit of gratitude is contagious—and living with Ruth was having its effect on Naomi. Naomi's sadness was gradually being replaced by thankfulness for Ruth's love and Boaz's kindness.

People do not listen to us when we tell them not to be discouraged or depressed. They close their ears to our logical arguments, and they are not interested in our success stories. They are convinced only by that which they cannot duplicate —reality in human experience. They will listen when we prove to them, through genuine change in our own lives, that Jesus Christ does change lives!

Thank You for helping me to realize, Father, that the problems I experience from day to day, when touched by Your love, will enable me to comfort others in similar situations. Help me to use those problems and experiences of suffering as stepping stones to a higher plane of living.

"WHAT IS THERE IN YOUR LIFE THAT YOU CANNOT EXPLAIN ON ANY BASIS OTHER THAN THE SUPERNATURAL?"[4]

A DIFFICULT SITUATION

Fear thou not; for I am with thee. . .I will strengthen thee; yea, I will help thee (Isa. 41:10, KJV). Read Ruth 3.

Now guide me, Father, as I go this evening
To find kind Boaz at the threshing floor.
I feel so brash and forward—oh, how different
These wedding plans from those I made before!
Then I was just a girl and I was courted;
Now custom dictates that I must propose.
Stay by my side, Lord, in this strange new venture:
I need to feel Your presence—very close.

—*Ruth*

What a difficult experience the night at the threshing floor must have been for the gentle, soft-spoken Moabitess! Imagine yourself in her place: stealing quietly across town, listening nervously to the sledgehammer pounding of her own heart as she prostrated herself on the dusty floor, choking back a sneeze so that no one would know she was there—no one but Boaz, who at midnight suddenly awoke from sleep, startled to find a young woman at his feet!

Sometimes, while following God, we find ourselves doing what seem to be strange things. . .and Satan whispers, "Whose idea was this anyway?" Yet in the midnight darkness, lying there unable to sleep, we receive the answer from God that all is well. . .and that He is still in control.

Thank You, Father, for the quiet assurance of Your still small voice.

"FAITH ONLY DEVELOPS UNDER PRESSURE. . .IN THE CRUCIBLE."[5]

REDEMPTION!

Religion that God our Father accepts as pure and faultless is this: to look after orphans and widows in their distress (James 1:27, NIV). Read Ruth 4.

Naomi was right; Boaz can be trusted
To follow through on all that must be done.
He has made the necessary sale arrangements
And with Naomi's property he has won
My hand and heart and all that's in my future—
I know he'll care for Naomi and for me.
How wonderful to know the God of Israel
Has touched my life in love so tenderly!
—Ruth

Boaz is not pictured as a dynamic personality, but his name means "strength"—the kind of quiet, reassuring strength that stands firm and is totally dependable through any crisis situation. According to the custom of the day, Boaz "redeemed" Ruth and Naomi. Redemption involved purchasing Elimelech's property and marrying Ruth in order to raise children to inherit the land and carry on her husband's name.

Boaz of Bethlehem is a "type" of Christ. Christ redeemed each one of us by buying our freedom from sin. Our gratefulness should surpass that of Ruth's. . .does it?

"I love Him. . .I love Him. . .because He first loved me. . . and purchased my redemption on Calvary's tree."[6] Thank You, Father, for loving me that much.

"IT IS REQUIRED OF A STEWARD, NOT THAT HE BE BRILLIANT, NOT THAT HE SUSTAIN A PUBLIC MINISTRY, BUT THAT HE BE FAITHFUL IN THE MINISTRY TO WHICH GOD HAS CALLED HIM."[7]

PENINNAH: USE AND ABUSE

I said to myself, I'm going to quit complaining! I'll keep quiet...But as I stood there the turmoil within me grew to the bursting point. The more I mused, the hotter the fires inside (Ps. 39:1-3, LB). Peninnah might have agreed with these statements of David's; Peninnah was a very frustrated woman.

Hannah and Peninnah, the two wives of the mild-mannered priest, Elkanah—what a contrast in personalities! Hannah lived up to the meaning of her name—"gracious." But what was Peninnah's problem? Peninnah's name means "coral," and her personality became just as sharp and cutting as the rock for which she was named.

Why did Elkanah choose two such different women? In fact, why did he marry two women? Many commentators agree that Hannah was Elkanah's first wife, in order of marriage as well as preference. Then why a second wife at all? Probably because Hannah was childless!

If this is true, we begin to understand Peninnah's behavior. She may have felt "used"—needed only to bear Elkanah sons to carry on the family name. When her function was fulfilled, she was more or less ignored by Elkanah.

As you read 1 Samuel 1 and 2 during the next two weeks, compare the loving relationship of Naomi and Ruth with this family relationship. Have you been guilty of "using" anyone in your family?

O. T. PASSAGE THIS WEEK: 1 Samuel 1:1-8

SPECIAL PRAYER NEEDS THIS WEEK:

ANSWERS TO PRAYER THIS WEEK:

PLAYING SECOND FIDDLE

For where envying and strife is, there is confusion: (James 3:16, KJV). Read 1 Samuel 1:1-8; Romans 5:1-10.

Hannah's first, and I'm second,
And it will be always so. . . .
I have borne Elkanah children,
But his love I'll never know.
As they whisper in the darkness,
I draw close to my young sons.
She is Rachel, I am Leah—
Elkanah loves the childless one.

—Peninnah

Bigamy—an impossible situation! How uncivilized, how insensitive to a woman's needs, we protest. Put yourself in Peninnah's place and imagine how long it would take *you* to become resentful. . .cold. . .hateful. . .especially if your husband ignored you after you had produced the children he wanted to carry on his name.

"We can rejoice. . .when we run into problems and trials for we know that they are good for us—they help us learn to be patient. And patience develops strength of character in us and helps us trust God more each time we use it until finally our hope and faith are strong and steady. Then, when that happens, we are able to hold our heads high no matter what happens and know that all is well, for we know how dearly God loves us, and we feel this warm love everywhere within us because God has given us the Holy Spirit to fill our hearts with his love" (Rom. 5:1-5, LB). But Peninnah didn't understand that!

Thank You, Father, for bringing me into a "place of highest privilege" through faith in Your promises. Thank You that I can look forward to becoming all You have in mind for me to be (Rom. 5:2).

"FORGIVENESS IS AN ACT OF THE WILL, AND THE WILL CAN FUNCTION REGARDLESS OF THE TEMPERATURE OF THE HEART."[1]

CRYBABY HANNAH!

What causes fights and quarrels among you? Don't they come from your desires that battle within you? (James 4:1, NIV). Read Romans 5:11-21.

I hate her! How I hate her!
Every time I see her tears
It reminds me that the future—
All those long and lonely years—
Will be spent beside this woman
Who has all I'm longing for. . . .
She is loved so dearly, yet
Still she reaches out for more.

—Peninnah

You probably have a Peninnah in your neighborhood—the aggressive, outspoken type of woman who lashes out verbally when she's angry and takes pride in "telling people off when they need it." And perhaps you also know a Hannah—quiet, holding her feelings inside, apt to cry instead of explode. Both personalities find it very difficult to understand the other.

Problems in our relationships often exist because of a lack of compassion for differing personalities and a lack of understanding of dissimilar backgrounds. It's important to remember that God loves my neighbor just as much as He loves me! Through Adam sin entered the *entire* human race—my neighbor and I are on the same level—and through Christ's righteousness—not mine or hers—we are offered forgiveness because of God's mercy.

Thank You, Father, for Your abounding grace that forgives so freely and gives me right standing with You. Help me to show Your forgiveness to others.

"GRACE THAT IS GREATER THAN ALL OUR SIN"[2]

RESENTMENT GROWS

You want something but don't get it. You. . .covet, but you cannot have what you want. You quarrel and fight (James 4:2, NIV). Read Romans 6:1-11.

> *If I cannot win Elkanah*
> *By the children I have borne,*
> *Then, I swear, I'll make her pay.*
> *Hannah—rose beside the thorn!*
> *And my thorns will prick her cruelly*
> *And I'll taunt her day by day,*
> *Reminding her that she is barren,*
> *That her curse is here to stay.*
>
> *—Peninnah*

Peninnah's misery found an outlet in her cruel treatment of Hannah. By hurting Hannah she felt she was somehow evening out the unfairness of the situation. Perhaps she could not face the fact that Elkanah was no longer attracted to her, and rather than place the burden of blame on his shoulders—or her own—it was easier to hate Hannah.

Hating and inflicting hurt are part of our old evil nature, the part that loves to sin. But that part of us was "crushed and fatally wounded" (Rom. 6:6, LB), when it was nailed to the cross with Christ. Is that evident in my life?

Thank You, Father, for putting those old evil desires behind me and allowing me to share Christ's new life. Thank You that I no longer need to be a slave to sin and its evil desires.

THE TRUTH WILL SET YOU FREE!

PERSONALITY CONFLICTS

*When you ask, you do not receive, because you ask with wrong motives
(James 4:3, NIV). Read Romans 6:12-23.*

> *That time of year is here again,*
> *Our trip to Shiloh—how I dread it!*
> *All that planning, washing, packing,*
> *And the journey is so hectic!*
> *Children tire of all that walking;*
> *Hannah's always in my way.*
> *Why can't she say what she's thinking?*
> *All she does is cry and pray!*
>
> *—Peninnah*

Hannah probably bit her tongue many times to hold back the angry words that often must have flooded her mind in response to Peninnah's taunts. There is no record that Hannah ever reacted to any of the cruel, biting words hurled at her—yet Peninnah probably would have felt better if Hannah had fought back. A fighter loves a fight!

"The tongue is a small thing, but what enormous damage it can do" (James 3:5, LB). In today's Scripture reading we are told not to let *any* part of our bodies become "tools of wickedness" to be used for sinning, but to give ourselves completely to God. Sin does not need to be our master!

Forgive me, Father, for using my tongue as a tool of wickedness. Purify my body as a living sacrifice, to be used in Your service. Thank You for freeing me from the enslavement of sin.

"TAKE MY LIFE, AND LET IT BE CONSECRATED, LORD, TO THEE."[3]

COMMUNICATION BREAKDOWN

Don't brag about being wise and good if you are bitter and jealous and selfish (James 3:14, LB). Read Romans 7:15-25.

Oh, Elkanah, how you've hurt me
Since the day I married you!
I gave you these sons and daughters
But to me you've been untrue. . . .
Why weren't you content with Hannah?
Why did you complicate my life?
I'd been happier still unmarried
Than to be "the other wife."

—Peninnah

If Peninnah had faced the situation squarely, she would have had to realize that Elkanah, not Hannah, was the real source of her frustration. Had she been able to talk about the situation with him, he might have been able to understand the reasons for her bitterness, and to do something about them.

Probably Elkanah and Peninnah never did "talk it out." Perhaps they wanted to, but couldn't, creating a very frustrating situation for all concerned. The apostle Paul also faced frustration in Romans 7, when he found that he didn't understand himself; he wanted to do right, but he couldn't. . .until Jesus Christ set him free.

Thank You, Father, for freeing me from my frustrating slavery to this deadly lowly nature. Thank You for Your Holy Spirit that guides us into all truth.

"GENTLE SHEPHERD, COME AND LEAD US, FOR WE NEED YOU TO HELP US FIND THE WAY."[4]

FRIENDLESS PENINNAH

For jealousy and selfishness are not God's kind of wisdom (James 3:15, LB). Read Romans 8:1-14.

Here we are, at last, in Shiloh.
Time to celebrate again. . .
But who feels like celebrating
When you're left without a friend?
No one wants to spend time with me.
I just cannot understand—
Everyone speaks well of Hannah
But I haven't got a friend.
　　　　　　　　　　　　　—Peninnah

There is no biblical record that Peninnah ever changed, so we think of her as going through life becoming increasingly bitter, always closing the doors to new friendships because of the accumulated hurts from the past. We can imagine the lines of sadness gouging themselves deeply into her face, leaving their unmistakable signs around her eyes and mouth, where the lines of laughter should have been.

Poor Peninnah—and the many others like her—always frustrated, always hurting others because of their own deep wounds. Sometimes the scars are carefully hidden, sometimes they are obvious. . .but they're always there. Have you told a present-day Peninnah that the Holy Spirit's power can free her from her vicious treadmill, and that "following after the Holy Spirit" (rather than her lower nature) "leads to life and peace"—the peace she needs so desperately?

Thank You, Father, for the power of Your love that can touch the deepest of wounds and heal it ever so gently and completely. Thank You for touching my life.

"HE TOUCHED ME. . .AND OH, THE JOY THAT FLOODS MY SOUL."[5]

HANNAH: DOESN'T ANYONE UNDERSTAND ME?

Hannah must have felt that no one understood her.

Elkanah, her husband, told her that his love should make up for her barrenness: "Isn't having me better than having ten sons?" (1 Sam. 1:8, LB). Peninnah, the other wife, was so driven by insecurity and jealousy that she had no desire to understand Hannah. Even Eli, the priest of Jehovah, called Hannah a drunk.

It's so difficult to be misunderstood! We cry out to be vindicated from the unwitting crimes heaped against our names. "You took me all wrong. . .I didn't mean it like that!"

Yet, in her hour of loneliness, it seems Hannah understood the issues at hand. Weak Israel, surrounded by the strength of her Philistine neighbors, needed a spiritual giant who could replace the inept and morally decayed leadership of the nation. The cry of Hannah's heart for a son was not only to fill the emptiness within her own mother heart, but also to fulfill Israel's need. When her prayer for a son was answered, she did not forget that need.

Hannah advanced from a state of depression and bitterness to a place of joyous certainty. Her trust in God was complete: "The Lord knows. . .and he will judge. . .for all the earth is the Lord's and he has set the world in order" (1 Sam. 2:3, 8, LB).

Perhaps the loneliness of being misunderstood developed Hannah's character. Certainly it taught her to look to God instead of people.

"I will lift up mine eyes unto the hills, from whence cometh my help. My help cometh from the Lord" (Ps. 121:1-2, KJV).

O. T. PASSAGE THIS WEEK: 1 Samuel 1; 2

SPECIAL PRAYER NEEDS THIS WEEK:

ANSWERS TO PRAYER THIS WEEK:

WOMAN OF A SORROWFUL SPIRIT

And now this word to all of you: You should be like one big happy family, full of sympathy toward each other, loving one another with tender hearts and humble minds (1 Pet. 3:8, LB). Reread 1 Samuel 1:1-8.

Oh, God, if only You would take
This curse of barrenness away from me!
My heart is heavy, even though I'm loved;
Elkanah just can't understand my need.
It's not because of envy that I pray
Nor urge to match Peninnah's style of life.
You know my heart—I simply want a son
Who'll spend his life in service, not in strife.
—Hannah

Peninnah's young offspring were being influenced to adopt wrong patterns of thinking and living because of the influence of their home environment. It must have grieved Hannah to see children—children she would have nurtured so carefully—being raised in an atmosphere of bitterness and dissension. How she yearned for a child of her own whom she could train to serve and glorify God!

"Actions speak louder than words." What am I teaching my children by my daily pattern of life? Am I aware that children learn what they see lived?

In the maelstrom of modern life, Father, help me to maintain a calm, uncluttered mind. . .and a heart that keeps Your values in first place.

CHILDREN LEARN WHAT THEY SEE LIVED!

DEEPENING DESPONDENCY

Don't repay evil for evil. Don't snap back at those who say unkind things about you. Instead, pray for God's help for them, for we are to be kind to others, and God will bless us for it (1 Pet. 3:9, LB). Read Psalm 62.

> *I know she thinks I hate her, but I don't.*
> *In fact, I understand the way she feels!*
> *It's true—Elkanah has been unfair to her,*
> *Inflicted wounds that even time can't heal.*
> *I wish I could break through the barrier*
> *That separates our hearts and thoughts and lives,*
> *Erase the years and all that lies between us,*
> *Break down the walls of prejudice and strife—*
> *But she won't let me try!*
>
> *—Hannah*

Each day of Hannah's life must have been an encounter with growing frustration. She could never escape Peninnah's taunting, sarcastic, cruel barbs. And the complicated relationship drove Hannah into periods of deepening despondency: "year by year. . .therefore she wept, and did not eat" (1 Sam. 1:7, KJV).

Am I allowing a person or people in my life to render me spiritually worthless? Are someone's words destroying my peace of mind? Am I waiting for my environment to change before I feel I can find happiness?

Help me to remember, Father, that all my expectations must be from You. You alone are my refuge, a Rock where no enemy can reach me.

"LEAD ME TO THE ROCK THAT IS HIGHER THAN I."[1]

MISUNDERSTOOD AGAIN!

If you want a happy, good life, keep control of your tongue, and guard your lips from telling lies (1 Pet. 3:10, LB). Read 1 Samuel 1:9-18.

Now even Eli, priest of God, accuses me
Of drunkenness within the holy place!
What are you telling me, my Lord?
Have I come here unclean to seek Your face?
Jehovah, give me grace and guard my tongue
As I explain to Eli what I've prayed. . .
And speak through him the words You have for me,
Help me accept the plans that You have made.
                    —Hannah

Hannah's attempt to seek Jehovah in the place of worship—to "draw nigh to God"—met with further discouragement. Her silent prayer was interpreted as a sign of drunkenness by Eli, the priest of God. *On sight* he put her in the same class with the prostitutes who hung around the temple (waiting for his own sons!).

At times in our lives our attempts to experience God's presence and be assured of His concern for us seem to be of no avail. Have you ever become so frustrated with your seeming inability to pierce the leaden skies that you gave up on prayer completely for a time?

Thank You, Father, for the story of Hannah and its living proof that prayers are answered. . .sometimes after the character development that may need to take place within me.

JESUS CHRIST WAS MISUNDERSTOOD!

SELF-CONSCIOUSNESS OR CHRIST-CONSCIOUSNESS

Turn away from evil and do good. Try to live in peace even if you must run after it to catch and hold it (1 Pet. 3:11, LB). Read 1 Samuel 1:19-28.

You have promised that my prayer has been heard;
You have spoken through Your servant, Lord, to me.
My heart rejoices in the Lord of hosts,
My soul cries out in praise and ecstasy.
The Lord alone gives life and love and peace.
Perhaps Peninnah cannot change her ways,
So I'll accept her as she is—and pray
The time will come when she'll have happier days.
                                                            —Hannah

The meaning of Hannah's name—"gracious"—was evident in her quiet and gentle spirit. Peninnah had made no secret of the fact that she heartily disliked Hannah, yet Hannah did not reciprocate in antagonism toward this woman with whom she shared her life in such a frustrating way. We can be sure that Hannah did not use her pregnancy as a tool to deepen Peninnah's jealousy and insecurity.

Am I constantly competing with people who should be my sisters and brothers in Christ? Do I make sure that everyone knows about my successes? Or am I able to just listen?

Father, please eliminate the constant self-consciousness in my life. I want Christ to be a reality—not I, but Christ who lives in me (Gal. 2:20).

"SELF-CONSCIOUSNESS IS THE FIRST THING THAT WILL UPSET THE COMPLETENESS OF THE LIFE IN GOD, AND SELF-CONSCIOUSNESS CONTINUALLY PRODUCES WRESTLING."[2]

A PROMISE MADE

For the Lord is watching his children, listening to their prayers (1 Pet. 3:12, LB). Read 1 Samuel 2:1-19.

> *Praise be to God! He has answered all my prayers*
> *And given me the son I've wanted so—*
> *A perfect child in mind and body too.*
> *The love I feel I thought I would never know.*
> *I have named him Samuel, meaning "asked of God."*
> *Each time I say his name I will recall*
> *The promise that I made to give him back,*
> *To give him to the One who heard my call.*
> *—Hannah*

Does Hannah's song remind you of the Magnificat (the song of Mary, mother of Christ)? Hannah never forgot for a moment the Source of her blessings—the Creator of all things, the Giver of life. She named her son Samuel so that his name would be a constant reminder that he had been given as a special blessing from the Lord.

It's so easy to take our blessings for granted, so easy to assume that what we enjoy today will always be ours. Unexpected tragedy has proved the opposite over and over again. "For what is your life? It is even a vapour, that appeareth for a little time, and then vanisheth away" (James 4:14, KJV).

Please remind me, Father, that every good gift comes from You. Help me not to become possessive of the children and the material things You have loaned to me for a little while to use in Your service.

"BEWARE OF ANYTHING THAT IS GOING TO SPLIT UP YOUR ONENESS WITH CHRIST."[3]

A PROMISE FULFILLED

Quietly trust yourself to Christ your Lord and if anybody asks why you believe as you do, be ready to tell him, and do it in a gentle and respectful way (1 Pet. 3:15, LB). Read 1 Samuel 2:18-21.

Well, Eli, do you know who this child is?
Do you remember when I knelt and prayed?
I made a promise then that I have kept
In memory of a love that will not fade.
I have learned that God is concerned about our needs;
I have learned that He will answer all our prayers.
His answers test our patience, wound our pride. . .
But always—if we wait—He shows He cares.
                                        —Hannah

Yesterday we observed that Hannah never forgot who was her Source. She also never forgot that her son was "on loan" to her from the Lord and that she had dedicated his life—before it began—to the God who had answered her prayer. Therefore when the time came to take little Samuel to the temple (what a heart-rending experience for any mother!), she was able to do so with peace of mind and heart . . .and the Lord blessed "barren Hannah" with three more sons and two daughters.

Trusting myself and my family to Christ means relinquishing my rights—and that's rough! We feel we must hang on desperately to everything we have accumulated in life lest we lose it. . .but it's when I learn to give my rights totally to God that He can return them as sacred privileges.

Help me, Father, to let go.

ANYTHING THAT DISTURBS REST IN CHRIST MUST BE DEALT WITH AT ONCE.

MICHAL: THE GIRL WHO
GOT HER OWN WAY

Since Saul was the first king in Israel, his daughters, Merab and Michal, were the first princesses. We know little about Merab other than that she was obedient to her father's orders; Michal, on the other hand, had an answer and an opinion in every situation. Perhaps, as the baby of the family, she had always gotten what she wanted as she was growing up.

Perhaps Michal was even attracted to David initially because he was Merab's betrothed—until father Saul forced Merab to marry another man, Adriel. But Michal was not to be put off! She wanted David and she was going to get him, no matter how father Saul felt about having the popular young David as his son-in-law.

"So Saul gave Michal to him" (1 Sam. 18:27, LB). But young, impetuous Michal had many lessons in life ahead of her. She got the handsome, charming young husband she wanted, but from that point on her life changed drastically!

Today read the familiar story in chapter 17 of 1 Samuel as an introduction to the story of Michal, and as you read, think about the ways in which the Lord has used circumstances and people in your life to shape your character.

Gothard points out: "If we respond to irritations in our lives with insight and proper action, we allow God to achieve His highest purpose in us—to reshape our lives as closely as possible to the ideal He has given us in the life of His Son."[1]

O. T. PASSAGE THIS WEEK: 1 Samuel 17—19; 24—25; 2 Samuel 3; 6

SPECIAL PRAYER NEEDS THIS WEEK:

ANSWERS TO PRAYER THIS WEEK:

YOUNG LOVE

And Michal Saul's daughter loved David (1 Sam. 18:20, KJV).
Read 1 Samuel 18.

> Oh, David, of all people we
> Were surely meant to share the throne. . . .
> I'll overlook your shepherd ways
> Until your background is outgrown.
> I'll teach you all you need to know
> While Saul my father is still alive,
> And then together we will reign—
> Oh, David, love, we will survive!
>
> —Michal

Everyone knew young David, son of Jesse—David the giant-killer! As Jonathan's best friend, he was a frequent guest in Saul's home, and before long he had found a place in Michal's heart as well. Who could forget the ruddy young shepherd who had advanced to commander of Saul's troops in such a short time?

"Love at first sight". . ."we were meant for each other"— how quickly those words are said, but how quickly they can be forgotten in times of stress! And how little most of us know of Calvary love. Amy Carmichael says: "If, in dealing with one who does not respond, I weary of the strain, and slip from under the burden, then I know nothing of Calvary love."[2]

Father, teach me to love when I am not loved or understood or even liked in return. Teach me the meaning of Calvary love.

LOVE BEGINS WHEN ANOTHER'S NEEDS BECOME MORE IMPORTANT THAN YOUR OWN.

MICHAL THE LIFESAVER

And Saul said unto Michal, Why hast thou deceived me so? (1 Sam. 19:17, KJV). Read 1 Samuel 19:1-17.

My love, I've saved your life today—
The stories I could tell!
I warned you of my father's wrath
And risked my neck as well.
I've lied for you, deceived for you;
My father hates me now.
Oh, David, hasten back to me;
Fulfill your marriage vows!

—Michal

Michal didn't seem to fear her father Saul's rages. Apparently she had never borne the brunt of his fits of anger. Perhaps she had observed him often enough, however, to become disgusted with his temperamental moods and to feel only contempt for him.

It's very difficult to respect or love a family member who is hypocritical in his daily life. People whom we have placed on pedestals inevitably topple off. Yet. . ."if I have not compassion on my fellow-servant even as my Lord had pity on me, then I know nothing of Calvary love."[3]

You know I have little or no patience with ＿＿＿＿＿, Father. I cannot understand certain things about him/her. Teach me the meaning of Calvary love.

"IF I SAY, 'JUST WHAT I EXPECTED,' IF A FALL OCCURS, THEN I KNOW NOTHING OF CALVARY LOVE."[4]

A NEW HUSBAND FOR MICHAL

For what glory is it, if, when ye be buffeted for your faults, ye shall take it patiently? but if, when ye do well, and suffer for it, ye take it patiently, this is acceptable with God (1 Pet. 2:20, KJV). Read 1 Samuel 24; 25:44.

> *I cannot do it—no, I won't!*
> *You cannot force me to!*
> *My husband, David, loves me still;*
> *He'll have revenge on you!*
> *Well, you may say I'm Palti's wife,*
> *But David's wife I'll be.*
> *I'm married to the future king*
> *And he'll come back for me!*
>
> *—Michal*

Temperamental Saul! His jealousy of David's growing popularity drove David into the wilderness. Then in 1 Samuel 24, Saul asked David's forgiveness for hunting him down like a wild animal. Yet in chapter 25, we find that Saul has forced lonely Michal to marry a man named Palti. In most cases women were considered mere chattel, or property to be used and moved at will like checkers on a board.

Imagine Michal's helpless anger! Imagine your feelings in a similar situation! How do you react when decisions with which you disagree are made for you, and you are left with the unpleasant results? How do you react when you "do well, and suffer for it" (1 Pet. 2:20)?

Father, I can't honestly say that I react patiently when I'm in situations like that. Forgive me for my inability to see past my nose, to immediately strike out in frustration. **"IF THE PRAISE OF MAN ELATES ME AND HIS BLAME DEPRESSES ME, THEN I KNOW NOTHING OF CAL—VARY LOVE."**[5]

HEARTBREAK

For even hereunto were ye called: because Christ also suffered for us, leaving us an example, that ye should follow his steps (1 Pet. 2:21, KJV). Read Colossians 2:6-10; 1 Samuel 25:39-43.

> *I can't believe this story's true—*
> *It's all a pack of lies!*
> *My father started this, I'm sure,*
> *And spread it by his spies!*
> *They're saying David took a wife*
> *While he's away from me.*
> *Two wives, you say? Impossible!*
> *I know it cannot be.*
>
> *—Michal*

Poor Michal! Her knight in shining armor had failed her! It must have been a mortal blow to the pride of the young princess. We can only imagine the emotions that stirred within her: jealousy, heartbreak, chagrin, embarrassment, depression, bitterness, contempt, hatred.

How do we conquer our negative emotions? "If I myself dominate myself, if my thoughts revolve around myself, if I am so occupied with myself I rarely have 'a heart at leisure from itself,' then I know nothing of Calvary love."[6]

Father, I'm so tired of thinking about *me, me, me* all the time—that old self-consciousness again. Help me to think of others and forget myself. Teach me the meaning of Calvary love.

CAN GOD TRUST ME WITH DISAPPOINTMENTS?

DESIRE FOR REVENGE

Who did no sin, neither was guile found in his mouth (1 Pet. 2:22, KJV). Read 2 Samuel 3:1-16.

Now he wants me back again
To add to his collection!
He's been as good as dead to me—
Now comes the resurrection!
Poor Palti loves me, it is true;
I hate to leave him now. . . .
But David calls, and I must go!
I'll pay him back somehow!

—Michal

Saul was dead, but his followers continued to fight David's forces. Their position, however, was weakening as David, now head of the Judean confederacy, rapidly gained strength. Finally Abner, leader of the opposing forces, sent messengers to David to discuss a deal, but David would not "talk" unless his wife Michal was returned to him (although by this time he had accumulated six other wives—and six sons!).

How would you react to such a humiliating situation? "If I avoid being 'ploughed under,' with all that such ploughing entails of rough handling, isolation, uncongenial situations, strange tests, then I know nothing of Calvary love."[7]

Forgive me, Father, for complaining about my lot in life so easily and so frequently. Forgive my martyr attitudes. Teach me the meaning of Calvary love.

DO I HAVE A HEART AT LEISURE FROM ITSELF?

A CRITICAL SPIRIT

Who, when he was reviled, reviled not again; when he suffered, he threatened not; but committed himself to him that judgeth righteously (1 Pet. 2:23, KJV). Read 2 Samuel 6.

> *I watched him dance out in the street*
> *With all the peasant girls. . . .*
> *I couldn't hold back my sheer disgust,*
> *Reproaches at him hurled.*
> *I thought somehow I would repay*
> *The blows he'd dealt to me. . . .*
> *But here I sit—ignored, alone,*
> *A princess—but not a queen.*
>
> *—Michal*

Loving, weeping Palti had been left behind, but Michal had become accustomed to living with a man whose major concern may have been their relationship. Contrast King David, who had just come from a thrilling worship experience and was oblivious to anyone or anything but his and his people's relationship with God.

Michal had developed a critical spirit, and all she could see was David's disgusting lack of royal dignity. She had no understanding of David's spiritual ardor. Does my spirit get in the way of God's work in lives around me?

Thank You, Father, for dealing with me on the issue of a critical spirit. If You did not see me through the righteousness of Your Son, my personal righteousness would be as unclean as filthy (menstrual) rags.

DOES MY CRITICAL SPIRIT GET IN THE WAY OF GOD'S WORK IN LIVES AROUND ME?

ABIGAIL: WHAT'S A NICE GIRL LIKE YOU DOING HERE?

A certain man in Maon, who had property there at Carmel, was very wealthy. He had a thousand goats and three thousand sheep, which he was shearing in Carmel. His name was Nabal and his wife's name was Abigail. She was an intelligent and beautiful woman, but her husband, a Calebite, was surly and mean in his dealings (1 Sam. 25:2-3, NIV).

The Living Bible describes Nabal as "uncouth, churlish, stubborn, and ill-mannered." What an introduction to a marriage! Perhaps you're asking, "Why did Abigail ever marry a guy like Nabal?"

Don't forget: in Abigail's time women didn't have the advantages we have today! In most cases (unlike Michal) they weren't given their choice of a husband. Women were often treated as chattels or pieces of property and had very few rights. As we discuss Abigail's appeal to David, we will realize that it was a very daring and risky venture.

The words of Galatians 3:28 express a revolutionary new way of thinking concerning the Jehovah-male-female relationship: "There is neither Jew nor Greek, there is neither bond nor free, *there is neither male nor female:* for ye are all one in Christ Jesus" (KJV, emphasis added).

Strange, isn't it, that many people today associate Christianity with repression of women? Jesus Christ came to set us free from bondage and gave us a position unparalleled in history!

"We are all the same—we are Christians; we are one in Christ Jesus. . .and all of God's promises. . .belong to us" (Gal. 3:28-29, LB).

O. T. PASSAGE THIS WEEK: 1 Samuel 25

SPECIAL PRAYER NEEDS THIS WEEK:

ANSWERS TO PRAYER THIS WEEK:

A GIRL'S DREAMS

Wine gives false courage; hard liquor leads to brawls; what fools men are to let it master them (Prov. 20:1, LB). Read 1 Samuel 25:2-42.

Imagine having servants
And clothes—whatever I choose!
I know there will be problems;
I'm told he likes his booze. . . .
But to think I'm going to marry
The wealthiest man around!
Yes, I'll be Mrs. Nabal,
The richest girl in town!

—Abigail

Abigail's early life may have been just the opposite of Michal's. Perhaps she came from a poor shepherd family and felt it an honor to be selected as the wife of wealthy Nabal. And perhaps she looked back later on her youthful fantasies and wished for the freedom of the hills once again—and the love she might have found in a shepherd's tent.

Nabal's personality problems were accentuated by his drinking problem. Proverbs says, "Strong drink is raging"— you'd never know it from those super-attractive television commercials, would you? How many families in your neighborhood have suffered the emotional and financial problems caused by the effects of liquor?

I promise, Father, never to expose my children (or other people's children) to the temptation of liquor within my home if it is within my power to avoid it. Help me to present my body as a living sacrifice to You (Rom. 12:1-2).

"IF THE CARE OF A SOUL BE ENTRUSTED TO ME, AND I CONSENT TO SUBJECT IT TO WEAKENING INFLUENCES. . .THEN I KNOW NOTHING OF CALVARY LOVE."[1]

HOSTILITY AT HOME

A dry crust eaten in peace is better than steak every day along with argument and strife (Prov. 17:1, LB). Read Proverbs 14:16-35.

Well, now I'm Mrs. Nabal,
But Nabal's lost his charm.
I never dreamed that I would feel
The brute strength of that arm.
It's not just me that he insults—
It's everyone in sight.
It seems he's always eager
To somehow pick a fight.

—Abigail

Whether or not it was evident to Abigail from the first days of their marriage, Nabal was a very difficult man to live with—"uncouth, churlish, stubborn, and ill-mannered" (1 Sam. 25:3, LB). The busy schedule of the sheep-shearing season probably served to aggravate his hostility toward the world in general.

Do you have a neighbor or a family member like Nabal? Sometimes you have no idea what he's bugged about—you just know he is, and he's taking out his frustrations on everyone in sight! How do I react in that situation?

Father, the way I usually react to _____ is not pleasing to You. Forgive me for my impatience, my lack of understanding. Teach me the meaning of Calvary love. **"IF STUPID PEOPLE FRET ME AND LITTLE RUFFLES SET ME ON EDGE. . .THEN I KNOW NOTHING OF CALVARY LOVE."[2]**

UNGRATEFUL NABAL

A quick-tempered man starts fights; a cool-tempered man tries to stop them (Prov. 15:18, LB). Read Proverbs 15:1-18.

Nabal has refused David—
How can he be so dumb?
We'll all be dead tomorrow
If something isn't done.
The servants want to know
What I think we should do.
O God of Israel, give me strength—
Our lives depend on You!

—Abigail

While hiding from Saul's insane jealousy in the wilderness of Paran, David had given the protection of his six hundred men to Nabal's shepherds, so that not one sheep was lost or stolen. David had the right, therefore, to ask Nabal for a contribution. But Nabal didn't see it that way!

Tim LaHaye, in his book *How to Cope with Depression*, points out that depressed people are usually ungrateful people. It's easy to just use people and then forget about *their* needs. "If the burdens of others are not my burdens too, and their joys mine, then I know nothing of Calvary love."[3]

There are so many people in my past, Father, who have helped me when I needed help desperately—and they probably think I've forgotten. Help me to show them my appreciation. And Father. . .thank You for Your love.

FRIENDSHIP INVOLVES RESPONSIBILITY AS WELL AS PLEASURE.

UNDERSTANDING THE SITUATION

A soft answer turns away wrath, but harsh words cause quarrels (Prov. 15:1, LB). Read Proverbs 15:21-33.

> *I have to face the fact—*
> *Nabal will never change—*
> *Accept him as he is,*
> *And keep him out of range.*
> *By making this decision*
> *And handling everything,*
> *Perhaps I'll save our household*
> *And please the future king.*
>
> *—Abigail*

What to do? In Abigail's hands lay the lives of her household, as well as the livelihood of the shepherd families around them. Abigail was "a woman of good understanding," and she realized and accepted her responsibilities.

Abigail was also realistic about her husband Nabal. She knew what he was and she accepted him as he was. We can't say that her acceptance changed Nabal, but it freed her from self-pity[4]—one of Satan's favorite traps. Can I accept my situation and trust God to work within that situation?

Father, I've been feeling sorry for myself because of some of the people I live with and work with. Please forgive me. Teach me the meaning of Calvary love. **"I CAN CHANGE NO OTHER PERSON BY DIRECT ACTION. I CAN CHANGE ONLY MYSELF; BUT AS I CHANGE, OTHERS TEND TO CHANGE IN REACTION TO ME. LORD, CHANGE *ME*!"[5]**

TAKING THE BLAME

When a man is trying to please God, God makes even his worst enemies to be at peace with him (Prov. 16:7, LB). Read Proverbs 16:1-20.

I take the blame for Nabal—
Please listen to what I say.
Don't carry through this murder
Or you will have to pay.
You don't want him to haunt you
When you are on the throne;
I know the Lord is with you,
But I am all alone.

—Abigail

What courage it required for Abigail to go out and meet David—a woman unprotected by her husband facing an angry unknown! In that day it was practically unthinkable. . .only Abigail's faith in the God of Israel could have sustained her and given her the calm wisdom that David quickly recognized and appreciated.

Do I rely on God in difficult situations. . .or do I collapse? What about the everyday problems? Do I search God's Word and seek His face each day, or do I "follow my instincts"?

Thank You, Father, for the example of Abigail, who tried to save her husband's life when it would have been much easier just to let him be slaughtered. I need Your compassion, Lord, for the ugly people in *my* life.

"IF I AM AFRAID TO SPEAK THE TRUTH, LEST I LOSE AFFECTION. . .THEN I KNOW NOTHING OF CALVARY LOVE."[6]

A VERY ANGRY MAN

Better a meal of vegetables where there is love than a fattened calf with hatred (Prov. 15:7, NIV). Read Proverbs 16:21-33.

*I tried to save our household
By pleading for our lives,
And then God intervened—
I now am David's wife.*

*Some people judge me harshly
For acting on my own
But—as we've named our son—
"God is my judge" alone.*

—Abigail

David accepted Abigail's much-needed peace offering. One victory was won, but the worst still lay ahead—facing an even angrier husband! Abigail decided to wait until morning to tell her drunken husband what she had done. (What a night she must have spent!) Nabal's anger was so great that it brought on a stroke. . .and he lay in a coma for ten days until he died.

It seems that we are given a valuable lesson on the danger of alcohol plus anger. Nabal's body could simply no longer stand the strain of years of this combination. Do I realize the effects of anger—either expressed outwardly or held in as resentment—on my body, mind, and emotions?

Father, help me to deal with my anger before it hurts others in its path. Help me to confess the resentment I've harbored so long. Teach me the meaning of Calvary love. **"IF I DO NOT GIVE A FRIEND 'THE BENEFIT OF THE DOUBT'. . .THEN I KNOW NOTHING OF CALVARY LOVE."**[7]

THE WOMAN OF ENDOR:
A WOMAN IN THE OCCULT

H. V. Morton describes the village of Endor: "To the east of the flat green plain of Esdraelon, or Armageddon, is a slight hill on whose slopes is a poverty-striken Arab village called to this day Endor. There are a few stone huts and caves, from one of which a thin stream of water flows into a narrow canal that guides it through the gardens.

"Old grain pits, tombs in the rocks and ancient water cisterns prove that the history of this village goes back into the mists of time.

"En-dor means the spring of Dor, or of the Dwelling. The stream of water that still trickles from the cave is the same stream that still ran there in the time of Saul and gave its name to the place where the Witch of Endor lived."[1]

Not only does the history of Endor go back into the mists of time, but also the practice of sorcery and magic. The practice had been popular in Egypt (Exod. 7:11; Isa. 19:3), but was strictly forbidden in Israel and was punishable by death (Exod. 22:18; Lev. 20:27). Yet Saul, the very king who had banned mediums and wizards from the land of Israel, consulted one for advice—the day before his death.

You may be interested in doing some further study on sorcery (also called magic, witchcraft, necromancy, or the occult). Related Scriptures include Numbers 23:23; Leviticus 19:31; 20:6; Isaiah 8:19; Jeremiah 29:8-9; Micah 3:7; Zechariah 10:2; Malachi 3:5; Galatians 5:19-20; 2 Thessalonians 2:9.

O. T. PASSAGE THIS WEEK: 1 Samuel 28

SPECIAL PRAYER NEEDS THIS WEEK:

ANSWERS TO PRAYER THIS WEEK:

WHAT KIND OF POWER?

I am glad to be a living demonstration of Christ's power, instead of showing off my own power and abilities (2 Cor. 12:9, LB). Read Deuteronomy 18:9-22.

It seems a special power is given to me. . .
For everything I speak seems to come true.
So far my instinct has been right in every case!
The people too believe a magic gift is mine—
They come to me for wisdom and advice,
Even to this ancient cave.

—Woman of Endor

Self-confidence is good if it is based on the premise that "I can do everything God asks me to with the help of Christ who gives me the strength and power" (Phil. 4:13, LB). Paul knew that when he realized his weakness, then he was truly strong—the less he depended on his own abilities, the more he depended on Christ.

Have you ever watched two children squabbling over a toy which had been given to both of them to enjoy? Any "natural" ability or gift we have is ours only because of God's goodness; to become "puffed up," therefore, because of that ability is very childish.

Thank You, Father, for the confidence You have given me as a result of my dependence on You. Thank You for Your total acceptance of me—my background, my personality, *myself*—through Your Son.

"AS LONG AS YOU ARE SELF-SUFFICIENT, YOU DO NOT NEED TO ASK GOD FOR ANYTHING."²

SIN'S SUBTLETY

For we wrestle not against flesh and blood, but against principalities, against powers, against the rulers of the darkness of this world, against spiritual wickedness in high places (Eph. 6:12, KJV). Read 1 Samuel 28:1-9.

King Saul has banned all mediums from the land,
And I'm in danger of my life if I am found. . .
But who is he against my greater power?
There is a force that guides me—
I've no fear!
Besides, the king will never find me in this cave.
—Woman of Endor

"The force" is often spoken of today in a very abstract way; in "Star Wars," it was pictured as neither good nor bad, but a little of both. Similarly, Satan is often pictured as a jovial, "the-devil-made-me-do-it," ordinary kind of guy. On the other hand, God is often treated as a tolerant godfather who is somewhat amused by our little shenanigans.

With the active help of the media, these subtle lies have found their way into Christian homes and organizations and make it very difficult for our children and youth to differentiate truth from fiction. How important it is that we spend time teaching them God's Word! Don't assume it's the job of the pastor and Sunday school teacher.

Please, Father, give me the wisdom and the strength I need to study and to teach—not just in formal schooling, but in the classrooms of everyday life.

SATAN IS THE MASTER OF SUBTLETY.

A REASON FOR DEPRESSION

Rebellion is as the sin of witchcraft (1 Sam. 15:23, KJV). Read 1 Samuel 15:1-30.

The people tell me Saul has disobeyed.
He will not do as Samuel directs.
They say that he's tormented night and day
By evil spirits that pursue him.
Could those same spirits be the ones
Who give me insight, tell me of the past,
And prophesy what lies ahead?
                    —Woman of Endor

Saul had been directed by the Lord (through Samuel) to "settle accounts" with the nation of Amalek for refusing to allow Israel to cross their borders during Israel's Exodus from Egypt. Saul not only disobeyed, but he lied about his disobedience as well—and then tried to cover his sin by promising to make special sacrifices! But Samuel replied sternly, "To obey is better than sacrifice, and to heed is better than the fat of rams" (1 Sam. 15:22, NIV).

Have you ever considered that fear and depression may enter your life for the very same reason—disobedience? Look back over any recent days of depression (discouragement is not the same as depression), and see if you can detect unconfessed sin.

Thank You, Father, for the clues Your Word gives us about the reasons for our problems. Help me to not only hear the Word, but do it.

"BEWARE OF ALLOWING ANYTHING TO SOFTEN A HARD WORD OF JESUS CHRIST'S."[3]

PARALYSIS OF FEAR

For God hath not given us the spirit of fear; but of power, and of love, and of a sound mind (2 Tim. 1:7, KJV). Read 1 Samuel 16:14-23.

Who is this coming to my cave by night,
Afraid of eyes that watch and then report?
But something tells me he is no ordinary man. . . .
Even though the lines of fear are heavy in his face
I must be sure he's not a spy of Saul's
Before I do the service that he asks.
                              —Woman of Endor

The scene in which Saul seeks the help of the woman of Endor is intensely dramatic. Aware that he has lost divine approval, and terrified by the powers amassed against him, the old king gropes in the darkness of his soul for some comfort—but can find none. He thinks of his dead counselor, Samuel, and wishes he were alive so he could go to him for comfort and advice.

How often we recognize the value of people in our lives after we have neglected to follow their advice! But Saul was now at the point of no return, and his way of getting help was against the laws of God. The ends do not justify the means.

Thank You, Father, for the many wise advisors You have placed in my path. Help me to remember that where there is no counsel, "the people fall" (Prov. 11:14)—and that includes me.

HAVE YOU REALLY LISTENED TO THAT ADVICE YOU ASKED FOR. . .OR DID YOU DISREGARD IT BECAUSE YOU DIDN'T AGREE?

A HOPELESS SITUATION

So why are you trying to find out the future by consulting witches and mediums? Don't listen to their whisperings and mutterings. Can the living find out the future from the dead? Why not ask your God? (Isa. 8:19, LB). Read 1 Samuel 28:10-20.

He wants old Samuel—and he says
No harm will come to me.
But there is something in his voice
That strikes cold fear in me.
This man is desperate—I'd best obey
Before he takes my life.

—Woman of Endor

In the darkness of the night Saul, disguised in a long cloak and accompanied by only two of his royal retinue, had climbed the slight volcanic hill to the dwelling of the woman of Endor. A man with only a few hours to live was about to question the spirits of the dead. . .how typical of a person with no hope!

It was because Saul could not pray that he had ceased to hope. God has promised that even before we call, He will answer us, and that while we're still praying, He hears (Isa. 65:24). Why, then, do we so often use prayer as a last resort?

Forgive me, Father, for the recent times in which I have willfully pursued my own way until I messed everything up, antagonized friends and family, and made myself totally miserable. And. . .thank You for still loving me in spite of myself!

"THINK OF THE LAST THING YOU PRAYED ABOUT— WERE YOU DEVOTED TO YOUR DESIRE OR TO GOD?"[4]

A SEANCE IN ENDOR

Saul died for his disobedience. . .and because he had consulted a medium, and did not ask the Lord for guidance (1 Chron. 10:13-14, LB). Read 1 Samuel 28:21-25.

> *It is the king—here in my cave—*
> *And I've transgressed the law!*
> *What will he do to punish me*
> *When he revives again?*
> *I will make sure he is well-fed;*
> *I'll kill the fatted calf. . . .*
> *Perhaps he'll forget what I have done*
> *And leave my home in peace.*
> *—Woman of Endor*

Whether the spirit the woman saw was really Samuel or not (there is much disagreement on this subject), the fact remains that the phenomena reported during this "seance" were the same as those known to modern spiritualists. When we see the woman of Endor not as a witch in a fairy tale, but as a real woman who believed herself to be—and convinced others that she was—in touch with an unseen world, we realize how very lifelike she is.

The woman appears very kind in her treatment of Saul. Nonetheless, she does nothing to deter him from going to his fate. But then, how could she? She, too, had no hope!

Thank You, Father, that we are "looking for that blessed hope, and the glorious appearing of the great God and our Savior Jesus Christ: who gave himself for us, that he might redeem us from all iniquity" (Titus 2:13, KJV).

IT IS POSSIBLE TO SINCERELY MISTAKE A POISON FOR A MEDICINE.

BATHSHEBA: TWO MISPLACED PERSONS

I chose you to be the leader of my people Israel when you were a mere shepherd, tending your sheep in the pastureland. I have been with you wherever you have gone and have destroyed your enemies. And I will make your name greater yet. . . . Your family shall rule my kingdom forever (2 Sam. 7:8-9, 16, LB).

God spoke these words through the prophet Nathan to David the king. Yet only a short time later, God sent the same prophet to reveal David's sins of adultery and murder! (Our opening readings for the next two weeks will be taken from Psalm 51, David's prayer of confession after Nathan's condemnation.)

"How could it have happened?" we ask. David, "a man after God's own heart"—how could such a man be guilty of adultery and then murder?

The times, of course, were different. God had warned Israel that wanting a king to rule over them was a mistake. He warned that kings would draft their sons, enslave their daughters, tax their increase, demand a percentage of everything they had. Kings were entitled to whatever they wanted in those days—and although Saul and David both started out humbly, we see pride and egotism in both their lives.

The tenth and eleventh chapters of 2 Samuel tell us that Bathsheba came into David's life during a war with the Ammonites. War—then why was the commander-in-chief at home in the City of David? Why indeed?

It seems obvious that this was a time in David's life when he was out of the will of God. He was not supporting his men as he should have been.

O. T. PASSAGE THIS WEEK: 2 Samuel 11

SPECIAL PRAYER NEEDS THIS WEEK:

ANSWERS TO PRAYER THIS WEEK:

THE PULL OF TEMPTATION

Have mercy upon me, O God, according to thy lovingkindness; according unto the multitude of thy tender mercies blot out my transgressions (Ps. 51:1, KJV). Read 2 Samuel 11; James 1:13-15.

> *It started when we moved nearer the palace.*
> *In all the city there was not a man so handsome as the*
>   *king.*
> *How could I block out from my mind the thought—*
> *The king lived practically next door to me!*
> *Another thought obsessed my mind for months:*
> *Someday we would meet by chance*
> *And, eyelids lowered, I would blush*
> *And then look up to meet his eyes. . .*
> *Those eyes that noticed everything.*
>   *—Bathsheba*

We have no way of knowing Bathsheba's feelings toward David, but this is certain: actions begin in the mind, with a tempting thought that flashes through and then is latched onto. Whether the thought of a possible seduction occurred only to David or to David *and* Bathsheba, it did begin as a thought!

Tempting thoughts are not sin in themselves, *if* we "resist the devil" and send them flying. If we dwell on those thoughts, however, and allow them to become patterns of thinking, eventually they will develop into wrong actions.

Help me, Father, to "clean house" in my mind *and* in my home. Help me to get rid of anything in either area that is not pleasing to You.

GOD WILL NOT TEACH US SELF-DISCIPLINE: WE HAVE TO DISCIPLINE OURSELVES.

A PATTERN FORMED

*Wash me throughly from mine iniquity, and cleanse me from my sin.
For I acknowledge my transgressions: and my sin is ever before me (Ps.
51:2-3, KJV). Read Matthew 5:27-32.*

I wanted him to see me. . .yes, it's true.
Perhaps I wouldn't admit it—
Even to myself—
But as I watched that regal body dance before the Lord,
I thought of what it would be like to be his queen.
And when Uriah left for war,
I asked if David, too, had gone.

—Bathsheba

When the wrong kinds of thoughts are allowed to stay,
they take root in the mind and begin to grow rapidly. King
David's wrong thoughts began with, or were accelerated by,
the sight of lovely Bathsheba taking a bath on her rooftop. He
had already accumulated umpteen wives, but lust is never
satisfied.

There are many kinds of wrong thoughts. A twinge of
jealousy may lead to bitterness and hatred. Giving in to self-
pity can cause nonstop depression. We need to ask the Holy
Spirit to examine our lives on a daily basis, checking for tell-
tale signs.

Help me, Father, to check wrong thoughts before they
develop into patterns. Show me in the mirror of Your Word
where my problems lie before they poison my spiritual life.
Thank You, Father, for the comfort of Your love.

**"DO NOT SAY—OH LORD, I SUFFER FROM WANDER-
ING THOUGHTS. *DON'T* SUFFER FROM WANDERING
THOUGHTS!"**[1]

NONKOSHER THOUGHTS AND ACTS

Against thee, thee only, have I sinned, and done this evil in thy sight:
that thou mightest be justified when thou speakest, and be clear when thou
judgest (Ps. 51:4, KJV). Read Matthew 15:10-20.

And so that evening when I bathed,
I realized he could see. . . .
The call came quickly, quietly:
"Come to the king."
I went.
I didn't have to ask the reason for his call.
I read it in his eyes.

—Bathsheba

In Jesus' day the Pharisees refrained from eating certain nonkosher foods for fear of defilement. Jesus pointed out that it's what we say and think, not eat, that makes us unclean. Obviously King David was thinking and saying all the wrong things.

Wrong patterns of thinking lead to wrong actions. At one point in our lives, we may say, "I could *never* do something like that!" Yet, days, months, or years later, we may find ourselves doing that very thing. What has happened? Wrong thoughts lead to wrong patterns of thinking that lead to wrong actions.

Forgive me, Father, for being pious and holier-than-thou. I'm no better than the people I've looked down on. Without You I am nothing. . .but. . .I can do *all* things through Your Son. Thank You, Jesus.

WRONG THOUGHTS LEAD TO WRONG PATTERNS OF THINKING THAT LEAD TO WRONG ACTIONS.

SHAPEN IN INIQUITY

*Behold, I was shapen in iniquity; and in sin did my mother conceive me
(Ps. 51:5, KJV). Read Exodus 20:14, 17; Leviticus 20:10; Malachi 3:5.*

I am with child.
I can't believe that this is happening to me.
Yet here I am, Uriah's wife,
With David's child inside my womb.
Have I gone mad?
What will I do?
What can I do?
I need Uriah's loyal arms.

—Bathsheba

Adultery in Israel was considered a major crime, punishable by death. Bathsheba's position was truly precarious. The child was obviously not her husband's, since he had been away too long, and David, as the king, could ignore her completely if he wished. Should she even let him know that she was carrying his child?

The ugly consequences of sin! It can look so attractive, so inviting, so fulfilling—until we see it for what it really is. What seems to be a beautiful relationship can suddenly turn into an ugly affair. The party that looks like so much fun can turn into a nightmare. Only the Holy Spirit can give us the discernment we need—and we must be willing to be shown.

Thank You, Father, for Your leading in my life. Keep me constantly on the alert for danger signs.

ROAD SIGNS ARE HELPFUL ONLY WHEN THEY ARE OBEYED.

LOVING MY NEIGHBOR

Behold, thou desirest truth in the inward parts: and in the hidden part thou shalt make me to know wisdom (Ps. 51:6, KJV). Read Deuteronomy 5:18, 21; Romans 13:9.

I have told the king I am with child;
He has called Uriah to come home.
Uriah is there with David now;
The men I love—and fear—
Are there together in one room.
How can I face Uriah now?
What will I say when we're alone?
Will he be able to detect
I've held and loved another man?
        —Bathsheba

"You must not burn with desire for another man's wife." "If you love your neighbor as much as you love yourself...you won't sin with his wife" (Deut. 5:21; Rom. 13:9, LB). David had failed the test of loving his neighbor—and Bathsheba's unexpected pregnancy was only the first of many tragic results of David's lust.

The laws of God have not changed over the years between then and now...and neither have the wages of sin. Sin leads to physical and spiritual death, because it necessitates separation from God. Separation from our Creator cuts us off from fellowship with Him and often from His children as well, and we are left in terrible isolation.

Thank You, Father, for this example that shows us so clearly the results of sin. Help me to remember it when I am tempted to disobey the guidelines You have established for my protection.

GOD'S LAWS ARE GUIDELINES ESTABLISHED FOR OUR PROTECTION.

A STUMBLING BLOCK

Purge me with hyssop, and I shall be clean: wash me, and I shall be whiter than snow (Ps. 51:7, KJV). Read Galatians 5:17-21.

Uriah would not come to me.
He said he couldn't leave his men,
Enjoy his home, and hold his wife
While others fight for Israel.
What will I do? I soon will show
This child that grows inside of me.
I bear the king's own child—and yet
I cannot let his people know.

—Bathsheba

"When you follow your own wrong inclinations your lives will produce. . .evil results" (Gal. 5:19, LB). As we discussed yesterday, Bathsheba's pregnancy was not the only result of David's lust. Think of the problems it must have caused in the nation: "If the king can have another woman, so can I". . ."He's God's representative, so God must no longer disapprove of adultery."

Whether we like it or not, other people are affected by our actions and our lives. If we call ourselves Christians, we are responsible to set an example in word *and* deed for those around us, *especially* within our own family (which seems the most difficult area!).

Father, I just can't do it on my own. The knowledge that others are watching my life scares me. I need Your strength, Your wisdom, Your love.

WHO'S FOLLOWING IN YOUR FOOTSTEPS?

BATHSHEBA: THE HUMBLING PROCESS

Time has passed; the years have gone by. David and Bathsheba have learned a valuable lesson—the need for confession of sin. "David spoke of this, describing the happiness of an undeserving sinner who is declared 'not guilty' by God. 'Blessed, and to be envied,' he said, 'are those whose sins are forgiven and put out of sight'" (Rom. 4:6-7, LB).

But what agony the two experienced before the joy of salvation was restored: hours of hating themselves and perhaps each other, reliving the nightmare of Uriah's murder, worrying about the child, despairing over the prophecies of the future.

How often they must have wished they could turn back the hands of the clock and undo the wrongs they had done!

But God promised, "If my people. . .shall humble themselves, and pray, and seek my face, and turn from their wicked ways; then will I hear from heaven, and will forgive their sin" (2 Chron. 7:14, KJV).

David humbled himself, and I feel sure that Bathsheba did also (if she too was at fault in the situation). Their second child, Solomon, was a symbol of God's blessing. His nickname, Jedidiah, meant "beloved of God," for God expressed His interest in the child through the prophet Nathan. God had forgiven!

If you feel that God has not forgiven you, perhaps you simply have not forgiven yourself. . .or someone else. "And forgive us our sins, for we ourselves also forgive every one who is indebted to us—who has offended us or done us wrong" (Luke 11:4, *Amplified*).

O. T. PASSAGE THIS WEEK: 2 Samuel 12

SPECIAL PRAYER NEEDS THIS WEEK:

ANSWERS TO PRAYER THIS WEEK:

URIAH BETRAYED

Make me to hear joy and gladness; that the bones which thou hast broken may rejoice. Hide thy face from my sins, and blot out all mine iniquities (Ps. 51:8-9, KJV). Read Psalm 32.

I look back on those days, my feelings mixed.
I've learned so many things since then—
And God has forgiven much.
I never will forget the shock
Of hearing of Uriah's death.
"Uriah's dead!"
    I had known him well,
My childhood sweetheart and my friend.
Excitement called and I had gone,
Betrayed him to a violent end.
        —Bathsheba

The announcement of Uriah's death must have rudely awakened Bathsheba from her fantasy world. Making secret love to the king one beautiful evening was a far cry from an unwanted pregnancy and a murdered husband.

At times it is necessary for a shepherd to break the leg of a stubborn lamb who persistently wanders away from the flock. After what seems to be an act of cruelty, the shepherd gently nourishes the lamb back to health, carrying it in his arms until the break is mended. Has it been necessary for the Good Shepherd to apply this discipline in my life—or will it be necessary?

Thank You, Father, for the way in which You have tenderly disciplined me when I was in such need of it. Help me to keep my eyes on You from this point on.

THE WRONG KIND OF DAYDREAMS TURN INTO NIGHTMARES.

FORGIVING MYSELF

Create in me a clean heart, O God; and renew a right spirit within me (Ps. 51:10, KJV). *Read Psalm 66:8-20.*

In just a few days David called,
This time for me to be his wife.
He had remembered, and he cared—
The king of Israel cared for me!

I loved him, hated him by turns.
I found I couldn't forgive myself
Or David either.
Uriah's face was in my dreams
Condemning me for what I'd done.
—Bathsheba

Bathsheba was probably exhausted at the end of each day, not so much by the increasing awkwardness of pregnancy as by the constant emotional conflict within herself. Memories of Uriah and their earlier happy days together must have haunted her nights—there was no rest to be had!

Bathsheba must have felt that she was locked into a cage with no way out. Marriage to David covered her shame to a certain extent, but she had to live with the constant oppression of her guilt. Is something from your past haunting you? Does confession need to be made?

Create in me a clean heart. . .renew a right spirit within me. If there is something or someone in my past that needs to be dealt with, bring it to my mind and then, Father, give me Your wisdom.

REMEMBER: WE ARE NOT SO MUCH PUNISHED *FOR* **OUR SINS AS PUNISHED** *BY* **OUR SINS.**

THE LONELINESS OF DISOBEDIENCE

Cast me not away from thy presence; and take not thy holy spirit from me (Ps. 51:11, KJV). Read Psalm 88.

As the child within me grew,
My shame increased each day as well.
I stayed within the palace gates;
Most days I stayed inside my room.
I couldn't bear to hear the talk;
I couldn't avoid the knowing looks.
I knew we'd disobeyed the Lord
And—worst of all—I couldn't pray.
                              —Bathsheba

"O Jehovah, God of my salvation, I have wept before you day and night. . . . Your wrath lies heavy on me. . . . You have made my friends to loathe me. . . . O Lord, I reach my pleading hands to you for mercy" (Ps. 88:1, 7-9, LB). If David felt this way, think of Bathsheba's emotions!

Knowing our friends are angry with us ties us in knots inside, but it's worse to know that we have disobeyed God and to feel that His wrath will be on us forever. Sometimes the burden of our sin is so great that we feel unable to pray, unworthy to approach a holy God.

Thank You, Father, that the doors of Your throne room are always open, and that we can bring our requests before the "mercy seat" at any time. Help me to show Your mercy and Your love to those around me.

SIN WILL BE REFLECTED IN YOUR FAMILY AND YOUR FUTURE.

FROM ADORATION TO CONDEMNATION

Restore unto me the joy of thy salvation; and uphold me with thy free spirit (Ps. 51:12, KJV). Read 2 Samuel 12; Jeremiah 3:20-25.

Our son is born. . . .
But still I feel a heaviness within.
Our sin has clouded both our lives.
The prophet Nathan has condemned us openly.
I fear that David soon will break beneath the strain.

O God, forgive us! We have sinned. . . .
Restore to us Your joy.

—Bathsheba

The public exposure of David's guilt by the prophet Nathan must have been a terrible experience for the man who was accustomed to being the most popular man in Israel. From adoration to condemnation is a long way down!

But God says, "Return, ye backsliding children, and I will heal your backslidings" (Jer. 3:22, KJV). It's important that we recognize ourselves for what we are—lost, wayward children—with none of the trappings of importance that we have picked up along the way. In God's eyes we are just children.

Thank You, Father, for letting me see myself from Your perspective. I've tried so hard to be "big," to be important—but I'm just Your child. And I'm so glad to be Your child. **REVIVAL IS LIKE SEEING YOURSELF IN A MIRROR BEFORE YOU'VE DONE ANYTHING TO YOURSELF.**

BELOVED OF GOD

Deliver me from bloodguiltiness, O God, thou God of my salvation: and my tongue shall sing aloud of thy righteousness. O Lord, open thou my lips; and my mouth shall shew forth thy praise (Ps. 51:14-15, KJV). Read 1 Corinthians 6:9-11.

> *We were forgiven! When the baby died,*
> *The past died too.*
> *Jehovah proved His love*
> *By sending us another son,*
> *A son who will someday rule*
> *The land of Israel—*
> *Solomon!*
> *His nickname says it all:*
> *"Jedidiah" means "beloved of God."*
> *—Bathsheba*

The exhilaration of forgiveness! The extraordinary joy of being totally cleansed! The certainty of total forgiveness enabled David to rise from the ground of mourning and meet his God in the place of worship.

"There was a time when some of you were just like that but now your sins are washed away, and you are set apart for God, and he has accepted you because of what the Lord Jesus Christ and the Spirit of our God have done for you" (1 Cor. 6:11, LB).

I too, Father, have experienced the beauty of Your forgiveness and Your cleansing. Help me to share that wonder with others. Please remind me, Father, of where I came from and where I've been, so that I might reach out a hand to someone who is still there.

FORGIVENESS IS THE PERFUME A FLOWER GIVES OFF AFTER IT HAS BEEN TRAMPLED UNDERFOOT.

NATHAN—GOD'S MOUTHPIECE

The sacrifices of God are a broken spirit: a broken and a contrite heart, O God, thou wilt not despise (Ps. 51:17, KJV). Read 1 Kings 1; Psalm 86.

Thanks be to God! The prophet intervened again.
The family problems he foresaw so long ago
Have come to pass—and mutiny
Still multiplies against the throne.
But thanks to Nathan, Solomon will reign!

God has used His mouthpiece many times
To show His judgment, speak His words,
And radiate His heart of love.

—Bathsheba

Over the years Nathan had been God's faithful messenger. He had denounced David publicly when to do so could have meant instant death. He extended the arm of God's forgiveness when Solomon was born. And now, years later, he warned Bathsheba that rebellious Adonijah (Solomon's half-brother) was about to usurp the throne when God had promised it to Solomon.

There are many times when it is difficult to be God's mouthpiece. There are unpleasant things that we must say as well as telling of God's love. In the decadent age in which we live, we need an example like that of Nathan when we flinch and hold back from speaking the words God wants us to speak.

Thank You, Father, that Your courage and Your power are available to us. "Tell me where you want me to go and I will go there. May every fiber of my being unite in reverence to your name. With all my heart I will praise you. I will give glory to your name forever, for you love me so much!" (Ps. 86:11-13, LB).

"THE LOVE OF GOD IS GREATER FAR THAN TONGUE OR PEN CAN EVER TELL."[1]

TAMAR: YOUR CHILDREN
ARE WATCHING YOU!

The Lord God of Israel says, 'I made you king of Israel and saved you from the power of Saul. I gave you his palace and his wives and the kingdoms of Israel and Judah. . . . Why, then, have you despised the laws of God and done this terrible thing? For you have murdered Uriah and stolen his wife. Therefore murder shall be a constant threat in your family from this time on, because you have insulted me by taking Uriah's wife. I vow that because of what you have done I will cause your own household to rebel against you. . . . You did it secretly, but I will do this to you openly, in the sight of all Israel' (2 Sam. 12:7-12, LB).

In a few short years King David had accumulated a harem. Six wives and six sons are listed in 2 Samuel 3; add the other unnamed wives and concubines and their children, along with Bathsheba and her son, and you have quite a royal family!

David's much-publicized adultery was certainly not lost on his sons. "Anything goes!" had become the favorite slogan of the palace. Our father the king did it. Why can't we? The story of Tamar and Amnon is a dramatic follow-up to David's spiritual failure; the very next chapter after the story of Bathsheba relates the consequences of David's sin.

Picture yourself, parent, in David's sandals. How could he chastise or properly discipline his children when he had so flagrantly disobeyed God's laws?

Is there an Amnon—or a Tamar—or an Absalom—watching *your* life? Can I teach young people to treat their bodies as the temples of the Holy Spirit (1 Cor. 6:19) if I, as a parent or an older Christian, have not offered my own body as a living sacrifice?

O. T. PASSAGE THIS WEEK: 2 Samuel 13; 18

SPECIAL PRAYER NEEDS THIS WEEK:

ANSWERS TO PRAYER THIS WEEK:

A SILVER SPOON IN MY MOUTH?

Better a dry crust with peace and quiet than a house full of feasting, with strife (Prov. 17:1, NIV). Read 2 Samuel 3:2-5; 5:13-16.

Being born a princess isn't what you might expect;
Living in a palace has its negative effects.
How could one man be a husband to so many different
women?
How could one man be a father to three dozen angry
children?
There are so many family feuds existing in this palace—
Each mother fighting with all the rest to give her child
importance;
The wives all hate each other and despise the
concubines. . . .
O God of Israel, only You can straighten out our lives.
—Tamar

King David's sons were growing up—and probably all of them had their eyes on the throne (or at least their mothers did!). Can you imagine the jealousy and intrigues that must have existed within the palace?

Each child—or each parent—wants to be kingpin. Homes are disintegrating as the divorce rate climbs higher each year. Outside of Jesus Christ we cannot be glad for others' successes, we cannot waive our own rights, we cannot submit to each other!

Please plant on the property of my life, Father, trees that will bear the fruits of Your Spirit: "love, joy, peace, patience, kindness, goodness, faithfulness, gentleness and self-control" (Gal. 5:22).

"IF THERE IS HARMONY IN THE HOME, THERE WILL BE ORDER IN THE NATION. WHEN THERE IS ORDER IN THE NATION, THERE WILL BE PEACE IN THE WORLD."[1]
—Author unknown

A HOME WITHOUT A SPIRITUAL LEADER

*Righteousness exalts a nation, but sin is a disgrace to any people (Prov.
14:34, NIV). Read Psalm 60.*

> It's no secret that Bathsheba is the one my father loves,
> All his other wives forgotten in his mad pursuit of love.
> Mother Maacah sits, despondent, in her room day after
> day.
> Brother Absalom is rebellious, always wanting his own
> way.
> I know my father is a good man—I remember earlier days
> When he cared about his children, and he taught us words
> of praise.
> But a spell has fallen on him, and I fear how it may end:
> King David disobeyed Jehovah, and His judgment will be
> sent.
>
> —Tamar

We are told nothing about Tamar's (and Absalom's)
mother, Maacah, except that she was the daughter of Talmai,
king of Geshur (a neighboring country to the north of Israel).
Perhaps David had married her only to insure his safety and
protection; after he met Bathsheba, if not before, he may have
lost all interest in Maacah and his other wives. Even before
the affair with Bathsheba, David was probably too constantly
involved with his wars to spend much time with his family.

A healthy, loving relationship between parents is a key
factor in a child's emotional development. A peaceful, happy
home life creates stability, while constant arguing or abuse is
likely to cause permanent feelings of insecurity in a child and
later an adult. Being ignored by a parent may have the same
results.

Help me, Father, not to vent my feelings of frustration on
innocent children. Help me to remember that verbal abuse—
or lack of attention—can be just as lethal as physical abuse.
"A GOOD LAUGH IS SUNSHINE IN A HOUSE."2

UNREQUITED LOVE?

A violent man entices his neighbor and leads him down a path that is not good (Prov. 16:29, NIV). Read 2 Samuel 13:1-16.

My half-brother Amnon watches me with lustful eyes.
I'm afraid to spend time with him, but I know he has his
*   spies,*
Always watching and reporting what I do and what I say,
And I fear what he would do to me if he would get his way.
He's the oldest of the king's sons, born to wife Ahinoam,
And he hates my brother Absalom—they're rivals for the
*   throne.*

—Tamar

The old, old story—Tamar was beautiful, and Amnon was attracted to her physical beauty. As the story progresses it becomes obvious that they had nothing in common spiritually. It's very possible that she knew how he felt, but did not share his feelings. Amnon was a very frustrated young man—frustrated both in his desire for the throne and in his desire for Tamar.

When we want something that it seems the Lord is withholding from us, there is a great temptation to cheat or steal or disobey or scheme in some way in order to get our heart's desire at any cost. In time, however, we may realize *why* God said "no."

I realize, Father, that sometimes in order to give me the desires of my heart (Ps. 37:4), You must first change my desires. Thank You, Father, for making me a new creature in Christ Jesus (1 Cor. 5:17).

"WHEN WE ARE IN AN UNHEALTHY STATE PHYSICALLY OR EMOTIONALLY, WE ALWAYS WANT THRILLS."[3]

LOVE OR LUST?

He who winks with his eye is plotting perversity; he who purses his lips is bent on evil (Prov. 16:30, NIV). Read 2 Samuel 13:7-18.

*Here's the bread that I have baked for you. . .perhaps a
little meat?*
You look at me so strangely. Are you well enough to eat?
*Amnon, why are you so foolish—you could marry me
some day!*
*Just the thought of it is shameful. Don't mistreat me in
this way!*
*Amnon, let me go, I beg you! You will suffer for this
crime. . . .*
*What will happen to me, Amnon? There's no place for me
to hide!*

—Tamar

What are the feelings of a girl who has been raped—by her own brother, nonetheless? Horror, anger, disgust, shame, self-pity, fear of the future and a possible pregnancy . . .Tamar was left "desolate" (2 Sam. 13:20). Obviously Amnon had not learned the difference between love and lust.

Lust is concerned for its own welfare, love for the happiness of its beloved. Lust is always greedy and eager to take from the other; love seeks to give. Lust grabs at fulfillment; love can wait.

I too, Father, have lusted after various things: admiration, importance, power, wealth, material possessions. Thank You that the desire for these things have faded in the light of Your love.

**THERE IS NOTHING YOU CAN DO. . .TO MAKE GOD
LOVE YOU MORE!**
**THERE IS NOTHING YOU CAN DO. . .TO MAKE GOD
LOVE YOU LESS!**
**HIS LOVE IS UNCONDITIONAL. . .IMPARTIAL. . .EVER-
LASTING. . .INFINITE. . .PERFECT!**

TAMAR'S RAPE AVENGED

Starting a quarrel is like breaching a dam; so drop the matter before a dispute breaks out (Prov. 17:14, NIV). Read 2 Samuel 13:19-39.

Absalom, now you have left me
And I sit here, desolate.
First our brother Amnon raped me
Then he cast me out in hate.
You don't understand my feelings—
Numbness now instead of strife.
There's no laughter left inside me. . . .
I can't live a normal life.

—Tamar

When Absalom heard about the rape, he told Tamar not to be upset about it: "It's all in the family anyway" (2 Sam. 13: 20, LB). Secretly, however, he began to plot Amnon's murder, and two years later he carried out his plan. The murder forced Absalom to flee to King Talmai of Geshur, his mother Maacah's father. In Absalom's eyes he was avenging his sister; in God's eyes it was one more sin.

"Two wrongs don't make a right"—but don't we sometimes justify our reactions by the act that prompted our responses? "You would have gotten angry, too, if. . . ." Why do we always compare our reactions to the responses of other people rather than to what Christ would have done?

Help me, Father, to stop evaluating my responses in the light of other people. Remind me to ask: "What would Jesus do?" Thank You, Lord Jesus, for the beautiful examples You have given me to follow.

TWO WRONGS NEVER MAKE A RIGHT.

DESOLATION

The Lord detests all the proud of heart. Be sure of this: They will not go unpunished (Prov. 16:5, NIV). Read 2 Samuel 18.

Absalom, my precious brother,
I just can't believe you're gone,
Lost in Ephraim's great oak forest
Like a frightened, running fawn.
And no matter what they tell me
Of rebellion and of war,
I still close my eyes remembering
Our dear childhood days once more.

—Tamar

"And Tamar lived in her brother Absalom's house, a desolate woman" (2 Sam. 13:20, NIV). Possibly she never married, never had children who might have healed the old wounds. Perhaps she mourned her disgrace all her life—and that sorrow, unchanged by Amnon's murder, was simply intensified by Absalom's rebellion and death. In her later years we can imagine her as a pathetic figure, still bound to the confines of Absalom's house, still mourning her loss of virginity and the tragic ruins of a once-great royal family.

God's father-heart must have grieved at the way in which His beautiful plan for this family had been distorted and warped. . .as He still grieves today for many other families.

Father, I see the horrible results that follow when Your plan is ignored. Chisel that lesson firmly into my heart and my home.

"LOTS OF FAMILIES ARE LIKE SAND DUNES—THEY ARE FORMED BY INFLUENCES, NOT PURPOSES."[4]

THE WOMAN OF TEKOA: HER WISDOM

Joab son of Zeruiah knew that the king's heart longed for Absalom. So Joab sent someone to Tekoa and had a wise woman brought from there (2 Sam. 14:1-2, NIV).

Have you ever noticed that some people are very free with their advice but no one listens? Conversely, some very quiet people are sought after for their valued comments.

A wise person gains much of his wisdom in the same way a doctor diagnoses a patient: by listening to a description of the problem, by checking the vital signs, by asking pertinent questions, by giving tests that reveal the nature of the problem.

The "wise woman of Tekoa" undoubtedly was a good listener. She felt the national pulsebeat as person after person told her of their concern and sorrow in seeing the divisions in the royal family. We can imagine their comments: "First, the affair with Bathsheba. . .then the rape of Tamar. . .then Absalom's revenge of Amnon and Absalom's escape to his grandfather's home outside of Israel—what is this country coming to? Israel needs a reconciliation between our leader and his son. Can't you do something, wise woman of Tekoa?"

But did she know Absalom well? Was she aware of his rebellious spirit? Probably not.

No matter how wise we are, there are things we cannot foresee, and we cannot depend on our own wisdom or intuition.

"If you want to know what God wants you to do, ask him . . .he is always ready to give a bountiful supply of wisdom to all who ask him" (James 1:5, LB).

Have you asked? In that special problem you're facing right now. . .have you asked?

O. T. PASSAGE THIS WEEK: 2 Samuel 14; 15:1-12

SPECIAL PRAYER NEEDS THIS WEEK:

ANSWERS TO PRAYER THIS WEEK:

PARENT IN PAIN

Lord, why are you standing aloof and far away? Why do you hide when I need you the most? (Ps. 10:1, LB). Read Luke 15:11-32.

King David's general, Joab, came to me one day for help.
His face was drawn and grave.
The king could have no peace, he said,
As long as Absalom was gone,
For David longed to see his son again.
And—in the meantime—
Affairs of state were going down the drain.
—The wise woman

David's heart must have been torn apart as he thought back over all the things that had happened since his sin with Bathsheba. Tamar had lost her vibrant smile. . .Amnon had lost his life. . .and he, the king, had lost two sons. How he wanted Absalom to come home—but could he pardon Absalom's crime?

The double role of father and king was not an easy one. Love and loneliness waged a war against the king's reputation for justice. Now as then parenthood carries with it many agonizing decisions. How we need God's wisdom in dealing with the all-new problems that face us each day!

There have been times, Father, when, like David, I felt that You were aloof and far away. I realize now that You were not hiding from me, but that You were teaching me lessons I needed to learn, refining and building my character. Teach me, Lord, to wait.

"PRAYER AND HELPLESSNESS ARE INSEPARABLE. ONLY HE WHO IS HELPLESS CAN TRULY PRAY."[1]

PLANNING THE PLEA

From a wise mind comes careful and persuasive speech (Prov. 16:23, LB). Read 2 Samuel 14:1-11.

> *We planned our strategy:*
> *I would pretend to be in mourning,*
> *Wearing robes of sackcloth,*
> *Tearing at my dirty, unkempt hair,*
> *Mourning one son I would never see again*
> *And pleading for another who, it seemed,*
> *Would follow him.*
> —*The wise woman*

General Joab decided to follow the example of the prophet Nathan, who had prefaced his appeal to David with a parable. Joab probably felt that David was so emotionally involved in the situation with Absalom that he could not see things objectively, and so he wanted to help David to see the story from a different perspective.

It certainly is possible to be so entangled in a problem that you can't see objectively. Often it's good to get away from the pressures for a little while, if that's possible. We can talk to some trusted Christian friends (not the type who will spread the word) or our pastor. Most important, we can spend time alone with God in prayer and in His Word, asking Him for guidance, but not demanding it immediately!

Guide me, Father, to Your people when I need advice and correction. Help me to be truthful as well as tactful with those who come to me for counsel. Remind me never to feel spiritually superior to someone who faces the same temptations I may also have faced in times past.

"OUR HELPLESSNESS IS ONE CONTINUOUS APPEAL TO HIS FATHER-HEART."[2]

CASE IN COURT

God will help the king to judge the people fairly; there need be no mistakes (Prov. 16:10, LB). Read 2 Samuel 14:12-20.

King David listened—and promised to protect my son
And myself too.
But that was not my true intent
For coming to the court.
I asked to speak again
And pled the case of Absalom.
I asked for his return.
King David asked if Joab sent me there.
I couldn't deny the truth.

—The wise woman

Even the wise woman of Tekoa, with all her skill in talking to people, must have "shivered in her shoes" when King David thundered the question: "Did Joab send you here?" Would she and Joab both suffer for their interference in royal affairs? It was very possible.

Have you ever intervened in a situation where you felt outside help was needed, only to be told, in no uncertain terms, to "butt out"? One real problem in Christian burden-bearing is knowing both how and when to speak up. Jesus Christ intervened in my behalf. . .in your behalf. Do we fully appreciate His concern for our messed-up lives?

I don't express my appreciation to You as I should, Lord Jesus. Thank You for entering this dirty world and taking on Yourself all its sin, as much as You hated that sin. Thank You, Lord Jesus, for suffering in my place.

"HELPLESSNESS BECOMES PRAYER THE MOMENT THAT YOU GO TO JESUS AND SPEAK CANDIDLY AND CONFIDENTLY WITH HIM ABOUT YOUR NEEDS."[3]

JOAB THE INTERCESSOR

Greater love hath no man than this, that a man lay down his life for his friends (John 15:13, KJV). Read 2 Samuel 14:21-33.

"Go. . .bring back Absalom!"
The words rang through the court,
And Joab bowed before the king
And blessed him for his words.
I wondered at this man's fidelity.
He thanked the king for bringing back his own!
—The wise woman

Joab knew that David longed to see Absalom; he also understood David's inability as king-judge to pardon his own son for the murder of another son. Joab tactfully solved David's painful predicament by taking the responsibility for Absalom's return on his own shoulders—and still made it to appear as though the king were doing *him* a favor.

What skill Joab had! Did he really love his uncle *that* much, or was he bent on keeping his position as David's commander-in-chief? Joab was a very unique person; we'll study his character more closely in chapter 37.

Give me discernment, Father, when people who say they love me are not being completely honest with me. Help me to do what is right rather than what seems the most practical thing to do.

"DIFFICULTIES ARE THE THINGS THAT SHOW WHAT MEN ARE."

—Epictetus

DAYS OF UNCERTAINTY

A sensible son gladdens his father. A rebellious son saddens his mother (Prov. 15:20, LB). Read 2 Samuel 18:18; Psalm 34.

Perhaps Joab suspected treachery.
Perhaps he saw what lay behind the prince's smile.
When Absalom returned, there was no "Welcome home!"
He wasn't even brought before the king;
Two years went by before they met again.
Joab refused to be the go-between.
*   —The wise woman*

Perhaps Joab realized the possible outcome of Absalom's return when the handsome, popular young prince re-entered Jerusalem. Perhaps the wise woman of Tekoa sensed the undertones beneath the hubbub of the curious crowd: "Look at Absalom! What a fine king he would be! David is growing old. . . ."

Why did David refuse to see Absalom for two long years? Was he uncertain how to handle the situation? Was he still grieving over Amnon's death? Was he afraid of Absalom's popularity? Warring emotions in the heart of the father-king!

I've experienced conflicting emotions as well, Father. I must simply agree with David: "I will praise the Lord no matter what happens. . . . Let all who are discouraged take heart. Let us praise the Lord together, and exalt his name" (Ps. 34:1-3, LB).

PRACTICE PRAISING!

BITTERNESS BREEDS REBELLION

The upright speak what is helpful; the wicked speak rebellion (Prov. 10:32, LB). Read 2 Samuel 15:1-12; 18:18.

At last the king has seen his son. . .
But intuition tells me that
The bitterness that has built up over years of pain
Will cause more grief 'til all is said and done.
Did I do right by pleading Absalom's cause?
—The wise woman

When did Absalom's rebellion begin? Was it when his father stopped loving his mother Maacah (perhaps in favor of Bathsheba?)? Was his personal ambition encouraged by his grandfather, king of Geshur, during his stay there? His rebellion grew to its full proportions during those two years of uncertain silence and separation in the City of David.

We are told that "no one in Israel was such a handsome specimen of manhood as Absalom, and no one else received such praise" and also that he "stole the hearts of all the people of Israel" (2 Sam. 14:25; 15:6, LB). His vanity was evident in the fact that he cut his beautiful locks of hair only once a year (also, he built a monument to himself!)—but his vanity *and* his hair were his undoing!

Thank You, Father, for helping me realize the potential danger of vanity and ambition. Thank You, Lord Jesus, for giving up all Your heavenly glory to become a suffering servant. Thank You that You have promised to fulfill my needs for significance and security as I follow Your plan for my life.

"RESENTMENT COMES FROM BELIEVING THAT MY NEEDS ARE THREATENED BY SOMETHING WHICH GOD HAS ALLOWED TO HAPPEN TO ME."[4]

ZERUIAH: THE MOTHER
WHO STOOD ALONE

Although you may not remember their names, you probably do know that David had older brothers who served in Saul's army and who were bypassed when Samuel anointed David to be the next king.

But do you know that, in addition to Jesse's eight sons, there were also two daughters in the family? Their names were Zeruiah and Abigail. Zeruiah was the mother of three young men who figured very importantly in David's battles: Joab, Abishai, and Asahel.

The three brothers all had something in common—their undivided allegiance to their Uncle David. Young Asahel was the swiftest runner in David's army; General Abishai counseled David to kill Saul early in the game; and it seems General Joab spent most of his life at David's battlefront.

The brothers' loyalty to David may indicate that their mother, Zeruiah, was very close to David during their childhood years. It's easy to imagine a young shepherd girl, tanned by the hot sun, keeping her favorite brother company during the long hours of watching the sheep.

When David mentions Zeruiah later, however, it is with a negative implication: "I can do nothing with these two sons of Zeruiah" (2 Sam. 3:39, LB). While hiding from Saul, David sent his mother and father into Moab for protection, but what about his sisters? Did the relationships within David's family continue once David became king, or were there problems within the family? Is there a reason why Zeruiah's husband's name is never mentioned?

O. T. PASSAGE THIS WEEK: 1 Samuel 16; 2 Samuel 2; 3:17-39; 11:14-25

SPECIAL PRAYER NEEDS THIS WEEK:

ANSWERS TO PRAYER THIS WEEK:

MEMORIES ARE MADE OF THIS

'Honor your father and mother'—which is the first commandment with a promise—'that it may go well with you and that you may enjoy long life on the earth' (Eph. 6:2-3, NIV). Read 1 Samuel 16; 1 Chronicles 2: 13-17.

> I'm Zeruiah, sister of the king.
> I am the mother of three sons:
> Joab, then Abishai, and last, Asahel,
> The strongest warriors in the land.
> I remember well the days
> When I would help young David tend the flocks—
> Our father's sheep—near Bethlehem.
> I roamed the rocky slopes with him
> And listened to him sing.
>
> —*Zeruiah*

Zeruiah and Abigail—two girls in a family with eight boys! It's almost inevitable that at least one of the girls would have preferred watching the flocks to learning weaving at the loom or helping to cook for the large, hungry family. Perhaps Zeruiah wandered the hills with David, making up songs about their father's great-grandparents Rahab and Salmon or his grandparents, Ruth and Boaz, who had also lived in Bethlehem.

One's ancestry in those days was a source of pride. Grandparents were considered a part of the immediate family and often lived in the same house with the rest of the family. To show disrespect for one's parents was unthinkable for a Jewish child.

Help me, Father, to teach my children respect as well as love for their parents and parents' parents. Help me to show them through my own example the meaning of honoring their parents.

"PERSONS ARE TO BE LOVED: THINGS ARE TO BE USED."[1]

FIGHT THE GOOD FIGHT

Fight the good fight of faith, lay hold on eternal life, whereunto thou art also called (1 Tim. 6:12, KJV). Read 1 Samuel 17:12-51.

I was so proud when I first heard the news—
My brother David killed the Philistine!
My pride increased as over many years
My brother's name became a household word.
I married and three sons were born to me;
I raised them to respect their uncle's words.
And though I could not fight our nation's wars,
I sent my sons to serve in David's band.
—Zeruiah

Zeruiah's husband (if she had one) is not even mentioned in Scripture; perhaps she became a widow early in life. Probably Zeruiah raised her sons on the tales of Israel's wars; "Uncle David" certainly played a major role in the boys' development, and perhaps they became soldiers at a very early age. The meaning of their names ("Jehovah is father". . ."God has made") indicate a strong belief in Israel's spiritual heritage.

The story is told of a mother who constantly complained of loneliness because her sons had gone off to sea. Someone pointed out to her that in a prominent place in their home there had always hung a large painting of a magnificent ship. The boys had grown up "in the shadow" of that picture. What dominates your home?

Help me to be aware, Father, of the influences exerted on the lives of those around me. Help me to write good things on the chalkboards of innocent children's lives. . .things that are pure and lovely, true and good and right (Phil. 4:8).

"BEING A MOTHER IS WHAT MAKES A REAL LIFE FOR A WOMAN, NOT APPLAUSE, YOUR PICTURE IN THE PAPER, THE ROSES AND THE TELEGRAMS YOU GET ON OPENING NIGHT."[2]

LITTLE BOYS GROW INTO MEN

Who can stretch forth his hand against the Lord's anointed, and be guiltless? (1 Sam. 26:9, KJV). Read 1 Samuel 26:1-25; 1 Chronicles 11:1-6, 20-21, 26; 27:7.

> *Joab was made commander of the army;*
> *Abishai took on three hundred men—*
> *And killed them (single-handed)—in the war;*
> *And Asahel, my youngest, was a runner*
> *Whom no one could out-distance anywhere.*
> *I'd raised my sons to serve the God of Israel.*
> *I raised my sons to fight in Israel's wars.*
> —Zeruiah

Zeruiah's sons apparently were active in David's battles right from the start. Joab was awarded his leadership post because he killed the first Jebusite (the original inhabitants of Jerusalem, as explained in 1 Chron. 11:3-6), and Abishai and Asahel were known as great warriors. It soon became evident that the three young men were eager to fight—even overly zealous at times, as when Abishai urged David to kill Saul.

If Zeruiah was forced to assume the double role of mother and father to her three sons, perhaps the gentleness of a mother's touch was lacking in their lives. Can't you just hear Zeruiah commanding: "Come on now, no whimpering, no crying! You're going to be a warrior for Israel!"

Thank You for pointing out, Father, that firmness needs to be balanced with gentleness. Remind me to allow children to be children.

A MOTHER NEEDS TO BE BOTH GENTLE AND FIRM.

LOSS OF A SON

Must the sword devour forever? Don't you realize that this will end in bitterness? How long before you order your men to stop pursuing their brothers? (2 Sam. 2:26, NIV). Read 2 Samuel 2:12-32.

My son, my son, beloved son Asahel,
You gave your life for Israel, my son!
The news came unexpectedly to me:
Young Asahel was dead, stabbed as he ran
Pursuing Abner, the commander of King Saul.
My brother's war with Saul was at an end,
For Saul was dead. . .but still the feud went on.
—Zeruiah

Asahel—swift and graceful as a deer, youngest of Zeruiah's sons, and perhaps closest to her heart. Now, for the first time, perhaps Zeruiah began to question Israel's wars and her brother's leadership. Asahel was dead—why hadn't David done something? But hot-headed Joab, her son Joab, had been in charge. . . .

Pain strikes deep when we begin to question our life-long allegiances. The moorings of our lives become shaky as those we love slip from their homemade pedestals. Even the basics seem illusory, deceptive.

"In times like these," Father, "I need an anchor. . . ." Thank You for being the one certain stability in my life. When everyone else fails me, I know You will still be there.
ONLY ONE ANCHOR IS INDESTRUCTIBLE.

FEAR BUILDS

And today, though I am the anointed king, I am weak, and these sons of Zeruiah are too strong for me. May the Lord repay the evildoer according to his evil deeds! (2 Sam. 3:39, NIV). Read 2 Samuel 3:22-39; 18:1-18; 21:15-17.

> *I fear now that my other sons will die*
> *For Joab has killed Abner in cold blood,*
> *And David has pronounced a curse on him*
> *—Not just on Joab, but on all his family.*
> *My brother, how could you do such a thing?*
> *My Joab killed for you—he'd die for you.*
> *But your wars take my sons away from me.*
> *   —Zeruiah*

Joab killed Abner to avenge the death of his brother Asahel, and also because he feared losing his position as commander-in-chief. (Joab knew David was considering Abner for the post.) David's public indictment of Joab washed his own hands of the murder in a continuing attempt to heal the breach between Judah and Israel and to bring them together under his leadership. To Zeruiah, however, David's curse on Joab's family—her family—must have seemed terribly unfair!

Many mothers, like Zeruiah, find it almost impossible to be objective about their children's behavior. It's so important for parents to discern a child's weaknesses early in that young life, so that they are able to help the child strengthen those traits through study and application of God's Word.

Help me not to be too busy, Father, to see the importance of helping to mold and shape young lives. Help me also to recognize and deal with problems instead of ignoring them or expecting others—the pastor, Sunday school teacher, or youth leader—to handle the situation.

WORKING WITH A CHILD'S WEAKNESSES CAN HELP HIM TO OUTGROW THEM; IGNORING HIS PROBLEMS ONLY PROLONGS THEM.

THE RESULTS OF WAR

In the multitude of counsellors there is safety (Prov. 11:14). Read 2 Samuel 19:1-8; 20:4-10.

Oh, Joab, how could you have killed Amasa
—Your cousin, only son of Abigail!
My sister's son, dead by the hand of Joab. . .
My brother's son, Absalom, lifeless too.
This bloody war has torn apart our family,
Yet David seems to mourn only his son.
We've all lost sons because of war, my brother.
My sons laid down their lives defending yours.

—Zeruiah

Joab was almost indispensable to David. Joab made command decisions (2 Sam. 20:14-22); he led the troops in battle (2 Sam. 20:23); he did the king's "dirty work" (2 Sam. 11:6-25); he brought back David's son (2 Sam. 14:1-22); he advised him in political decisions (2 Sam. 24:3-4). He even made sure Absalom's rebellion had ended (by killing Absalom!) and then advised David how to keep his kingdom from falling apart (2 Sam. 19:1-10)!

Some of Joab's counsel was sound (2 Sam. 24:3-4), but it seems his advice dominated the political arena. Probably everyone was afraid to oppose him. (It was a good way to get a dagger in your middle!) Have you allowed yourself to be unduly influenced by someone whose life is not consistent with biblical principles? Watch your step!

Thank You, Father, for showing me the danger of being dominated by wrong philosophies of life. Help me to build my thought patterns—and hence my behavior—on Your Word. **"DISCERNMENT IS GOD'S CALL TO INTERCESSION."**[3]

RIZPAH: "'TIL DEATH DO US PART" —AND THEN SOME!

She is mentioned only twice in the Scriptures, but her story is a poignant one. Once you've discovered Rizpah, you'll never forget her!

The meaning of Rizpah's name is "hot coal," and this may have been descriptive of her temperament during her early years as Saul's concubine.

A bit of history is necessary here. . . . Years before, Joshua had made peace with the Gibeonites (check Joshua 9) and had promised them protection in return for their servanthood. Perhaps in an effort to compensate for his disobedience in sparing Agag, king of the Amalekites (whom God had ordered Saul to destroy), Saul killed some of the Gibeonites, thus breaking Joshua's covenant before the Lord. God showed His displeasure by sending a famine on the land years later. (God doesn't settle all His accounting within thirty days!) After David, who was then king, inquired of the Lord as to the reason for the famine, he then asked the Gibeonites what he could do to rid the nation of guilt. Their reply was to exchange the lives of Saul's sons for the lives of their own people, so David gave them two of Saul's sons and five of his grandsons.

Here is where Rizpah comes in—she was the mother of Saul's two remaining sons (Jonathan and two others had been killed in the war with the Philistines along with Saul). This week we will trace the story of Rizpah's reaction to the hanging of her sons.

One characteristic of Rizpah's personality comes through clearly—her faithfulness to her family, living or dead. Faithfulness is also one of Jehovah's major attributes. In this day of broken promises and broken homes, Rizpah is a Bible character worthy of emulation.

O. T. PASSAGE THIS WEEK: 2 Samuel 21:1-14

SPECIAL PRAYER NEEDS THIS WEEK:

ANSWERS TO PRAYER THIS WEEK:

LIFE AS A CONCUBINE

There is neither Jew nor Greek, there is neither bond nor free, there is neither male nor female: for ye are all one in Christ Jesus (Gal. 3:28, KJV). Read 1 Samuel 9:1-24.

Saul was my life—my very life—
A handsome giant of a man.
He filled my life, my heart and soul;
I was his favorite concubine.
I watched his sons and daughters grow,
I loved his daughters like my own. . . .
Merab and Michal—they loved and lost,
And I could understand their woes.

—Rizpah

Concubines usually came from one of four backgrounds: (1) a Hebrew girl bought from her father (!); (2) a Gentile captive taken in war; (3) a foreign slave bought from her owner; (4) a Canaanite woman bound or free. The rights of (1) and (2) were protected by law (Exod. 21:7; Deut. 21:10-14), but (3) was unrecognized and (4) prohibited. Free Hebrew women also might become concubines.[1]

In this day of ERA, it's difficult for us to even imagine the life of a concubine. We also find it easy to forget that the verse for today was written many years ago. Jesus Christ was the original women's liberator!

How thankful I am, Father, for the equality Your Son renewed on Planet Earth. Please impress that equality on my mind in situations where I unwittingly look down on others, spiritually or in any other way.

"WHEN ONCE THE CONCENTRATION IS ON GOD, ALL THE MARGINS OF LIFE ARE FREE AND UNDER THE DOMINANCE OF GOD ALONE."[2]

CONSEQUENCES OF DISOBEDIENCE

When they knew God, they glorified him not as God, neither were thankful. . . . Wherefore God also gave them up to uncleanness through the lusts of their own hearts (Rom. 1:21, 24, KJV). Read 1 Samuel 16:14-23.

My sons—Armoni and Mephibosheth!
I idolized those boys of mine.
They were my link to Saul,
His image recreated.
And in the days when terror overtook him,
Spirits heavily oppressed him,
My sons reminded me of better days.
                              —Rizpah

As we read yesterday, Saul had been the most handsome man in Israel—and he was humble as well as handsome. That had all changed, however, in a few years of position and power; Saul was disobedient to God's orders (given through Samuel) on several occasions and then even attempted the age-old sin of "cover-up"! Finally, God's Spirit left Saul, and "an evil spirit. . .troubled [terrified] him" (1 Sam. 16:14, KJV). But Rizpah still had her sons (2 Sam. 21:8)!

When man persists in refusing to honor God and to give thanks for His blessings, God gives him over to the impurity he desires, and he suffers the consequences of his sin. The wages of sin is always death!

There are so many around me, Father, who are spiritually dead—dead in their sins. Thank You for "quickening" me, for bringing me to life, when I was "dead" (Eph. 2:1). Help me to share Your abundant life.

"THE THING GOD INTENDS YOU TO GIVE UP, IF EVER YOU ARE GOING TO BE A DISCIPLE OF JESUS CHRIST, IS YOUR RIGHT TO YOURSELF."[3]

THE IRONY OF WAR

Who knowing the judgment of God, that they which commit such things are worthy of death. . . (Rom. 1:32, KJV). Read 2 Samuel 1:1-16.

The news came back that Saul was dead!
He had killed himself—
He wouldn't give in—
And Jonathan had been killed too!
My sons were safe. . . .
I held them tight,
So thankful that they had survived,
My only hope for future days.

—Rizpah

Now that Saul was dead, Rizpah had only her sons to lean on as the support of her declining years. Perhaps she even dreamed that they would someday attain to their father's throne, for a concubine's sons were considered to be full-fledged members of the family.

Saul killed himself rather than be captured and tortured by the Philistines. He fell upon his sword. . .and so was killed by the same instrument of war which he had used to kill so many. What tragic irony! Later the Philistines beheaded him in triumph (1 Sam. 31).

I realize, Father, that I will only receive from life in return for what I have given. When I lapse into self-pity, help me to remember Your suffering. When I withdraw into my turtle shell of depression, force me out! Help me to reach out to others with Your love.

ARE YOU A MRS.DOASYOUWOULDBEDONEBY OR A MRS. BEDONEBYASYOUDID?

A PROBLEM WITH ABNER

Being filled with all unrighteousness, fornication, wickedness, covetousness (Rom. 1:29, KJV). Read 2 Samuel 3:6-18.

Who would have thought the loyal Abner,
Captain of the hosts,
Would desecrate Saul's memory by defiling me?
I was afraid of his brute strength and of his power,
So I complained to Ish-Bosheth. . . .
But he feared Abner too.

—Rizpah

Was Rizpah seduced or raped by Abner—or was Abner unjustly accused? We only know that Ish-Bosheth (the reigning king of Israel) accused Abner of fornication. If it did occur, it seems logical that Rizpah, acting in respect of her dead husband's memory, had brought her case to Israel's leader.

Perhaps the entire situation was a false charge against Abner. In any case, he certainly reacted to Ish-Bosheth in a rather arrogant or impatient manner. Perhaps Abner was coveting Saul's throne as well as his concubine!

Thank You, Father, for pointing out to me through Your Word how dangerous the sin of covetousness can be. It starts so small—with a longing glance at what someone else has—but it can become such a monster! Thank You for Your power to deliver me from it.

"'ONE THING THOU LACKEST'—THE LOOK OF JESUS WILL MEAN A HEART BROKEN FOREVER FROM ALLEGIANCE TO ANY OTHER PERSON OR THING."4

A GOD OF JUSTICE

And just as they did not see fit to acknowledge God any longer, God gave them over to a depraved mind, to do those things which are not proper. . ."covenant breakers" (Rom. 1:28, NASB; 1:31, KJV). Read 2 Samuel 21:1-6; Joshua 9:3-27.

> *The famine lasted three long years—*
> *And finally David asked the Lord*
> *The cause of it.*
> *We had broken contract with our friends,*
> *The Gibeonites (whom Saul had killed),*
> *And we must pay for broken vows;*
> *With Saul's own sons we would pay the price.*
> *This was the edict of the king.*
>
> *—Rizpah*

The ancient gods of the heathen were bloodthirsty and could only be appeased by the shedding of human blood in sacrificial orgies. This type of "propitiation" is not to be confused with the expiation or atonement which Jehovah demanded in return for the covenant-breaking of Saul's "bloody house."

What form of justice does the God of the New Testament request of us? Simply that we accept the Atonement which Jesus Christ has made for *our* sins through payment by His shed blood on the cross of Calvary. ("The life of the flesh is in the blood," Lev. 17:11, KJV). Christ's death alone is a propitiation for sin.

Thank You, Lord Jesus, for the way in which You voluntarily forfeited Your life so that I could have life. Thank You for Your mercy and Your grace when I deserved only punishment. Thank You for the Atonement that makes me "at one" with You, the justification that cleanses me "just-as-if-I-had-never-sinned."

"THE REVELATION OF GOD IS THAT HE CANNOT FORGIVE; HE WOULD CONTRADICT HIS NATURE IF HE DID. THE ONLY WAY WE CAN BE FORGIVEN IS BY BEING BROUGHT BACK TO GOD BY THE ATONEMENT."[5]

FAITHFUL UNTO DEATH

With my mouth will I make known thy faithfulness to all generations
(Ps. 89:1, KJV). Read 2 Samuel 21:7-14.

So there they hang, beloved dead,
Awaiting rest—without a grave.
All that is left of Saul's and mine
Is here upon this wretched rock.
I've kept the scavengers away;
I've watched my sons through night and day,
Just as I watched them years ago
When they were babies in my arms.
                                        —Rizpah

Rizpah did not rebel against the execution of her sons, but her mother-heart kept right on loving in death as it had in life. She loved so much that she stood guard over her sons' bodies (and those of Saul's grandsons as well) for several months. What a pathetic figure in her loneliness—but superb in her faithfulness!

We are not told whether Rizpah lived to see the much-desired results of her faithfulness—an honorable burial (so important to the Israelites) for her beloved dead—but in the last mention of Rizpah's name she is again called the "concubine of Saul," even though Saul is now long dead. Rizpah's faithfulness is unsurpassed in human history!

"Great is Thy faithfulness, Oh God my Father, There is no shadow of turning with Thee; Thou changest not, Thy compassions they fail not; As Thou hast been Thou forever wilt be."[6]
GREAT IS THY FAITHFULNESS!

ABISHAG: AN UNUSUAL JOB DESCRIPTION

These are the last words of David: 'The oracle of David son of Jesse, the oracle of the man exalted by the Most High, the man anointed by the God of Jacob, Israel's singer of songs: The Spirit of the Lord spoke through me; his word was on my tongue' (2 Sam. 23:1-2, NIV).

King David was growing old! At seventy years of age, he had lost his energy, his drive—and his body heat! The once vigorous king spent his days as well as nights shivering beneath the warmest covers in the kingdom.

Was it custom or a last-ditch effort to please an aging king that inspired David's servants to organize a beauty contest? Purpose: to search out a beautiful girl whose assignment would be to serve as nurse and companion to the king. Perhaps her beauty would cheer him and make life pleasant once again!

The girl chosen to be David's "bed-warmer" was Abishag of Shunem, a small town located near Jezreel, the fortress Ahab later made famous. Probably Abishag came from a modest, unassuming background, but she met all the qualifications and she was very beautiful.

Perhaps winning the beauty contest was exciting at first, but how did Abishag feel after several weeks "on duty"? Was she frightened by the family feuds? Was her job a door to other opportunities or a dead-end street? Whatever happened to Abishag?

O. T. PASSAGE THIS WEEK: 2 Samuel 22; 23:1-7; 1 Kings 1; 2:13-25.

SPECIAL PRAYER NEEDS THIS WEEK:

ANSWERS TO PRAYER THIS WEEK:

THE NEED FOR AUTHORITY

The first to present his case seems right, till another comes forward and questions him (Prov. 18:17, NIV). Read 1 Kings 1:1-4; 2 Samuel 22:1-20.

Who would have thought that I would live in this palace,
A simple country girl with sun-tanned skin?
My home was humble and my parents were poor.
I grew up in the plains of Jezreel outside Shunem,
Free to enjoy the beauty of the open fields.
The outside world seemed very far away
And palace life seemed but a dream.
                                                    —Abishag

Although Israel's outlying areas—like Shunem—were somewhat isolated, everyone in the nation was aware of the fact that their king, the great King David, was in the last years of his life. In many Israelites' minds this question was uppermost: who would be the next king?

To Abishag, however, the battle for the throne was probably not very meaningful at all—until she became personally involved with the royal family! Our priorities can change radically from one day to the next as tragedy strikes or our moorings give way.

Thank You, Father, for the assurance that no matter what happens, You have promised to be with me always. Thank You for the peace of heart and mind that is an outcome of that assurance.

"BEWARE OF THE INCLINATION TO DICTATE TO GOD AS TO WHAT YOU WILL ALLOW TO HAPPEN IF YOU OBEY HIM."[1]

DOMINATION OR PROTECTION?

Show proper respect to everyone. . .fear God, honor the king (1 Pet. 2:17, NIV). Read 2 Samuel 22:21-51.

They came to find a virgin maiden
Whose youth and warmth could cheer the aged king.
The thought was glamorous—life in the palace!
But what would happen after David died?
I wasn't sure of my own feelings
But my mind was made up for me.
I had been chosen as the one
To nurse the aged king.
I had to go.

—Abishag

As usual, we are told nothing of Abishag's reaction to being chosen as the king's "bed-warmer." Did she consider it an honor or did she resent this interruption of her life? Was there a young man at home to whom she had to bid farewell—perhaps permanently? Can you imagine the modern reaction to a situation like this?

But Abishag had been called to a task. She had to set aside her personal feelings and respond to a higher duty. Perhaps as she did so, she found God's will for her life in a way she would never have imagined.

Thank You for showing me, Father, that although I may not always relish the tasks to which You've called me, You are using those very tasks, those menial, mundane chores, to develop my character and to conform me to the image of Your Son.

"WHENEVER THERE IS ANY ELEMENT OF PRIDE OR OF CONCEIT, JESUS CANNOT EXPOUND A THING."[2]

SUBMIT YOURSELF!

Submit yourselves to your masters with all respect, not only to those who are good and considerate, but also to those who are harsh (1 Pet. 2:18, NIV). Read 2 Samuel 23:1-7.

So I'm companion-nurse to old King David.
Sometimes I feel imprisoned in this place.
True—it's a palace, yet a prison
Whose bars are made of linen and fine lace!
It's hard to watch a good man die,
Especially this great king.
But when he speaks those words of praise,
My heart begins to sing.

—Abishag

Although our "country girl" must have yearned for the fragrance of the rose of Sharon on the plains of Jezreel, she was probably also fascinated by the grandeur of the aged monarch she had been called to serve. The magnetic charm that had drawn people to him for so many years must have remained intact, for the Spirit of the Lord—the Source of David's charisma—still shone through the old king's last words of praise.

"The Spirit of the Lord spoke through me, his word was on my tongue. . .when one rules over men in righteousness. . . he is like the light of morning at sunrise on a cloudless morning. . . . Is not my house right with God?" The old king had repented of his sins and God had renewed "a right spirit within him" (Ps. 51:10).

Help me, Father, to realize that just as I will need love and concern as I grow older, it is my responsibility—my opportunity—to provide that consideration for those who have loved me. . .and others as well.

"AS LONG AS WE ARE NOT QUITE SURE THAT WE ARE UNWORTHY, GOD WILL KEEP NARROWING US IN UNTIL HE GETS US ALONE."[3]

INSIDE INFORMATION

Now we ask you, brothers, to respect those who work hard among you, who are over you in the Lord and who admonish you. Hold them in the highest regard in love because of their work (1 Thess. 5:12-13, NIV). Read 1 Kings 1:5-27.

Bathsheba has come to speak to David.
The prophet Nathan has warned her of a mutiny.
Adonijah, David's eldest, has crowned himself the king.
Priest Abiathar, General Joab—many others
Are in league with him.
I fear that Adonijah is too handsome for his good;
His father, old King David, never tells him "no."
He's always gotten his own way
Through force or flattery.

—Abishag

Abishag's position as an "insider" allowed her to be aware of some of the royal decisions before they were released to the public. She probably heard Bathsheba's conversation with David, and perhaps the king confided in her during the long hours they spent together.

Have you ever been in a situation where "inside information" is available to you? What do you do with that knowledge—bathe it in prayer, or use the information as prime gossip to undercut the power of the person in authority? "Consider what a great forest is set on fire by a small spark" (James 3:5, NIV).

Help me, Father, to keep my tongue under control. It's such a temptation to pass on juicy bits of gossip under the sanctimonious pretext of sharing "prayer requests." Teach me to pray more and talk less.

THE WORDS YOU SPEAK IN TIME WILL ECHO IN ETERNITY.

WHAT DOES THE FUTURE HOLD?

A son who mistreats his father or mother is a public disgrace (Prov. 19:26, LB). Read 1 Kings 1:28-53.

> *My heart leaps high in gratitude,*
> *For Solomon is king!*
> *And Adonijah has bowed low,*
> *He's finally given in!*
> *When David dies, I'll be passed on*
> *As part of the estate*
> *To Solomon, King Solomon!*
> *He now decides my fate!*
>
> *—Abishag*

Custom dictated that the new king would inherit his father's concubines; although Abishag was still a virgin (David had no sexual relations with her), she probably would have fit into this category. Abishag may have feared becoming Adonijah's concubine, knowing his reputation for getting his own way (1 Kings 1:6). Perhaps she even nourished a secret admiration for Solomon!

Let's take a moment to review the man-woman relationship. Instituted by God as a beautiful "one-flesh" union (Gen. 2:24), it was degraded (by man) into polygamy in its varying forms. (Is modern divorce and re-marriage a form of polygamy?) Not until Jesus Christ came to earth was womanhood once again elevated to her original status.

Thank You, Father, for the new life You have given me in Christ. Thank You for the opportunities You provide to tell others of my liberation through Your love.

LIBERATION OPENS THE DOOR TO A NEW FIELD OF SERVICE.

SYMPATHIZING WITH A REBEL

Submit yourselves for the Lord's sake to every authority instituted among men. . .to punish those who do wrong and to commend those who do right (1 Pet. 2:13-14, NIV). Read 1 Kings 2:13-25.

But Adonijah was determined he would win—
If not by force, then through a subtler way.
Deceitfully, he went to see Bathsheba
And asked my hand since David now was dead;
And she, naively unsuspecting,
And wishing to reward what she thought love,
Requested Solomon to grant this one small favor
To pacify his older brother's needs.

—Abishag

Adonijah used a woman's sympathy in his second effort to gain the throne. He acted as though he were resigned to losing the kingdom and was asking for the one thing that would brighten up his life—Abishag as his wife. Bathsheba obviously felt sorry for him and was overly generous in her rather awkward position as mediator. She did not realize the danger of the concession to a rebel; in giving Abishag to Adonijah, Solomon would practically have been handing over the kingdom!

As women we need to be fully aware of our tendencies toward gullibility. Our emotions can influence us to be sympathetic toward the wrong causes, and that sympathy can encourage the growth of problems in other lives and may undermine our own spiritual straightforwardness. Never sympathize with a rebel!

Thank You, Father, for this word of caution. Please enable me to discern a rebellious spirit and then give me wisdom in dealing with it.

"DISOBEDIENCE IN MIND TO THE HEAVENLY VISION WILL MAKE YOU A SLAVE TO POINTS OF VIEW THAT ARE ALIEN TO JESUS CHRIST."[4]

BATHSHEBA: AS VIEWED BY HER SON

In Proverbs 24, two verses dealing with the home stand out: "Through wisdom is an house builded; and by understanding it is established: and by knowledge shall the chambers be filled with all precious and pleasant riches" (vv. 3-4, KJV).

The commentator Matthew Henry points out that the entire collection of Proverbs reminds us of phases in the life of Bathsheba. References are made to "the adulterous woman" in the beginning of the book, possibly referring to Bathsheba's earlier days, but happily the book ends with the oft-quoted passage on "the virtuous woman," tying in with Solomon's positive feelings about his mother in her later years.

On one of his "Insight for Living" radio programs, well-known author and speaker Chuck Swindoll told of a man who was asked what translation of the Bible he preferred. His reply was memorable: "I like my mother's translation best. Hers was the most convincing translation I ever encountered. . .because *she translated it into life!*"

To quote Swindoll again: "A mother has a nine-month advance on understanding a child." She has built-in wisdom and sensitivity concerning the needs of that little bundle. And if she grows in maturity as a mother along with the child, she will continue to be sensitive to the child's needs. She will not always understand the child completely, but her intuitive concern, guided by the Holy Spirit, will usually overshadow any lack of training in psychology.

What are the riches with which the rooms of a house can be filled by every mother? Let us list a few: beautiful, love-filled memories; open, understanding relationships.

O. T. PASSAGE THIS WEEK: Proverbs 31

SPECIAL PRAYER NEEDS THIS WEEK:

ANSWERS TO PRAYER THIS WEEK:

A VIRTUOUS WOMAN

A woman who fears and reverences God shall be greatly praised (Prov. 31:30, LB). Read Proverbs 31:1-9.

I dedicate you to the Lord,
My son; please listen to these words:
These attributes your wife must have:
Faith that's like a healing salve
To soothe the hurts and mend the breaks
Resulting from life's give-and-take.
For faith gives strength and confidence,
Yet tenderness and common sense.
*   —Bathsheba*

This passage is introduced as "the wise sayings of King Lemuel. . .taught to him at his mother's knee" (LB). Some authorities identify this man, King Lemuel, as a prince of Massa (a neighboring country in the Arabian desert) whose mother was a daughter of Israel.

Other interpreters are of the opinion (and I like this one!) that Lemuel was Solomon himself, *Lemuel* meaning "one that is for God" or "devoted to God." This is in keeping with Solomon's other nickname, mentioned in an earlier study of Bathsheba—*Jedidiah*, "beloved of the Lord." Supposedly *Lemuel* was a fond, endearing name which Bathsheba may have called Solomon when he was a child, and their relationship was so precious to the king that he was not embarrassed to call himself by that name as an adult.

Thank You, Father, for my mother and the great influence she has had on my life. Help me to be as aware of her needs as she has been of mine.

AN OUNCE OF MOTHER IS WORTH A POUND OF CLERGY.

*   —Selected*

BEAUTY OF SPIRIT

She will not hinder him, but help him all her life. . . . Charm can be deceptive and beauty doesn't last (Prov. 31:12, 30, LB). Read Proverbs 31:10-18.

> *What, my son, son of my vows,*
> *You say you look for beauty next?*
> *Beauty of spirit is the key*
> *Or else your marriage will be vexed.*
> *She needs to use her talents well*
> *To benefit your family name;*
> *Working together, you will find*
> *Your goals and victories are the same.*
> *—Bathsheba*

Obviously Solomon had great respect for his mother Bathsheba, as is evidenced by his treatment of her in 1 Kings 2 (giving her a seat on his right hand in the court and promising to give her whatever she asked—although in that particular situation Solomon realized the impossibility of fulfilling his promise). Again, in the Song of Solomon, we are told that Bathsheba crowned Solomon on his wedding day, showing his respect for her and his wish for her to share his happiness (Song of Sol. 3:11).

Undoubtedly Bathsheba had great hopes and dreams for her beloved son, and for some years it probably seemed as though all her dreams had come true. Wisdom and wealth, power and popularity—Solomon had it all!

Thank You, Father, for these lessons in what is truly valuable in Your sight. Help me to learn to be a virtuous woman—not only in my speech, but also in my life.

LIKE A HOPE DIVINE IN A TROUBLED WORLD IS THE THOUGHT OF A MOTHER'S CARE. . .NO PAYMENT IS ASKED FOR ITS GIVING, NO SELFISHNESS PROMPTS ITS PRAYER.

LOVING IS GIVING

She will richly satisfy his needs. . . . He praises her with these words:
'There are many fine women in the world, but you are the best of them all!'
(Prov. 31:11, 28-29, LB). Read Proverbs 31:19-31.

> Well, son, I've listed several things
> To look for in a wife. . .
> But one thing's most essential, son,
> Or you will live in strife.
> She must know how to love you, son,
> To love unselfishly,
> To love you when the chips are down
> And love you laughingly.
>
> *—Bathsheba*

As we read the last chapter of Proverbs, we can picture mother Bathsheba reflecting on her life with Uriah and David as she warns her son of the pitfalls of life: "Give not thy strength unto women, nor thy ways to that which destroyeth kings" (Prov. 31:3, KJV). Bathsheba, of course, was not speaking against her own sex, but rather cautioning her son to save himself for the marriage relationship.

If only Solomon had followed her advice, how different his life—and Israel's future—could have been!

Thank You, Father, for the patterns in love You have provided in my life. Help me to learn from them and from You. Teach me the meaning of Calvary love.

SHARED, IT INCREASES IN RICHNESS: DIVIDED, 'TIS FULL IN EACH PART. FOR GOD HAS HIDDEN A LOVE LIKE HIS OWN IN THE DEPTHS OF THE MOTHER HEART!

A GENEROUS SPIRIT

She is energetic, a hard worker, and watches for bargains. . .and generously gives to the needy (Prov. 31:17-18, 20, LB). Read Matthew 6:24-34.

> A generous spirit goes with love,
> Concern for others' needs.
> An industrious worker she must be—
> People judge us by our deeds!
> Your wife should know your earning power,
> Understand your limitations,
> Or you'll eat steak half of the year. . .
> With the other half on rations!
> —Bathsheba

Much emphasis in Proverbs is placed on helping the poor and needy. If "the virtuous woman" was a description of Bathsheba, perhaps she used memories of the past wisely in reminding herself to be especially aware of problems outside the palace walls. Perhaps she always remembered what it was like to live on a young soldier's income, and it's possible she looked after the welfare of Uriah's parents and her own.

A definition of "pure religion" is given us in James; it's not teaching Sunday school, reading the Bible several hours a day, or even praying for long periods (not that there is anything wrong with any of those things!). The secret of "undefiled religion" is this: "to visit the fatherless and widows in their affliction, and to keep oneself unspotted from the world" (James 1:27, KJV).

Remind me, Father, always to be aware of the needs of others.

THERE IS NOTHING HUMAN SO IRRESISTIBLE OR SO UNSELFISH AS MOTHER LOVE.

MUTUAL RESPECT

She goes out to inspect a field, and buys it. . . . When she speaks, her words are wise (Prov. 31:16, 26, LB). Read Matthew 25:14-30.

> *A wife with good sound business sense*
> *Can help you reach your goals.*
> *You can share decisions with your wife*
> *And still fulfill your roles.*
> *Her ability is not a threat. . . .*
> *Learning together is the theme.*
> *You'll find you'll grow along with her*
> *As she achieves her dreams.*
> *—Bathsheba*

The fact that the prophet Nathan (in 1 Kings 1) had gone to Bathsheba with the news of Adonijah's revolt is a good indication that she had become highly respected in the palace and in Israel. It's not likely that Nathan would have discussed the problem with her had he not trusted her wisdom, good judgment, and spiritual healing.

Can you be trusted? Do you handle problems sensitively, calmly—or do you lash out at others when frustrated? Do you look to God for wisdom in a crisis situation, or do you panic? Have you learned from your mistakes as Bathsheba obviously did?

Thank You, Father, that You *can* turn our mistakes into learning experiences that are steppingstones to higher planes of living. Help me to forget "those things which are behind" and reach forth "unto those things which are before" (Phil. 3:13, KJV).

A MISTAKE IS NOT A WASTE OF TIME IF I LEARN FROM IT.

SUBMISSION TO EACH OTHER

Her husband can trust her. . . . She is a woman of strength and dignity, and has no fear of old age (Prov. 31:11, 25, LB). Read Ephesians 5:21-33.

> *Working together is the key*
> *To family happiness.*
> *A lot of love, a lot of prayer—*
> *The Lord will do the rest!*
> *You're head of the house; learn how to lead*
> *With love, so tactfully.*
> *Submit to each other, and you will find*
> *The key to authority.*
>
> *—Bathsheba*

Bathsheba's conversation with David in 1 Kings 1 evidences an aura of mutual respect between the aged king and the woman who had attracted him so many years before. Bathsheba's physical loveliness was now enhanced by her beauty of spirit, and we can imagine that, as she came into his presence, the old king still looked at her with love in his faded eyes.

David and Bathsheba—they had sinned together, repented together, agonized together, and received spiritual healing together. Now Bathsheba would live to see the son of their union rule Israel. Did she live long enough to witness the tragedy of Solomon's apostasy? For her sake as a mother, we hope not.

Father, our family members need to learn to submit to each other and to You. Break our stubborn wills as Your loving heart was broken. Thank You for this excellent advice from Your Word.

"SURRENDER IS NOT THE SURRENDER OF THE EXTERNAL LIFE, BUT OF THE WILL; WHEN THAT IS DONE, ALL IS DONE."[1]

THE SHULAMITE: SOLOMON'S BELOVED

It has always been a puzzlement to me that the wisest man who ever lived could have been so remarkably stupid in one area of his life. That he possessed seven hundred wives and three hundred concubines is unbelievable enough. But that he married heathen women who taught him the worship of their gods is a contradiction in his God-given wisdom.

Earlier we mentioned that some commentators feel that Abishag may have been the lovely girl around whom the Song of Solomon revolves. The girl is identified as a Shulamite; Abishag's home was Shunam, and the backgrounds seem similar. It is very possible that Solomon took Abishag as his wife after his refusal of Adonijah's request for her hand; perhaps love for Abishag was partial reason for Solomon's anger at Adonijah.

In 1 Kings 3:1 we are told that Solomon, probably as a means of strengthening his alliance with Egypt, married the daughter of Pharaoh, later building her an extravagant palace. First Kings 3:3 mentions that "Solomon loved the Lord." Apparently his marriage to the Egyptian princess came before the days of his apostasy. Why, then, the "unequal yoke"?

Commentator Matthew Henry suggests the possibility that Pharaoh's daughter may have been "a sincere convert (for the gods of the Egyptians are not reckoned among the strange gods which his strange wives drew him into the worship of), and that the Book of Canticles (Song of Solomon) and the 45th Psalm were penned on this occasion, by which these nuptials were made typical of the mystical espousals of the church to Christ, especially the Gentile church."[1]

The Song of Solomon serves as a beautiful allegory of Christ's love for His heavenly bride.

O. T. PASSAGE THIS WEEK: 1 Kings 3; 7:8-12.

SPECIAL PRAYER NEEDS THIS WEEK:

ANSWERS TO PRAYER THIS WEEK:

WEDDED BLISS

Come out, you daughters of Zion, and look at King Solomon wearing the crown with which his mother crowned him on the day of his wedding, the day his heart rejoiced (Song of Sol. 3:11, NIV). Read 1 Kings 3:1; Song of Solomon 3:6-10.

> *The glory of my wedding day,*
> *Unmatched by any in its pomp and majesty!*
> *I rode in Solomon's royal chariot*
> *With bodyguards surrounding us.*
> *And Solomon murmured magic words of love.*
> *I gave no thought to what I'd left behind—*
> *The glories of rich Egypt couldn't compare to this.*
> *   —The princess*

Although Pharaoh's daughter came from the most powerful, wealthiest country in the world at the time, what Solomon offered her could not be surpassed. He owned forty thousand stalls of horses, countless chariots, endless arrays of servants with gold drinking vessels. The extravagance of the wedding preparations knew no bounds, and his cedar chariot boasted silver posts, a golden chassis, and a purple canopy.

What is the meaning of all this for us? Perhaps the bridegroom's chariot is representative of salvation, the vehicle which enables us to approach our heavenly home. It is made of the finest, longest-lasting materials, and the blood of the covenant is the cover or shelter. The center of the plan of salvation, or its focal point, is "paved with love"—the love of Christ which surpasses human knowledge.

Thank You, Father, for this vivid unfolding of Your love. Thank You for its beautiful picture of my heavenly Bridegroom who is waiting for His bride.

"THE LOVE OF GOD MEANS CALVARY, AND NOTHING LESS."[2]

LITTLE FOXES

*The little foxes are ruining the vineyards (Song of Sol. 2:15, LB).
Read Song of Solomon 2; 1 Kings 4:29-34.*

Don't they realize that I'm a royal princess?
The people in Jerusalem do not bow down to me;
They even murmur "heathen one" when I walk by.
If I were home, my father would decree to have them killed!
But, though they hate me, Solomon is loved.
His wisdom is revered by all
And he can do no wrong.

—The princess

If we contemplate Israel's past years of bondage to Egypt, we can visualize public reaction to Solomon's marriage to the Egyptian princess. Shock and disbelief may have greeted the announcement (I wonder how Bathsheba felt). As time went by, however, the marriage was probably tolerated, Solomon forgiven—but perhaps the princess was treated with cold contempt.

How often has this situation been repeated within the body of Christ? So many Christians sit back and condemn another Christian for marrying an unbeliever (and this is not an attempt to condone "mixed marriages"), but make no effort to reach that unsaved person with the love of Christ. How easily we forget where we've been!

Thanks for reminding me again, Father, of where I was when Your loving hand reached down to me and pulled me up and out. I could never have made it on my own, Father. . .and I still can't.

"GOD DOES NOT TELL YOU WHAT HE IS GOING TO DO; HE REVEALS TO YOU WHO HE IS."[3]

LIVING IN THE LAP OF LUXURY

His cedar-paneled living quarters surrounded a courtyard. . . . (He designed similar living quarters, the same size, in the palace which he built for Pharaoh's daughter. . . .) These buildings were constructed entirely from huge, expensive stones, cut to measure (1 Kings 7:8-9, LB). Read Song of Solomon 3:1-5; 5:2-8.

> *My palace is complete—and oh, what beauty!*
> *Luxury even greater than my home in Egypt—and all*
>   *mine!*
> *Now I can be surrounded by my own handmaidens. . .*
> *And my gods!*
> *My husband's always working on the Temple,*
> *He has no time for me.*
> *Isis and Osiris, give me strength*
> *To fight this God Jehovah*
> *Who demands such loyalty.*
>
> *—The princess*

When her gorgeous new home was completed, Solomon moved his wife "from the City of David sector to the new palace he had built for her. For he said, 'She must not live in King David's palace, for the Ark of the Lord was there and it is holy ground'" (2 Chron. 8:11, LB). What a man of contradictions Solomon was! He felt it was "kosher" to marry heathen wives, as long as he kept them away from "holy ground." Didn't Solomon realize that he was defiling another one of God's temples—his own body (1 Cor. 3:16-17)?

If the princess had converted to Judaism, it's very likely that now, having her own quarters, she would have gone back to worship of her childhood gods (probably Isis and Osiris).

Forgive me, Father, for the times I've been cold and insensitive to the needs around me. Forgive me for being wrapped up in myself and my involvements. Teach me the meaning of Calvary love.

WE CANNOT EXPECT THOSE AROUND US TO LOVE OUR GOD IF WE DO NOT SHOW HIS LOVE BY THE WAY WE LIVE.

HUMILIATED BY A HAREM

All night long on my bed I looked for the one my heart loves; I looked for him but did not find him (Song of Sol. 3:1, NIV). Read Song of Solomon 6:1-12.

> *Our love was beautiful, O Solomon,*
> *You whom I loved completely, joyously. . . .*
> *But many were the nights I spent in misery*
> *While other wives enjoyed your company.*
> *I never could be sure where you were going*
> *Or which night you would choose to spend with me.*
> *And now my palace walls are prison walls to me.*
> *—The princess*

How the princess's disillusionment with Solomon must have grown as he accumulated one wife and concubine after another! At the time of the writing of the Song of Solomon the king had sixty wives and eighty concubines (which leads me to think that the Canticles were not written about either Abishag or Pharaoh's daughter). Obviously Solomon saw no reason for this arrangement to interfere with any new attractions.

What poor examples we can be of the creed we preach! Many of Solomon's proverbs deal with the need for love within a home, but his concept of love was obviously *eros* (self-fulfilling love). . .not *agape* (self-giving love)!

Please help me, Father, to keep my mouth shut when I feel like preaching at others. Help me to live my life in such a way that they will be won without a word.

"THE HOLY SPIRIT CANNOT BE LOCATED AS A GUEST IN A HOUSE; HE INVADES EVERYTHING."[4]

ENDURE. . .PITY. . .EMBRACE

Let us behave decently. . .not in orgies and drunkenness, not in sexual immorality and debauchery, not in dissension and jealousy (Rom. 13:13, NIV). Read 1 Kings 11:1-13; Jeremiah 7:29-31; 1 Kings 10:1-10.

In spite of all my king has preached about Jehovah
And all the proverbs that his wisdom has produced,
He has begun to worship other idols,
The idols his new wives have introduced.
Ashtoreth, Chemosh, and Molech,
Have groves and temples on the Hebrews' land.
I have no respect for Solomon's great wisdom. . . .
Let Sheba's queen bow down and kiss his hand!
                    —The princess

Perhaps Solomon's idol worship began as an indulgence to one of his favorite wives—something he didn't take seriously at the time but which, as it grew, made greater and greater inroads into his life, until "his wives turned away his heart" (1 Kings 11:3, KJV). The gods Solomon worshiped are described (in the Living Bible) as "depraved" and "unutterably vile." Ashtoreth-worship demanded the participation of young virgins, and worship of the other "deities" involved child sacrifice.

"Sin is a monster of such awful mien. . .that to be hated needs but to be seen. . .but seen too oft, familiar with its face . . .we first endure, then pity, then embrace." (Unknown)

Father, please sweep my life clean of the sins that have crept in the door when I wasn't looking. Purify my life with the Lysol of Your Word. . .on a daily basis.

"THERE ARE MOTIVES I CANNOT TRACE, DREAMS I CANNOT GET AT—MY GOD, SEARCH ME OUT."[5]

LOSS OF CONTROL

Put on the armor of light. Clothe yourselves with the Lord Jesus Christ, and do not think about how to gratify the desires of the sinful nature (Rom. 13:12, 14, NIV). Read 1 Kings 11:14-25.

My maids bring rumors to me that
My friend Hadad is returning to his home
And will lead Edom against Israel.
I grew up with the son of Hadad, and I know
His father hates the house of David, so perhaps
I'll have revenge against this land,
This land that hates me and its faithless king.
                                                    —The princess

Some years earlier, David and Joab had slaughtered most of the Edomite males—all except the boy Hadad (a member of the royal family) who had fled to Egypt with some servants. Hadad later married the sister of Queen Tahpenes, and their son (Genubath) was brought up in Pharaoh's palace. Because of Solomon's apostasy, God allowed Hadad to return to Edom and to grow in power.

"The Lord stirred up an adversary"—Hadad, then Rezon, and later Jeroboam, who overthrew the Davidic dynasty—all because a once-wise king started to play around with sin, and eventually lost control.

Help me to always remember, Father, that no sin can be toyed with. Thank You for this story of a very foolish king who once had everything a man could desire...and who lost it all because He forgot about You.

"GOD WILL NEVER REVEAL MORE TRUTH ABOUT HIMSELF UNTIL YOU HAVE OBEYED WHAT YOU KNOW ALREADY."[6]

ZERUAH: A PROUD MOTHER

Saul, Solomon, and David had each reigned over Israel for forty years; for a total of 120 years the nation had been united under the kings for whom the people had begged. Now, however, God's judgment was to fall on Solomon for his unfaithfulness.

"Thus saith the Lord, the God of Israel, Behold, I will rend the kingdom out of the hand of Solomon, and will give ten tribes to thee: . . .because that they have forsaken me, and have worshiped Ashtoreth the goddess of the Zidonians, Chemosh the god of the Moabites, and Milcom the god of the children of Ammon, and have not walked in my ways,. . ." (1 Kings 11:31, 33, KJV).

These words were spoken to Jeroboam, an industrious, efficient young soldier whom Solomon had appointed as head of the entire labor force of the house of Joseph (the tribes of Ephraim and Manasseh). By tearing a robe into twelve pieces and giving all but two of the pieces to Jeroboam, the prophet Ahijah dramatically symbolized the break-up of the nation of Israel.

Why was Jeroboam chosen? He was not of royal stock; his father was Nebat (probably an official under Solomon). As a young man, Jeroboam must have worked hard to support his widowed mother Zeruah. . .and did so well that he became the official representative of the working man.

Jeroboam—a man of great promise who seemed slated for great things! God had promised, through the prophet Ahijah, to build "a sure house," to keep the crown permanently in Jeroboam's family *if*. . . .

There is an *if* in every life!

O. T. PASSAGE THIS WEEK: 1 Kings 11:26-43; 12; 13:1-10, 33-34.

SPECIAL PRAYER NEEDS THIS WEEK:

ANSWERS TO PRAYER THIS WEEK:

MOST LIKELY TO SUCCEED

The father of a righteous man has great joy; he who has a wise son delights in him (Prov. 23:24, NIV). Read Psalm 37:1-7.

My son—I am so very proud of him!
He has worked so hard to save our home
And take good care of me.
If only Nebat could have known
Our son has done so well!
Young Jeroboam—now appointed by the king
To head the labor force;
Everyone speaks so well of him.

—Zeruah

King Solomon had decided to rebuild Fort Millo, a part of the fortified wall of Jerusalem, and Jeroboam had been made overseer of the heavy work assigned to the house of Joseph. From his vantage point on the construction site the young foreman may have been able to see the newly constructed temple in all its glory; and perhaps he dreamed what it would be like to lead the people of Israel in worship there.

Determination, discipline, and a dream—all three are prerequisites to success! Undoubtedly Jeroboam had them all, for the Lord told him: "You will rule over all that your heart desires" (1 Kings 11:37, NIV) provided the desires were in keeping with God's plans for his life and the future of the nation. And God will give us our hearts' desires when our hearts are right with Him.

I understand now, Father, why some of my prayers were answered with a "No." At the time I thought those prayers weren't being answered at all, but now I realize You *did* hear. Thank You, Father, for giving me new desires.

"GOD HAS NOT GIVEN US HIS PROMISES AND THE PRIVILEGE OF PRAYER IN ORDER THAT WE MIGHT USE THEM TO POUND A DEMANDING FIST UPON THE TABLE BEFORE GOD AND COMPEL HIM TO DO WHAT WE ASK."[1]

TAKEN BY SURPRISE

Humble yourselves before the Lord, and he will lift you up (James 4:10, NIV). Read 1 Kings 11:26-43.

My mind is reeling from this sudden shock. . .
My son—my only son—will be the future king!
The kingdom is taken from the house of David
And given to my son!
But what will Solomon do?
Oh, Jeroboam, you may be
In danger of your life!
Escape—before he hears the news
And has you killed!

—Zeruah

One day as Jeroboam was walking outside of Jerusalem (possibly on a lunch break!), Ahijah of Shiloh caught sight of him and pulled him aside. The prophet was wearing a new garment, but in a dramatic gesture he tore the cloth into twelve pieces and gave ten to Jeroboam as a pledge that Jehovah had destined him to be king over ten of the twelve tribes. This was not to take place, however, until after Solomon's death. . .and his reign would last only as long as his behavior was pleasing to the Lord.

What a surprise the announcement must have been to the newly promoted construction worker! God was saying—and still is—that humility is much more important than status; integrity than wealth in God's eyes.

Forgive me, Lord, for sometimes wanting to be "important." I want what's really important in *Your* eyes, and I know that significance comes in serving others as I worship You.

"THE GREAT CHARACTERISTIC OF A SAINT IS HUMILITY."[2]

THE LAND OF BONDAGE

The daughters of the nations shall lament. . .for her, even for Egypt, and for all her multitude, saith the Lord God (Ezek. 32:16, KJV). Read Ezekiel 32:1-16.

My son has left our native Israel
And gone to Egypt.
I'm happy for his safety, but
I fear for him.
I think of our ancestor Joseph
And of Potiphar's wife.
Will Jeroboam be able to withstand
Temptations that will face him there?

—Zeruah

In some way Solomon found out about Ahijah's prophecy. Perhaps Jeroboam found it difficult to keep the news to himself and lost control of his better judgment *and* his tongue. At any rate, Solomon soon tried to kill him, and Jeroboam was forced to flee to Egypt, where he was influenced by Solomon's enemy, King Shishak.

It's very possible that if Jeroboam had kept his mouth shut, he might have been able to stay in Israel until Solomon's death, wisely preparing for leadership among his own people. Instead, he spent the intervening time in Egypt, the place of physical bondage in times past and generally designated as a type of spiritual bondage. (Ezekiel's prophecy sentences Egypt to eternal doom.)

Thank You for this lesson, Father, in the wisdom of silence. Help me not to put my tongue in motion before my brain and my heart are in gear. Remind me to spend less time talking to people and more time talking to You.

WE CAN EXPECT TO ENCOUNTER IRRESISTIBLE TEMPTATION WHEN WE ARE "OFF LIMITS" SPIRITUALLY.

A CHANGED MAN

And Aaron said unto them,. . . These be thy gods, O Israel, which brought thee up out of the land of Egypt (Exod. 32:2, 4, KJV). Read Exodus 32.

My son is back, but with him he has brought
An Egyptian wife.
My heart is broken, for she does not fear Jehovah.
The Egyptian calf-god Apis is her god.
Jeroboam laughs at all my fears.
He's changed so much—his love and faith are gone.
My son, my son, what has happened to you?
—Zeruah

The Bible does not tell us that Jeroboam met his wife during his stay in Egypt, but it is a very likely possibility. It seems that his life was pleasing to the Lord before the time spent in Egypt, but there is a definite downward trend from that point on. Who or what would have been more likely to draw him into the Egyptian idol worship than a persuasive Egyptian wife?

The quotation "These be thy gods, O Israel," harks back to an earlier day of idolatry led by Aaron, Moses' brother. The children of Israel had not been able to wait out the forty days Moses spent on Mount Sinai awaiting the Ten Commandments. They wanted a god-leader immediately, and so Aaron had pacified their demands with a golden calf, molded from their own jewelry.

I see the parallels in my own life, Father—the tendency to be fickle and impatient, unstable and demanding. Forgive me for my unfaithfulness. Thank You that You never change. **IMPATIENCE IS A TELL-TALE SIGN OF SPIRITUAL IMMATURITY.**

HALF-HEARTED RELIGION

Whereupon the king took counsel. . .and said. . ., It is too much for you to go up to Jerusalem: behold thy gods, O Israel, which brought thee up out of the land of Egypt (1 Kings 12:28, KJV). Read 1 Kings 12.

*My son has adopted his wife's gods
And built two golden calves.
He fears the temple worship trip
Will steal the people's minds and hearts
And give them back to Rehoboam.
So he has built the altars where
He sacrifices to those calves.
Jehovah, wake him to his sin
And show my son that You are God!*
— Zeruah

Jeroboam was afraid that if the people went up to Jerusalem to worship, they would be won back to the house of David (Rehoboam) and would reject him as their leader. He therefore established a center of worship at each of the two extremities of the kingdom—Dan in the north and Bethel in the south. In defiance of the second commandment he set up a golden calf in each of the two places of worship, quoting Aaron's words from the past.

Jeroboam used Aaron's familiar words to add credibility to his half-old, half-new religion, as though he still desired to worship Jehovah under the image of the calf. But God cannot tolerate a divided worship; He does not want only half of our hearts. "Choose you this day whom ye will serve!" (Josh. 24:15, KJV).

Thank You, Father, for this lesson in total commitment. Forgive me for my half-heartedness in serving You. "Take my life, and let it be consecrated, Lord, to Thee."[3]
THE GOD OF THE UNIVERSE CANNOT MAKE HIS HOME IN ONLY HALF A HEART.

UNHEEDED WARNING

Yet if thou warn the wicked, and he turn not from his wickedness, nor from his wicked way, he shall die in his iniquity; but thou hast delivered thy soul (Ezek. 3:19, KJV). Read 1 Kings 13:1-10, 33, 34.

God gave my son another chance.
He struck the arm that sacrificed,
Then made it whole again.
But Jeroboam's withered heart
Refused to comprehend,
It could be healed just like his arm
If he would just repent.
But the prophet has gone—
And my son has gone
Back to his sacrilege.

—*Zeruah*

Jeroboam not only established "high places" of worship which lacked the ark and the Shekinah (the visible majesty of the divine presence as in a cloud of glory), he also allowed Israelites who were not of the tribe of Levi to be priests, and he participated in the altar services himself. Jeroboam was probably dedicating his newly constructed altar when the prophet of Judah came to give him a warning from the Lord.

Jeroboam took the warning seriously while his arm was crippled, but as soon as the miraculous healing took place, he "returned not from his evil way," but continued in his idol worship. How easy it is to turn to God in times of crisis, but to forget His existence when things are going our way!

Help me, Father, to absorb the rebukes You have given me into my way of life.

THERE IS NO POINT IN WORSHIP UNLESS WE KNOW THE GOD WE ARE WORSHIPING.

JEROBOAM'S WIFE:
NO OSCAR FOR HER ACTING!

Only one isolated incident in the life of Jeroboam's wife is given in the Scriptures, and it doesn't tell us much about her. We have imagined that she was an Egyptian girl whom Jeroboam met during his escape to her country, and that she influenced him to introduce calf worship to the Jewish culture.

We can visualize the king relaxing at home in the palace at Tirzah, a town noted for its beauty that became the capital of the ten tribes. Perhaps physically he was enjoying the luxuries which accompanied kingship, but his mind was at work on the problem of keeping his people faithful to him. It may have been his wife who, questioning the reason for his preoccupation, suggested building the local places of worship as a boost to their popularity.

Jeroboam's words to his wife in 1 Kings 14 denote an attitude of respect for her and her ability: "Arise, I pray thee, and disguise thyself, that thou be not known to be the wife of Jeroboam; and get thee to Shiloh: behold, there is Ahijah the prophet, which told me that I should be king over this people" (v. 2, KJV).

This introduction to Ahijah seems to tell us that the queen was not familiar with the old prophet, although he had been a prominent figure in Jeroboam's earlier life. Obviously the royal family had had little time for true spiritual advisors, but now they were at a crisis point in their lives and they needed help!

Oddly enough, Jeroboam was confident of the old prophet's spiritual perceptiveness but he didn't consider that that same closeness to God would cause him to see through the queen's disguise. . .all the way through to her unbelieving heart!

O. T. PASSAGE THIS WEEK: 1 Kings 14:1-18

SPECIAL PRAYER NEEDS THIS WEEK:

ANSWERS TO PRAYER THIS WEEK:

IN-LAW PROBLEMS

The Lord will destroy the house of the proud: but he will establish the border of the widow (Prov. 15:25, KJV). Read Ruth 1:1-14.

Zeruah hated me
From the first moment I set foot
On Israel's soil.
She watched me fiercely as a hawk
—A mother hawk—
Protecting her young brood.
Zeruah thinks I'll be the ruin of her handsome son.
Why can't she let her son alone?
He's my protector now.

—Jeroboam's wife

Unfortunately, conflicts between mothers and daughters-in-law are more familiar than the beautiful relationship we studied in the Book of Ruth. Assuming that Jeroboam's wife was a "heathen" Egyptian, imagine the queen's reaction to her mother-in-law! She probably thought of Zeruah as narrow-minded and totally outdated. Perhaps there was no giving, no tolerance, no trying to understand from either side.

All that to say this: our environment does not determine our reactions—WE determine our reactions! I *choose* to love, hate, or simply tolerate; I *choose* to be content or not to be content; I *choose* commitment or lack of it!

Teach me, Father, to be content in whatever state I am, as long as You're there with me. Teach me tolerance and understanding. Thank You for the total commitment You showed me at Calvary.

BLOOM WHERE YOU'RE PLANTED!

SINGLENESS OF HEART

The contentions of a wife are a continual dropping (Prov. 19:13, KJV). Read Ruth 1:15-22.

What God is this—demanding singleness of heart
From those who worship Him?
Why worship only one God
And trust in Him to save you?
It seems to me
You've got a better chance
With two or three.
The old king saw the light. . .
He worshiped many gods.

—Jeroboam's wife

Jeroboam's wife had just as much of an opportunity to embrace the worship of the one true God as Ruth had had, but there is no record that she exerted any positive influence over her husband's life. Nor is there any record that Jeroboam made any effort to introduce his wife to the worship of Jehovah.

In many ways, sadly enough, Solomon's life was probably seen as a stamp of approval on the pagan customs of the nations around him. Again we see how one's life—more so than that person's teachings—affects the lives of others.

Make me constantly aware, Father, of the influence I exert on those around me. Help me to do everything as unto You—even the most menial tasks that I enjoy the least. **"IT REQUIRES THE INSPIRATION OF GOD TO GO THROUGH DRUDGERY WITH THE LIGHT OF GOD UPON IT."**[1]

A GODLY INFLUENCE

Hear counsel, and receive instruction, that thou mayest be wise in thy latter end (Prov. 19:20, KJV). Read 2 Timothy 1:3-14.

> *The years have passed, and I have borne two sons.*
> *Zeruah has done her best to influence them.*
> *She tells them constantly about her God,*
> *Old stories of a Moses and an Abraham—*
> *I cannot see the sense in all of it,*
> *But "Bijah" listens to her stories closely,*
> *Loves her dearly—I wished he loved me so.*
> *—Jeroboam's wife*

A grandmother's godly influence has often made the difference in the life of a child who knew no other spiritual heritage. Just as Timothy in the New Testament was deeply affected by his mother and grandmother's teachings, so Jeroboam's son Abijah may have been influenced for good by grandmother Zeruah: "In him there is found some good thing toward the Lord God of Israel in the house of Jeroboam" (1 Kings 14:13, KJV).

Children growing up in today's world often miss out on the opportunity to spend time with grandparents. Perhaps you have the opportunity to take the place of a much-needed family member in a child's life. Pray about it, and take advantage of the opportunity if the Lord leads you!

Thank You, Father, for each and every area of ministry You have planned for me. Sometimes it is difficult to know where I am needed most. Please make my priorities clear to me.

"WHEN THE LORD DOES A THING THROUGH US, HE ALWAYS TRANSFIGURES IT."[2]

A STUBBORN WILL

It is an abomination to kings to commit wickedness: for the throne is established by righteousness (Prov. 16:12, KJV). Read Psalm 34:11-22.

Abijah is sick—our oldest son,
The one I treasure most,
The heir-apparent to the throne.
Suppose we lose him now!
The court physician shakes his head,
Says he can do no more.
If I could take him to my home—
But he's too sick to go.

—Jeroboam's wife

Jeroboam had persisted in his contempt of God and the true religion. God had sent him one warning in the form of the Judean prophet with the message of doom, but the broken altar and withered arm were soon ignored by the agnostic king. Now God chose to strike again—this time at Jeroboam's hope for the future, his oldest son.

There's a song that says: "Whatever it takes for my will to break, that's what I'll be willing to do." Those words were not true in Jeroboam's life; he seemed determined that nothing would break his will, even though his future—and the nation's future—was headed for destruction. Is your will pliable in the hands of God?

Thank You, Father, for breaking my will. I see now how necessary it was. You have promised me "the mind of Christ" in exchange for my stubborn will.

"I CANNOT GIVE UP MY WILL; I MUST EXERCISE IT. I MUST WILL TO OBEY."[3]

A LAST RESORT

Arise, I pray thee, and disguise thyself, that thou be not known to be the wife of Jeroboam; and get thee to Shiloh: behold, there is Ahijah the prophet (1 Kings 14:2, KJV). Read 1 Kings 14:1-9.

Zeruah played her little game—
She talked to Jeroboam yesterday.
So now he's sending me to see the prophet,
To inquire of that old man about our son.
What does he know?
My husband thinks because the prophet gave him good news once
He'll give good news again.
But Jeroboam's scared—afraid to make the trip himself.
                                        —Jeroboam's wife

What made Jeroboam decide to send his wife to speak to the old prophet? We can guess that it was his mother's influence, in hopes that contact with the man of God might have an effect on her son's life. Perhaps Jeroboam felt that the old man could not disappoint him, regarding him as a sort of talisman that had brought him good luck in the past and would bring him good luck again.

Going to the prophet was a form of prayer. Many people today regard prayer as an emergency measure to be used when all else fails. What an insult to God that is! Prayer has been called "the breath of the soul." In other words, without prayer the soul is lifeless.

Forgive me, Father, for the times when I have used prayer as a last resort. Forgive me for the many days that have been powerless and lifeless because I ignored You. Thank You for the blessed privilege of prayer that brings me before Your throne through the power of Jesus' name.
PRAYER IS THE BREATH OF THE SOUL.

STEPS OF DEATH

Arise thou therefore, get thee to thine own house: and when thy feet enter into the city, the child shall die (1 Kings 14:12, KJV). Read 1 Kings 14:10-18.

How did that old man know I was the queen?
Who gives him knowledge of the deep unknowns?
He has predicted that our son will die
As soon as I get home!
His prophecy came true before—
Should I turn back and beg for mercy?
No! I will not fear that blind old man
Or his lone God!

—Jeroboam's wife

Did the queen take the old prophet's words seriously, or did she laugh them off? In a matter so serious as the life of her oldest child, it seems that there must have been a strange uneasiness clutching the heart of Abijah's mother as she sped back to her home. As the beauty of Tirzah came into view, perhaps she fought back the impulse to turn back. As she entered the iron gates of the palace—or perhaps the threshold of the sick child's room—Abijah took his last breath.

We are not told whether this incident changed the lives of the royal couple in any way. We only know that when Jeroboam's second son, Nadab ascended the throne, he "did evil in the sight of the Lord, and walked in the way of his father, and in his sin wherewith he made Israel to sin" (1 Kings 15:26, KJV). Apparently their hearts were hardened so that nothing could soften them.

Thank You, Father, for making very clear the effects of a parent's sin on a child's life. Thank You that the opposite is also true. Help me to train and to teach my children Your principles of life.

"PART OF THE CALLING OF A PARENT IS TO HELP A CHILD 'UNSEAL HIS ORDERS'—DISCOVER WHAT IT IS THAT GOD MEANS HIM TO BE AND DO."[4]

THE WIDOW OF ZAREPHATH

Sandwiched between the stories of two queens who lived in luxury is the tale of a poor widow who lived at "Wit's End Corner." At the time her story is told, her total material possessions consisted of a handful of flour and a little cooking oil in the bottom of a jar. She was about to combine those two ingredients into a small cake as a last meal for herself and her son. . .when Elijah the prophet entered her life.

The widow's home country, Phoenicia, along with Israel, had just suffered two and a half years of drought as a result of God's punishment for the wickedness of their rulers.[1] (Ahab, the seventh king of Israel, had married Jezebel, the daughter of the Phoenician priest-king Ethbaal, and the ungodly couple was now ruling Israel.) The poor widow was probably severely undernourished, and when she met the prophet Elijah, we can imagine that she was a picture of misery, with her clothes hanging loosely about her emaciated body.

Elijah had also come from a background of discouragement. Having recently fled from Jezebel's wrath after she had attempted to destroy all the prophets of Jehovah, he was able to understand the widow's feelings and yet give to her a message of faith and hope. But before she could understand that message, she had to obey God. . .through the words of a dirty, hungry prophet.

Edith Deen writes, "The wonder of it all was that this widow, though humble and impoverished, had been willing to accept from the prophet a knowledge of God, which Jezebel, a proud and merciless queen, had fought so bitterly. A queen would go down to her death fighting God, while a widow, a Phoenician too, would come back to health and plenty because she had faith to believe in God."[2]

O. T. PASSAGE THIS WEEK: 1 Kings 17

SPECIAL PRAYER NEEDS THIS WEEK:

ANSWERS TO PRAYER THIS WEEK:

A MAN OF GOD

Behold, I have commanded a widow woman there to sustain thee (1 Kings 17:9, KJV). Read 1 Kings 17:1-10.

I cannot even find two sticks to build a fire—
There is no gleaning in the fields these days!
All I have left is a bit of meal and a little oil,
Before my son and I both starve.
But who is this approaching, wearing camel's hair,
A leather girdle, and a prophet's mantle too?
He's coming up to me—what can I give this man?
*   —The widow of Zarephath*

The word of the Lord had come to Elijah while in hiding, telling him to leave Israel and go to Zarephath (eight miles south of Sidon on the road to Tyre), where the Lord had already provided a place for him. The widow's words to Elijah—"as the Lord thy God liveth" (v. 12)—indicate that she recognized him immediately as a prophet, probably from his clothing.

Even though the Lord had told Elijah to get out of Jezebel's way, even under penalty of death, Elijah was still recognizable as a man of God. Is my witness that clear to anyone who spends time with me? Do my words and my actions mark me as one who knows God?

Help me, Father, to make a lasting impression on those I meet—not an impression of me, Lord, but of *You* shining through me. Help me to remember to listen to You before I speak, to check with You before I act and react.

WHAT DO PEOPLE WHO'VE MET ME ONCE REMEMBER ABOUT ME?

POSITIVE ASSURANCE

Fetch me, I pray thee, a little water in a vessel, that I may drink (1 Kings 17:10, KJV). Read 2 Corinthians 8:12-15.

He asked me for a drink. . . .
At least that's one thing I can give.
I've managed somehow just to save
Some drops of water here and there.
I'll give this man what he has asked;
Perhaps—who knows?—he'll bless my home.
—The widow of Zarephath

God had supplied Elijah's physical needs for some time in an almost unbelievable way because he had obeyed God's command; now God had directed Elijah to Zarephath and, even in the midst of drought and famine, the prophet approached this poverty-stricken woman with the positive assurance that God could and would supply both their needs.

You and I would have hesitated to ask someone so obviously penniless for help. We judge by external appearances because we feel dependent on human resources in time of need. We totally ignore the fact that God is our Source and that He can provide for us in any way He wishes.

Father, how I need to learn to trust You completely! Why do I continually turn to people and things when You are there? Forgive me for my lack of faith.

OUR SOURCE IS NOT LIMITED IN HIS RESOURCES.

TRUST AND OBEY

Bring me, I pray thee, a morsel of bread in thine hand (1 Kings 17:11, KJV). Read 1 Kings 17:12-16; Luke 8:4-21.

He asks for bread. . .but I have none to give.
I have enough to bake just one cake
That's even too small for my young son!
I cannot give my son's last crumbs
To this strange man. . . .
But how can I say no?
Perhaps he'll put a curse upon my house!
                    —The widow of Zarephath

The Phoenician religion, Baal-worship, was noted for its cruelty and inhuman practices. Since priests were very influential in Phoenician culture (the king of Phoenicia, Ethbaal, had formerly been a priest), the widow may have been somewhat fearful of refusing the prophet's request.

The words "As the Lord thy God liveth," however, tell us that the widow had some knowledge of Jehovah. But the real test was ahead; would she obey Him (through the prophet)? That test confronts each one of us, as is illustrated in the parable in today's reading. What happens in our lives after we hear the Word?

There are areas in my life as well, Father, in which it is difficult for me to obey, even though I have heard Your words of direction many times. Help me especially, Father, in this area: _____ .

"WE CAN DISOBEY GOD IF WE CHOOSE, AND IT WILL BRING IMMEDIATE RELIEF TO THE SITUATION, BUT WE WILL BE A GRIEF TO OUR LORD."[3]

SHARING THE BURDEN

Behold, I am gathering two sticks, that I may go in and dress it for me and my son, that we may eat it, and die (1 Kings 17:12, KJV). Read Galatians 6:2; Matthew 7:7-12.

> *I would like to honor your request. . . .*
> *I would like to give you of our food. . . .*
> *But you don't understand my plight—*
> *I only have enough for two.*
> *I cannot bear to see my own son starve;*
> *If I don't eat, I'll leave my son alone.*
> *I simply do not have enough to give.*
> *—The widow of Zarephath*

Perhaps it was difficult for the widow to unburden herself to this man she had just met. Perhaps up to that point she had been too proud to admit to anyone the misery of her poverty—or perhaps she had asked others for help and had been rejected. Whatever the past, now she decided to throw caution to the winds and tell all.

Are you afraid to ask God for your deep inner needs? "Ask, and it shall be given." Are you too proud to seek His will for you? "Seek, and ye shall find." Are you too encumbered by your past to knock on His door to the future? "Knock, and it shall be opened unto you."

Thank You, Father, that You *are* my heavenly Father and that You are ready and waiting—just for the asking—to give the best of gifts. Wipe out my fear, my pride, my self-sufficiency.

THE SOUL WOULD HAVE NO RAINBOW HAD THE EYES NO TEARS.

FACING YOUR FEARS

Fear not; go and do as thou hast said: but make me thereof a little cake first, and bring it unto me, and after [ward] make for thee and for thy son (1 Kings 17:13, KJV). Read Mark 12:38-44.

> *He says "Fear not" with utmost confidence,*
> *But is it right for me to obey him?*
> *And yet I'm not obeying this old man—*
> *A power that's far greater drives him on,*
> *Gives him the courage to buck Jezebel,*
> *Gives me a sudden faith in Israel's God.*
> *I will obey. . .I will not fear. . .*
> *I will face life anew.*
>
> *—The widow of Zarephath*

By telling the prophet that she and her son would die of starvation after their last meal, the widow put into words—and faced squarely—her greatest fear. Elijah listened calmly, then said in essence: "But that's not a problem for my God! If you'll just do what the Lord is asking you to do—through me—I can guarantee you that the Lord will meet all your needs!"

Sometimes it's helpful to make a list of all our fears. Put at the top the ones that haunt you the most frequently. Then write across that list: "My God shall supply *all your need* according to his riches in glory by Christ Jesus" (Phil. 4:19, KJV).

Help me, Father, to face my fears, especially the subtle ones that oppress me subconsciously. Provide someone with whom I can share them who will be able to help me lovingly but truthfully. Help me to reach out to others who also have problems with the truth of Your Word.

THERE ARE 365 "FEAR NOTS" IN THE BIBLE—ONE FOR EVERY DAY OF THE YEAR.

FAITH RENEWED

Have you come here to punish my sins by killing my son? (1 Kings 17:18, LB). Read 1 Kings 17:17-24; Psalm 118:1-9.

He saved my son, gave us new life—
But what has happened now?
Is this a punishment for past sin,
Have I disobeyed somehow?
Yet I forget so easily. . .
His God is my God too!
I put my son into His hands;
I've found Him to be true.

—The widow of Zarephath

The widow had acted on the promise that neither the barrel of meal nor the cruse of oil would be exhausted before the drought ended, and because of her faith she had seen a handful of ingredients multiply into a year's plentiful supply for herself, her son, and the prophet. But now her son—possibly due to disease caused by malnutrition—had died, and her faith wavered.

Why is it that we can watch God work miracles in our lives and the lives of others and then suddenly doubt His power in a time of personal crisis? An excellent way to combat our "memory loss" in this type of situation is to keep a running record of prayer requests and answers to those requests complete with dates for each. If you have been keeping one, why not get it out and review what God has done for you.

Forgive me, Father, for forgetting Your many answers to prayer. Your lovingkindness is forever!

DISCOURAGEMENT SHOWS DISAPPOINTED TRUST IN SOMETHING OR SOMEONE OTHER THAN GOD.

JEZEBEL: SAMARIA'S SEX SYMBOL

What's in a name? Sometimes nothing, but in the case of Jezebel, the name is packed with evil significance and is used as a symbol of lewdness in the Book of Revelation 2:20. I've never heard of a mother since that time who named her baby daughter "Jezebel."

Do you know the facts about this woman with the unsavory reputation? She lived in the ninth century B.C. and was the daughter of the Phoenician priest-king, Ethbaal, who murdered his own brother in cold blood. Ethbaal's lack of conscience seems to have been handed down to his daughter Jezebel.

As a king's daughter, Jezebel's wish had been her servants' command, and no ethical or moral implications were considered. Her marriage to Ahab was probably the result of an alliance between Ethbaal and Ahab's father, Omri. Her husband's obvious weakness of character contributed to her ruthlessness. (Although Ahab had a harem, no other wives are mentioned—only seventy sons!) A smaller kingdom than her father's and a childish monarch for a husband provided a fertile playground for this willful woman.

Jezebel's religion cost Ahab a lot of shekels; she supported (that means fed!) 450 prophets of Baal and 400 priests of Asherah. Her worship of these evil deities provided the religious basis for her activities, for she subscribed wholeheartedly to the philosophy of pleasure and self-centeredness.

The worship of Asherah, writes Nancy Tischler, encouraged the "life of the flesh, a life to which Jezebel apparently committed herself freely until that very flesh was trampled by horses and her body became 'as dung in the field'."[1]

O. T. PASSAGE THIS WEEK: 1 Kings 16:29-33; 18; 20; 21

SPECIAL PRAYER NEEDS THIS WEEK:

ANSWERS TO PRAYER THIS WEEK:

EXTERMINATION ORDERS

Queen Jezebel had tried to kill all of the Lord's prophets (1 Kings 18:4, LB). Read 1 Kings 16:29-33; Romans 1:18-27.

They must be totally wiped out!
I cannot tolerate their kind!
They seek to ruin my life here
And they confuse the people's minds.
Their god is sanctimonious—
He won't allow them any fun—
But they'll be gone when I am done!
—Jezebel

Archaeology has confirmed that Baal and Asherah (translated "grove" in the KJV) were the patron god and goddess of sex. Robert Boyd writes: "The hillsides (or high places) were dotted with 'groves' (or Asherim), which were hand-carved, sex-cult objects—tree stumps on each side of an altar—one conspicuously displaying the privates of a man and the other exhibiting in like manner the sex organs of a woman. Baal's sister and mistress, Anat, engaged Baal in sexual relations, thus causing the worshippers of Baal to promote fertility in 'sacred sex acts'. As the religious leaders of Baalism publicly practiced immoral sex acts, the people of Canaan gave vent to their lustful passions, and adultery became the norm in the land."[2]

Perhaps we should think about similar activities in today's world.

I realize, Father, that man has always "changed the truth of God into a lie" (Rom. 1:25, KJV), that man has taken the beautiful gifts that You have provided and made them dirty. Thank You, Father, for Your patience. Thank You that Your goodness led me to repentance.

"WHEREVER I KNOW I AM UNCLEAN, HE WILL PUT HIS FEET; WHEREVER I THINK I AM CLEAN, HE WILL WITHDRAW THEM."[3]

REACTION TO THE MT. CARMEL BATTLE

Ahab told Queen Jezebel what Elijah had done (1 Kings 19:1, LB).
Read 1 Kings 18.

Ahab, you must be kidding me!
You let him get away with that?
Where is your backbone, silly king?
Why didn't you kill that alley rat?
You had him there within your power,
With all your people as support;
Since you didn't kill him, now I must—
Tomorrow is his day in court!

—Jezebel

To Jezebel and the Canaanites, Baal alone was *the* god. He was the god of nature and the god of war, as well as the god of procreation. The followers of Baal erected temples and altars on hilltops or "high places" near their villages where they offered sacrifices and performed their rites. They offered their children as human sacrifices—burnt offerings to Baal. They worshiped demons; they used idols, incense stands and prayer beads in their rituals; and they paid homage to serpents and to other creeping things.

The dramatic struggle between the God of Israel and the god Baal is told in today's reading; the "contest" on Mount Carmel was held to decide which deity was the "lord of nature." Baal, represented by 450 prophets, failed to "make it rain." God, represented by just one of His servants, succeeded.

It is easy to see how stupid the Israelites were in preferring heathen gods to You, Father, but sometimes it is not as easy to see that I, too, put other "gods" before You. Point out those wrong priorities in my life and help me get them out of the way so that You are free to work.

"GODS" ARE NOT NECESSARILY MADE OF WOOD OR STONE.

MARRIED TO A BABY

Are you the king of Israel or not? (1 Kings 21:7, LB). Read 1 Kings 20; 21:1-7.

What is the problem, Ahab dear?
Your appetite's usually prodigious!
They say you will not eat or drink—
Your fast is certainly not religious!
You say you want a vineyard now,
But Naboth won't give it to you?
What is your problem, spineless king?
Just let me tell you what to do.

—Jezebel

In the wars recorded in 1 Kings 20, God demonstrated to Ahab that He was God of both the plains and the hills, and that He was the God of war as well. It becomes obvious in chapter 21, however, from Ahab's reaction when he didn't get his own way (Naboth would not sell him the vineyard he wanted) that Ahab would never be a leader, spiritual or otherwise. His way of handling a problem was refusing to eat and lying in bed with his face to the wall—just like a pouting child!

Jezebel's personality was very much like her father Ethbaal's—aggressive, violent, willing to do anything to reach the desired goal. How she must have despised Ahab's weakness! Do you find yourself being scornful of someone who seems weaker? Or do you pout when you don't get your own way?

Help me, Father, to face problems constructively. . .not with violent anger, and not with defeatism. Remind me that every problem is teaching me growth of character if I allow You to work through it.

GOLD IS REFINED IN INTENSE HEAT.

HATRED OF GOD'S LAWS

I'll get you Naboth's vineyard (1 Kings 21:7, LB). Read 1 Kings 21:8-16; Romans 1:28-33.

I never would have thought it, but
Ahab's encumbered by tradition!
The do's and don'ts old Moses gave
They made the law and called religion.

I'll teach those peasants who's in charge
And pious Naboth will be shamed.
I'll write a letter to the mayor
And tell him Naboth must be framed.

—Jezebel

Notice the fanatical zeal with which Jezebel set about accomplishing her self-assigned project. The Jewish laws infuriated her, since in Phoenicia nothing could countermand the king's wishes. She decided to make Naboth a public example of what would happen to anyone who defied the king or queen.

We see that same fury against God's laws in unbelievers today. The world is full of "greed and hate, envy, murder, fighting, lying, bitterness, and gossip." All around us we see "backbiters, haters of God, insolent, proud braggarts, always thinking of new ways of sinning and continually being disobedient to their parents" (Rom. 1:29-30, LB). How easy it is to slip into those patterns!

I realize more and more, Father, that the days are coming when the fury of the world will be directed much more vehemently against Your people. Help me to prepare for that onslaught with Your Word firmly tucked away in my heart. **FREEDOM IS NOT THE RIGHT TO DO WHAT WE WANT, BUT THE POWER TO DO WHAT WE OUGHT.**

SOLD OUT COMPLETELY

You have sold yourself to the devil (1 Kings 21:20, LB). Read 1 Kings 21:17-29; Romans 2:1-4.

The nerve of that impertinent man,
Defying Jezebel the queen!
He called me murderer and thief—
Doesn't he know I reign supreme?
He even prophesied my death—
Oh, wouldn't he be overjoyed!—
He cursed our entire family,
Said all of us would be destroyed.

—Jezebel

Elijah's confrontation of Ahab was direct and unafraid: "I have come to place God's curse upon you because you have sold yourself to the devil. The Lord is going to bring great harm to you and sweep you away" (1 Kings 21:20-21, LB). Several verses later we read that "no one else was so completely sold out to the devil as Ahab, for his wife Jezebel encouraged him to do every sort of evil" (v. 25).

The potential for wickedness within ourselves is frightening! Each one of us, no matter how good we think we are, has the "Jezebel possibility." "When you say they are wicked and should be punished, you are talking about yourselves, for you do these very same things" (Rom. 2:1, LB). Thank God for His redemptive power to save us from ourselves!

Thank You, Father, that You do save "to the uttermost." Thank You for loving me at a very unlovely time in my life. Remind me of those times when I tend to look down my nose at others who are going through similar problems.

GOD LOVES THAT PERSON YOU CAN'T STAND JUST AS MUCH AS HE LOVES YOU.

A HORRIBLE END

Her body would be scattered. . .so that no one could tell whose it was (2 Kings 9:36, LB). Read 2 Kings 9:1-37.

Elijah is getting his revenge—
His God has claimed my oldest son,
Jehu has murdered yet another,
And now he says I had better run!
I'll never run; I am the queen!
Jehu's just a rebellious slave!
I won't quit fighting you, Jehu,
Till one of us is in the grave!

—Jezebel

But Jezebel's body never found refuge in a grave. She was thrown from a window (by Jehu's orders) by her own servants, and when they finally got around to collecting her remains, the dogs of the area had eaten all but the skull, the feet, and the palms of her hands. (Ahab had been killed in battle about ten years earlier, and the dogs of Samaria also licked his blood, just as prophesied.) Her oldest son, Ahaziah, died from a fall out of a window, and her second son, Toram was murdered by Jehu. Jezebel's daughter, Athaliah, became queen of Judah. . .we'll deal with her later.

God was patient with Ahab and his family, but He could not tolerate Jezebel's love of sin. In Revelation 2:20 we are warned against a Jezebel who teaches God's servants that "sex sin is not a serious matter" (LB). We need that warning today!

Thank You, Father, for Your Word that clearly distinguishes right from wrong and also clearly warns of the results of disobedience. Thank You that "the gift of God is eternal life through Jesus Christ our Lord" (Rom. 6:23, KJV).

INFLATION HASN'T CHANGED THE WAGES OF SIN . . .IT WILL ALWAYS BE DEATH.

THE PROPHET'S WIDOW:
FAILURE AND FAITH

Elijah's successor, Elisha, was as much unlike the older prophet as the still small voice described in 1 Kings 19, differed from the tempest and the earthquake. Elijah was a man of fire; Elisha was mild-mannered and diplomatic. Yet Elijah's mantle fell on Elisha.

This week we will be studying the story of Elisha's encounter with a widow very similar to the widow of Zarephath. This woman had been married to one of the "junior prophets," or prophets in training. But now he was dead, and she was in trouble with his greedy, grasping creditor. This prophet's life, too, must have seemed a failure.

As Mildred Tengbom reminds us, "God gives us opportunities to discover how real our faith is. But who of us *wants* to be stretched in this way? We want a strong faith, but we shrink from the growing process. We'd rather be left alone and allowed to go our own comfortable way—our needs amply supplied, our loving family surrounding us, our snug life at church affirming us, our sensitivity to right and wrong a bit blunt, and our conscience not deeply disturbed.

"We may be satisfied with our status quo, but God is not. He forever encourages us to explore further both our depths and His. And we can explore our depths only as we understand how much of our faith is real and how much is only imagined. And how do we know which is which until our faith is tested?

"God knows. Our testings are not for His benefit, but for ours, that we may understand aright just where we truly stand and, realizing afresh our complete and utter helplessness, turn to Him."[1]

O. T. PASSAGE THIS WEEK: 2 Kings 4:1-7

SPECIAL PRAYER NEEDS THIS WEEK:

ANSWERS TO PRAYER THIS WEEK:

ANOTHER WIT'S END CORNER

Hear me, Lord! Listen to me! For I groan and weep beneath my burden of woe (Ps. 55:2, LB). All these things are against me (Gen. 42:36, KJV). Read 2 Kings 4:1-7.

> *If only he were here to tell me what to do!*
> *He always took care of the bills—*
> *I handled things at home.*
> *Isn't it enough, O God,*
> *These boys have lost their father?*
> *Surely you won't let them lose*
> *Their mother and their freedom too!*
> *I cannot bear this all at once!*
>
> *—The prophet's widow*

That terrible feeling of helplessness. . .another lonely widow in desperate need! She had even more problems than the widow of Zarephath and her son—this widow had two sons, and her husband's death had not only left her penniless, but in debt as well. Her creditor was threatening to take her two sons as slaves if she couldn't pay him; legally he was allowed to do just that.

There are times when I feel boxed-in, cornered—like an animal of prey surrounded by frenzied hunters and their maddened, yelping dogs. Everything—and everyone—seems to be against me, and I cannot see a way out.

Thank You, Father, for reminding me that I am not alone in having problems. Help me to remember that when I feel weakest, I am most likely to depend on Your power and strength.

"I HAVEN'T THE RIGHT TO CHOOSE THE WOOD OF MY CROSS."[2]

MIXED EMOTIONS

In thee, O Lord, do I put my trust. . . . Bow down thine ear to me (Ps. 31:1-2, KJV). Read Psalms 31:1-10.

Who can I talk to? Who will hear?
And who will have an answer for me?
I must not panic—that won't help—
I must stay calm for my boys' sake.
That awful man! When he returns,
He'll take my boys if I can't pay!
—The prophet's widow

It seems impossible to remain calm and simply trust God when everything inside you is at the point of panic. The widow was being hard pressed by her creditor, and each noise in her house sounded like his knock at the door—perhaps coming to take her boys! She missed her husband terribly, but that loving grief may have been mixed with a growing feeling of resentment toward his memory for having left her in this situation.

Bittersweet emotions are extremely hard to deal with. I can love someone dearly and yet feel like I almost hate him/her at times. Both emotional extremes tear at my inner being and leave me utterly confused. . .and in my confusion I become like a wounded dog, snapping and barking at the people I love most.

Your love, Father, is the only completely stable force in my life. Thank You for teaching me to rely on You and You alone. . .but I keep forgetting. Please keep teaching.

"WHEN THE RISK OF BEING JUDGED OR BETRAYED ARISES, THEN THE TEMPTATION COMES TO RUN AWAY FROM IT BY KEEPING BACK CERTAIN CONFIDENCES."[3]

POINT OF DESPERATION

Let me not be ashamed, O Lord; for I have called upon thee (Ps. 31:17, KJV). Read Psalm 31:11-24.

Elisha! He's the one I need to see!
He's wise and good—he'll take the time
To listen to my problems. . .and
He'll have some words of good advice.
He understands how poor we are.
I needn't be ashamed.
He has great faith.

—The prophet's widow

It seems this widow felt little or no hesitancy about asking for help. Elisha's reputation as a wise and loving person was well established. He could be trusted with her problem, and the widow seemed confident that Elisha would have an answer. Why? He was in touch with Jehovah!

Do people sense the indwelling of the Holy Spirit in your life? Can they come to you when they are in trouble? Or are they embarrassed to confide in you? Do you know how to listen with understanding. . .or are you an "I-told-you-so" friend? Do you know how to love without coddling?

Father, help me to be a true friend. Remind me that just being there—whether or not I have the right words to say—is so important. Help me to share my faith through my life as well as my words.

TRUTH WITHOUT LOVE IS HARSH; LOVE WITHOUT TRUTH IS HYPOCRISY.

WHAT'S THAT IN YOUR HAND?

Be of good courage and he shall strengthen your heart, all ye that hope in the Lord (Ps. 31:24, KJV). Read John 6:5-13.

My husband's dead, as you well know.
I'm left alone with my two boys.
We owe some money—if I don't pay
Only God knows where we will go.
What do I have?
                    Why, nothing, sir. . .

Except one jar of olive oil.
                    —The prophet's widow

Elisha's questions were pointed: What can *I* do for you? What do *you* have? Then, without any hesitation, the prophet instructed the widow how to use the one possession she had for God's glory.

How many times have you heard someone say—or perhaps you've said it—"I can't do that. I don't have any talent. When the Lord was handing out gifts, He forgot about me." God showed the widow through Elisha that even a little jar of olive oil can become a miracle, just as Jesus used two fish and five barley loaves to feed five thousand people.

Thank You, Father, that I can do all things that You ask of me through the strength which Your Son gives me (Phil. 4:13). Remind me also that any strength I might consider my own comes from You. . .and *every* gift.

"TRUE FAITH NEVER MAKES GOD THE SERVANT."[4]

GOD'S KIND OF VISION

Whatsoever he saith unto you, do it (John 2:5, KJV). Read John 2:1-11.

I don't understand what Elisha said,
But we must obey the man of God!
Run, boys, to all our neighbor's homes
And borrow some pots and pans—
As many as you can carry home,
As many as they will let you have.

—The prophet's widow

The widow could have questioned Elisha's directions or reacted against them: "What will my neighbors think? They'll wonder why I want all these pots! They'll think I've gone crazy! What if Elisha's scheme doesn't work—I'll be the laughingstock of the village!" But the widow said none of these things; she simply did what Elisha had told her to do, without question!

The rational, logical thing to do is not always what God wants us to do. We are usually so limited by our tunnel vision that the peripheral vision God waits to give us is entirely lost to our eyes. When Jesus says, "fill the water pots," fill them!

Help me, Father, to seek You first. . .to seek Your thinking through Your Word. There were times, Father, when I did things directly contradictory to Your orders as laid out in Your Word and then wondered why I didn't have Your blessing. Thank You for forgiving me.

THE RATIONAL, LOGICAL THING TO DO IS NOT ALWAYS WHAT GOD WANTS US TO DO.

PAYING MY DEBT

Bring ye all the tithes into the storehouse. . .and prove me now here-with. . .if I will not open you the windows of heaven, and pour you out a blessing, that there shall not be room enough to receive it (Mal. 3:10, KJV). Read Luke 17:11-19.

We've filled one pot—now two—and three!
Boys, bring them quickly. . .be careful, don't spill!
I've never seen so much olive oil!
The Lord is bountiful, praise His name!

He has provided enough so we can pay
The debt we owe—and enough left over
To meet our needs for the coming days.
*   —The prophet's widow*

Try to visualize the almost ecstatic woman pouring. . .and pouring. . .and pouring. . .an unbelievable supply of the precious, highly marketable fluid. Each drop meant food, clothing, rent—all those items that were so necessary to existence—but I'm sure she was quick to heed Elisha's advice and pay her debt before anything else was taken care of.

How much more important to pay our debt to the Lord! He is not beating on our door demanding payment. He loving-ly searches our hearts, asking gently that we give Him what is only His due share of our time, our talent, our possessions. . . and our gratitude. Nine out of ten lepers forgot to thank Jesus; do I thank Him enough?

Help me, Father, not to hold back from giving because of selfishness or fear. Thank You for Your supreme gift of love at Calvary.

IF WE BELIEVE IN JESUS, IT IS NOT WHAT WE GAIN, BUT WHAT HE POURS THROUGH US THAT COUNTS.

THE SHUNAMMITE WOMAN: LOVING AND GIVING

Do you remember what Rachel said to Jacob when the realization of her barrenness became more than she could bear? "Give me children, or I'll die!" (Gen. 30:1, NIV). Rachel felt that a life filled with the shame of barrenness was not worth living, even though she had the faithful love of her husband.

In the oriental culture barrenness was not only a cause for regret, but for reproach. It was believed that the man confides the living seed to his wife; if she does not return it in the form of a child, she has killed it. In the light of this belief, bitterness in barrenness is understandable.

The Shunammite woman profiled in 2 Kings 4:8-37 was also barren. She had never been able to bear a child and now her husband was old, so there seemed to be no possibility of a child in their future. Yet there is no mention—nor even any overtones—of bitterness in this woman's life. Instead she is described as a "great woman."

What made the difference between these women?

The answer may lie in Hebrews 11, the "faith chapter." The names of Abel, Enoch, Noah, Abraham, Sarah, Isaac, Jacob, Joseph, Moses, Rahab, Gideon, Barak, Samson, Jephthah, David, and Samuel are mentioned as men and women who were heroes and heroines in the Hall of Faith. We are told that time would fail the writer to tell of others who "through faith subdued kingdoms, wrought righteousness, obtained promises. . . . Woman received their dead raised to life again" (vv. 33, 35, KJV).

That last statement may refer to the Shunammite woman.

O. T. PASSAGE THIS WEEK: 2 Kings 4:8-37; 8:1-6

SPECIAL PRAYER NEEDS THIS WEEK:

ANSWERS TO PRAYER THIS WEEK:

THE SECRET OF HOSPITALITY

Do not forget to entertain strangers, for by so doing some people have entertained angels without knowing it (Heb. 13:2, NIV). Read 2 Kings 4:8-10; Acts 16:13-15.

I am not married to a king;
God has not called me to be a queen.
But I am content with what I have—
My heart overflows in gratitude.
By giving to the man of God
I am giving back to God Himself.
—The Shunammite woman

Shunem was a city in the tribe of Issachar (southwest of the Sea of Galilee) that lay along the road between Samaria and Carmel, a road that Elisha often traveled. Probably Elisha had been accustomed to staying in some obscure inn in the town, but this kind woman found out that he needed a place to stay and urged him to eat with her family. The friendship blossomed and soon the woman and her husband, after talking it over, decided to build the prophet a small room so that a quiet place would be available for meditation and rest whenever he wished.

The Shunammite woman gives us a lesson in hospitality. The secret of hospitality is not lavish entertainment or showing off one's home, but genuine concern for the needs of the friend.

I remember many times, Father, when I worked myself into a tizzy getting ready for guests. . .until I was so tired I couldn't enjoy our time together. Help me, Father, to relax in Your love and to radiate that love.

ENTERTAINMENT SHOWS OFF POSSESSIONS; HOSPITALITY SIMPLY SHARES.

THE SECRET OF HAPPINESS

I have learned. . .to be content (Phil. 4:11, KJV). Read Psalm 128.

We have built Elisha his own room
So he will have a place to stay. . .
And now he wishes to repay
Our love and gratitude to God.
But we don't want a place at court
Or even favors from the king.
We are content to live on here
And take our living from the land.
—The Shunammite woman

Elisha seems to have acted as an advisor to the king, and apparently he was so well respected that he could have gotten the Shunammite farmer an office of some kind, or presented a petition or complaint in the family's favor. In gratitude for their hospitality, Elisha offered his services in their behalf, but his hostess said simply: "I dwell among mine own people." In other words, "I am happy where I am."

No wonder she was such an excellent hostess! She was not trying to impress anyone or improve her position. She was simply contented with her life. Am I content? Or am I constantly trying to change things?

Forgive me, Father, for the nagging discontent, for the restlessness of heart, for the envy of others who seem to have it better than I do. Teach me to be truly content.

REMEMBER: HAPPINESS IS IN WANTING WHAT YOU HAVE, NOT HAVING WHAT YOU WANT.

AFTER ALL THESE YEARS

He who receives you receives me. Anyone who receives a prophet. . .
will receive a prophet's reward (Matt. 10:40-41, NIV). Read 2 Kings
4:11-17.

He tells me God will grant a son.
Can I believe such news as this?
I hesitate to think such thoughts;
I have accepted barrenness.
And yet—he is a man of God!
Why would he lie to me, his friend?
*   —The Shunammite woman*

The Shunammite woman was taken aback by the prophet's promise of a son: "Nay, my lord, thou man of God, do not lie unto thine handmaid" (2 Kings 4:16, KJV). She was not actually accusing Elisha of lying, as is obvious from her tone of respect; like Sarah, her reaction was a natural one, since she was considered barren, and her husband was old.

Nothing is impossible when you put your trust in God (Matt. 17:20; Luke 1:37). Extraordinarily difficult circumstances can be handled by an extraordinarily powerful God! We forget so easily that our God is the Creator of the universe and that He is unlimited in His resources.

Forgive me, Father, for my discouragement, for my inability to see beyond circumstances. Open my eyes to the possibilities faith makes visible or at least believable. Help me, Father, to be thankful for the testing of my faith.

"WE MAY BE SATISFIED WITH OUR STATUS QUO, BUT GOD IS NOT. HE FOREVER ENCOURAGES US TO EXPLORE FURTHER BOTH OUR DEPTHS AND HIS."[1]

TRAGEDY STRIKES

Let him ask in faith, nothing wavering (James 1:6, KJV). Read 2 Kings 4:18-37.

Our son—pride of his father's heart!
Oh, how he gladdened both our lives—
Now struck down. . .by the hand of God?
I begged Elisha not to lie.
Would God bestow then take away?
I cannot speak to anyone
Except the man who speaks with God.
                    —The Shunammite woman

The Shunammite woman had been blessed with the son for whom she had not even asked, and undoubtedly the boy was the apple of her eye. But unexpectedly, with the swiftness of a bolt of lightning, his body degenerated from buoyant health to the numbness of death. . .within one day! His mother's mind must have been numbed as well—bewildered, dazed by the harshness of the blow.

She would not speak with anyone except Elisha about the boy's death—not her husband, not Elisha's servant. The urgency of the matter demanded that it be resolved by God Himself (through Elisha). She would settle for no less.

I, too, feel dazed and bewildered by the sudden attack of forces I do not understand. Help me, Father, to trust—implicitly—when I can see neither rhyme nor reason in my life. . . and to look only to You for answers.

"TRUE FAITH IS ALIVE, AND ANYTHING LIVING IS NOT STATIC. IT MUST EITHER GROW OR DIE."[2]

A LIVING MIRACLE

Beloved, think it not strange concerning the fiery trial which is to try you, as though some strange thing happened unto you (1 Pet. 4:12, KJV). Read 1 Peter 4:12-19.

Why did God choose to take my son,
Then bring him back to life again?
I could not understand His plan
But now the mystery unfolds.
Our testimony opened doors
That let us tell our neighbors how
God had performed these miracles
Because He is Jehovah God.
                    —*The Shunammite woman*

The epilogue to the story of the Shunammite woman in 2 Kings 8 tells us that, because of famine, it was necessary for her to leave her home and live in the land of the heathen Philistines for seven long years. The fact that her son was a living, breathing miracle must have had a great impact on her household and everyone with whom they came in contact during those lonely years. The god of the Philistines could not raise people from the dead—only Jehovah!

Christians are not promised immunity from tragedy. Rather, it is the way in which the Holy Spirit enables them to face tragedy that brings glory to God. "Faith, painfully enough, is a plant that seems to require periodic fertilizing and pruning by testing and tension in order for it to remain healthy and sturdy."[3]

Oh, Father, how that pruning does hurt! But thank You for the assurance that all things do work together for good to those who love You, and that in this way You are conforming me to the image of Your Son (Rom. 8:28-29). I realize it is not necessary for me to understand *why. . .*now.

"FAITH IS A PLANT THAT SEEMS TO REQUIRE PERIODIC FERTILIZING AND PRUNING BY TESTING AND TENSION IN ORDER FOR IT TO REMAIN HEALTHY AND STURDY."

THE REWARDS OF GIVING

But rejoice, inasmuch as ye are partakers of Christ's sufferings; that,
when his glory shall be revealed, ye may be glad also with exceeding joy (1
Pet. 4:13, KJV). Read 2 Kings 8:1-6.

We are back in our homeland again,
Just as I knew we would be.
God has proven in mysterious ways
His power and His strength.
He has even given back our land—
My son will have a home.

—The Shunammite woman

Elisha had directed the Shunammite woman to leave her beloved country until the famine ended, and she was rewarded for her obedience. She could have showed reluctance to leave out of fear that her property would be taken over by an intruder (which evidently it was), but because she obeyed without question, God arranged that her petition to the king came at the same time that Elisha's servant Gehazi was telling the king about her. Impressed by the confirmation of her story, the king directed: "Restore all that was hers, and all the fruits of the field since the day that she left the land" (v. 6, KJV).

"Give, and it shall be given unto you; good measure, pressed down, and shaken together, and running over" (Luke 6:38, KJV).

Thank You, Father, for this lesson in the importance of giving. Thank You that You gave freely, fully in Calvary love. **LOVE IS NOT SATISFIED WITH JUST SAYING "I LOVE YOU." LOVE MUST ALSO GIVE.**

A WICKED QUEEN vs.
THE DAUGHTER OF A KING

When Athaliah the mother of Ahaziah saw that her son was dead, she proceeded to destroy the whole royal family of the house of Judah (2 Chron. 22:10, NIV).

The story of Athaliah, daughter of the infamous Jezebel, and her struggle for power is reminiscent of a Gothic horror tale. (When our four-year-old heard the story, he persisted in calling Athaliah "the wicked witch.") On the side of good is Jehosheba, the daughter of Jehoram (but not the daughter of his queen, Athaliah). Jehosheba was not concerned about power for herself; rather her name is recorded for posterity as a woman who was brave enough to defy the powers of evil without fear for her own safety.

Athaliah's attempt to exterminate the royal seed (2 Kings 11) was satanically inspired. The Old Testament records many such attempts to destroy the blood line of the promised Messiah. The Egyptian, Assyrian, and Babylonian captivities, with the accompanying dangers of assimilation (intermarriage and interbreeding) of the Jewish people, were all attempts to keep the promised Seed from His appointed task.

But God was and is in control! With His infinite power He overruled man's cooperation with Satan and actually fit it into His plan for human redemption.

God's promises that the throne of David would be everlasting and that David's physical seed would sit on his throne found fulfillment in the Person of a Son of David—Jesus Christ, the promised Messiah.

O. T. PASSAGE THIS WEEK: 2 Chronicles 21:4—22:9; 2 Kings 11; 12:1-16

SPECIAL PRAYER NEEDS THIS WEEK:

ANSWERS TO PRAYER THIS WEEK:

AN EVIL KING FROM A RIGHTEOUS FAMILY

Tremble, O women of ease; throw off your unconcern. Strip off your pretty clothes—wear sackcloth for your grief (Isa. 32:11, LB). Read 2 Chronicles 21:4-11.

Athaliah, queen of Judah!
Even as a child I hated her.
She had no time or love for children
And we had none for her.
I watched her work in horror
She and my father, hand in hand,
Killed all his brothers in cold blood.
She laughed as each ax fell.

—Jehosheba

Although he was the son of Jehoshaphat and the grandson of Asa, both of whom were righteous kings, Jehoram was influenced by his infamous in-laws, Ahab and Jezebel, and corrupted by his wife Athaliah. (His other wives are not mentioned by name.)

What grief Jehoram must have caused his godly parents and grandparents! Why do we find it so easy to be influenced by the forces of evil? Second Corinthians 11:14 gives us the answer: "Satan himself is transformed into an angel of light" (KJV). . .and how attractive he appears to be!

Help me, Father, to be aware of the evil influences in my life that are subtle enough to appear to be good. Sometimes they just seem to creep up on me. Help me to break off relationships that are spiritually unhealthy.

"JESUS CHRIST NEVER TRUSTED HUMAN NATURE, YET HE WAS NEVER CYNICAL, NEVER SUSPICIOUS, BECAUSE HE TRUSTED ABSOLUTELY IN WHAT HE COULD DO FOR HUMAN NATURE."[1]

A HORRIBLE END TO A TERRIBLE CAREER

Beat your breasts in sorrow (Isa. 32:12, LB). Read 2 Chronicles 21:12-20.

My father died an awful death—
Agony of mind and body both.
But Athaliah didn't weep;
Her son would now be king!
As the queen mother she would exert
More power than a queen.
So Ahaziah took the throne
But Athaliah ruled the land.

—Jehosheba

Jehoram was so evil that "the Lord stirred up the Philistines and the Arabs. . .to attack [him]." They "carried away everything of value in the king's palace, including his sons and his wives" (2 Chron. 21:16-17, LB). Only the youngest son—Ahaziah—escaped.

Jehoram died of a horrible disease: "His bowels fell out" (v. 19, KJV). The rotten stench of his physical condition was symbolic of his spiritual condition: "his whole life was one constant binge of doing evil" (v. 6, LB). He had failed to provide leadership in his family and in the nation.

Thank You, Father, for pointing out once again that the wages of sin have not changed from that time to this. Thank You for releasing me from the power and oppression of sin. Help me to appropriate *Your* power through the life of Your Son (Rom. 5:10).

THE WAGES OF SIN NEVER CHANGE.

END OF AHAB'S DESTINY

Your joyous homes and happy cities will be gone (Isa. 32:13, LB).
Read 2 Chronicles 22:1-9.

Marauding Arabs killed his brothers,
Left only Ahaziah.
Would Judah have fared better
If he had been taken too?
Ahab's family were his council,
Athaliah his advisor.
He reigned in utter wickedness. . .
And he was killed by Jehu.

—Jehosheba

Athaliah had been queen for eight years; her reign as queen mother lasted only one year, for Ahaziah was killed while visiting his Uncle Joram, king of Israel, with whom he had made an unholy alliance. God appointed Jehu to end the evil dynasty of Ahab; He had had enough.

Athaliah was a savage, bloodthirsty woman who cared about nothing but power—and forcing those under her to conform to her way of life. Do you find yourself expecting others to act the way you act. . .think the way you think? Do you put them down (at least mentally) if they disagree with you. . .and cross them off your list of friends?

Help me, Father, not to become infatuated with the taste of power. Help me to be tolerant of others and to realize that I too can be wrong.

WHEN WAS THE LAST TIME I REALIZED THAT I WAS WRONG ABOUT SOMETHING?

AN INSANE CRIME

Palaces and mansions will all be deserted (Isa. 32:14, LB). Read 2 Kings 11:1-12.

Athaliah could not be content
With just nine years of rule,
And Ahaziah's death aroused
An instinct deep within. . . .
A beastly, driving killer instinct
Raged through the palace grounds.
Is she insane, this woman
Who seeks to rule our land?

—Jehosheba

Fanatically devoted to Baal worship, Athaliah tried desperately to prevent anyone—even her own offspring—from interrupting her vicious rule. To insure her continuation as queen she perpetrated an unbelievable evil scheme; she tried to kill all her young grandsons.

Chambers writes: "When God wants to show you what human nature is like apart from Himself, He has to show it you in yourself. If the Spirit of God has given you a vision of what you are apart from the grace of God (and He only does it when His Spirit is at work), you know there is no criminal who is half so bad in actuality as you know yourself to be in possibility."[2]

Father, "I know that in me. . .dwelleth no good thing" (Rom. 7:18, KJV). I can never despair of anyone else because I know what Your power has done in my life. I thank You and praise You for Your miracle of love.

"GOD'S SPIRIT CONTINUALLY REVEALS WHAT HUMAN NATURE IS LIKE APART FROM HIS GRACE."[3]

THE TRAINING OF A KING

Look, a righteous King is coming (Isa. 32:1, LB). Read 2 Kings 11:13-21.

A woman, crazed by power, has killed her own offspring.
Young Joash, lone survivor of all the royal line,
Is Judah's future and our only hope.
Have mercy, O Jehovah—let this young prince survive.
                                        —Jehosheba

Jehosheba (also called Jehoshabeath) stepped onto the scene with a daring rescue of one of her nephews—baby Joash, just one year old. She kidnapped him from among the rest of the king's children who were waiting for execution and hid him and his nurse in a temple storeroom. During the prince's top-secret six-year stay in the temple, Jehosheba and her husband, the priest Jehoida (see 2 Chron. 22:11), prepared young Joash for his future leadership role.

This godly couple was so concerned for the future of their nation that they were willing to risk their lives in the rescue and training of a child who would become their king. As long as Jehoida lived, Joash reigned well. Are we as parents and teachers as concerned about the training of children?

Father, help me to be willing to make the sacrifices that are necessary for me to be the kind of parent and/or teacher You want me to be. Help me to give up the pleasures of this world so that I can teach young people the true joys of life. **REMEMBER GOD'S SECRET OF PARENTAL DUTY: SACRIFICING THE STIMULUS AND EXCITEMENT AND ENJOYMENT OF THE WORLD AND OF THE FLESH. . .FOR BETTER THINGS.**

TREASON! TREASON!

Your own breath will turn to fire and kill you (Isa. 33:11, LB). Read
2 Kings 12:1-16.

"TREASON!" she cried, "TREASON!"
As Joash took the crown.
She had rushed toward the temple
When she heard the trumpets sound.
"TREASON!" she cried, "TREASON!"
But no one raised a hand
To give her help—this woman
Who had defiled the land.

—Jehosheba

The noise of overjoyed people shouting and blowing trumpets brought Athaliah to the temple, perhaps for the first time. What a shock it must have been to the screaming ex-queen as she witnessed the coronation and realized that her fifteen years of rule had come to a sudden end!

"So they dragged her to the palace stables and killed her there" (2 Kings 11:16, LB). Her own servants had no more pity on her than her mother's servants had had when Jezebel was thrown down from a window. The end of a life filled with hatred and evil is not mourned. The grandson who survived, Joash, rebuilt the temple and reinstated the worship of Jehovah. . .but he did not destroy the shrines on the hills at which Athaliah had worshipped.

Thank You, Father, for the example of Jehosheba—a woman who was content without prestige or power. Let me never forget this terrible lesson of a mother and daughter without God in their lives. May my life, like Jehosheba's, counterbalance the Jezebels and Athaliahs of today.

"WHEN GOD WANTS TO SHOW YOU WHAT HUMAN NATURE IS LIKE APART FROM HIMSELF, HE HAS TO SHOW IT YOU IN YOURSELF."[4]

HULDAH: SHE WASN'T AFRAID TO SPEAK UP!

Josiah stands out in striking contrast to his father Amon and grandfather Manasseh, who were noted for their shedding of innocent blood and their encouragement of idolatry (2 Kings 21:16, 21). Josiah's initial attempts at reform were accompanied by his repair of the Temple, during which time the "book of the law" was found. When Shaphan the scribe read the law (the core of the Book of Deuteronomy) to Josiah, the king's concern and contrition quickened him to drastic action against the heathen practices Israel had acquired from the neighboring Canaanites.

Before Josiah took action, however, he sought for confirmation of his own reactions to the reading of the law. Probably his mother Jedidah had known Huldah, wife of Shallum, keeper of the palace wardrobe; in any case, it is obvious that Huldah was well-known and highly respected in Jerusalem. When Josiah requested his scribes and trusted advisors to "inquire of the Lord" concerning the book of the law, they went to Huldah.

Interesting, isn't it, that a woman should be consulted? Jeremiah was living during this time, but perhaps he lived at a distance and could not be readily consulted. Zephaniah also prophesied during Josiah's reign; perhaps he was still fairly unknown. Shaphan, as scribe, must have been fairly knowledgeable, and Hilkiah, as high priest, was certainly familiar with the Scriptures. . .yet Hilkiah and Shaphan, accompanied by their associates, went to Huldah for God's message.

Huldah must have been a very special woman. Let's learn more about her.

O. T. PASSAGE THIS WEEK: 2 Kings 22; 2 Chronicles 34

SPECIAL PRAYER NEEDS THIS WEEK:

ANSWERS TO PRAYER THIS WEEK:

A UNIQUE POSITION

Do not fret because of evil men or be envious of those who do wrong; for like the grass they will soon wither, like green plants they will soon die away (Ps. 37:1-2, NIV). Read 2 Kings 21.

Sometimes I wonder at this special gift
The Lord Jehovah has bestowed upon me.
The other women seem content
To sweep and cook and sew,
But I have always felt the urge to pray
And study sacred books of law.
I've read of Miriam and of Deborah
Whom God used to lead Israel. . . .
My one desire is to be used of Him.

—Huldah

As the wife of Shallum, the keeper of the king's wardrobe, Huldah probably would have been quite familiar with palace happenings and news of the entire land of Israel. Instead of listening eagerly to court gossip, however, undoubtedly Huldah combined her awareness of current events and knowledge of Hebrew law in effective intercession for her wayward nation.

God places each one of us in a unique position. There is no one more capable of intercession in a particular situation—your family, your husband, your co-workers—than yourself. Have you exercised the invaluable right of intercessory prayer this week. . .yesterday. . .today?

Thank You, Father, for reminding me that my place in life is special in Your eyes. Remind me to come to You when I am so frustrated with relationships that I feel like running away from those who need me.

"GOD GIVES US THE GIFT OF DISCERNMENT SO THAT WE MAY TAKE THE BURDEN OF SOULS BEFORE HIM AND THAT, IN RETURN, HE MAY GIVE US THE MIND OF CHRIST IN EACH SITUATION."[1]

THEN AND NOW

Trust in the Lord, and do good; so shalt thou dwell in the land, and verily thou shalt be fed (Ps. 37:3, KJV). Read Titus 2:1-8.

I've taught the women who have come
To learn of God and His commands.
Some are concerned about our land;
Some do not worship heathen gods.
But there are many who defile
Themselves and others with their filthy ways.
They even worship shameful idols
In God's holy place.

—Huldah

Josiah's father and grandfather had patronized the Canaanite ways of worship and had appointed pagan priests to burn incense on the high places to Baal, to the sun and moon, to the constellations and all the starry hosts (1 Kings 23:5). A carved image of the goddess Asherah had been set up in the Temple itself, and some of the women did weaving for Asherah in that holy place. Most unbelievable—and to Huldah, heart-rending—must have been the fact that in the house of God were the quarters of the male shrine prostitutes!

Compare this description of the cobbled streets of Jerusalem to the busy avenues of a United States metropolis. Compare the ancient worship of the sun, moon, and stars to modern interest in astrology, signs of the zodiac, and horoscope readings. Compare the perverted practices of Baal and Asherah worship with today's domination of the media by the same subject—sex. Make these comparisons and you will find many parallels!

Thank You, Father, for pointing out that it was just as difficult to serve You in Huldah's day as it is today. Thank You for the beauty that only You can restore in the midst of an ugly world.

"DO NOT FORECAST WHERE THE TEMPTATION WILL COME: IT IS THE LEAST LIKELY THING THAT IS THE PERIL."[2]

A BURDENED HEART

Delight yourself in the Lord and he will give you the desires of your heart (Ps. 37:4, NIV). Read 2 Kings 22:1-13.

And how my heart yearns for the children,
Little ones who are not taught of God's great love—
His love for them and for our nation Israel.
Some children have been sacrificed to Molech,
Passed through the fire in honor of a heathen god.
The God of Israel's heart must break to see these terrible
*   sins;*
His wrath will surely fall upon this land.
                   —Huldah

According to Jewish tradition, Huldah taught publicly in a school as well as teaching and preaching to women. To some of the children, the Hebrew tradition may have been only one religion among many; an increasing number of the youth must have been drawn into the obscene rites and rituals that were growing increasingly popular in Israel.

Huldah possessed two great qualities—righteousness and prophetic insight. Did her own purity of heart and life result in feelings of condescension toward those whose lives were impure? No, I believe that Huldah's heart was heavily burdened, especially for the youth of Israel, and that she did all she could to warn those around her of impending doom.

Father, give me a burden for those who do not know You. Help me not to be afraid to speak out. Let my delight in You be so obvious that my life will glorify You even when I am making no conscious effort to witness.

CHRIST IS THE GREAT INTERCESSOR; WE SHOULD FOLLOW IN HIS STEPS.

TOTAL COMMITMENT

Commit your way to the Lord; trust in him (Ps. 37:5, NIV). Read 2 Kings 22:14-20.

Hilkiah, Shaphan, you must give me time
To read this book and then to seek God's face.
This nation's disobeyed His laws so long,
The laws we have already heard and known.
And now here is another book of rules—
Our God will punish those who disobey.
                                        —*Huldah*

"Archaeological discoveries throw interesting light on the possible reason for the repairmen's finding the book of the law during their labors on the temple. It is possible that this was the copy of the Pentateuch which had been placed in the cornerstone of the temple several hundred years earlier in the days of Solomon when he directed the building of the temple. From archaeological discoveries we now know that it was customary to place documents in the foundations of ancient buildings."[3]

Huldah, a mere woman, was being asked to check on the validity of a nearly 300-year-old document! Remember the two great qualities Huldah possessed? Because she possessed purity of heart she was able to use her prophetic insight wisely; prophetic power is only given to those who love God with all their hearts.

Thank You, Father, for the way in which You used this woman simply because she loved You and committed her life to You. Help me to pattern my way of life after hers.

EVEN AT OUR WEAKEST POINT, WE CAN EXPERIENCE THE POWER OF GOD WHEN WE SIMPLY LET GO.

CHANNELS ONLY

He will make your righteousness shine like the dawn, the justice of your cause like the noonday sun (Ps. 37:6, NIV). Read 2 Chronicles 34:14-29.

Our God says He was grieved with Israel.
Now grief has turned to anger,
Sorrow's given way to righteous wrath.
God will destroy this city and its people
Because His people have forsaken Him.
Josiah, who repented, He will spare;
The king won't live to see his country's doom.
　　　　　　　　　　　　　　—Huldah

Huldah not only confirmed the authenticity of the book of the law; she also told of Israel's future. It is noteworthy that in the short passages relating Huldah's prophecy the scribe repeated a phrase four times: "Thus saith the Lord!" Huldah did not think of herself as a person of great authority or wisdom, but only as a channel of God's Word.

Each of us can be a channel as well, if we allow God to speak through us. It's so easy to become infatuated with the sound of our own voices and to stop listening for His "still, small voice" (1 Kings 19:12). That Voice can best be heard in the silence of meditation as we build our thought patterns on the foundation of God's Word.

Thank You, Father, for this lesson in the beauty of a quiet spirit. Calm my spirit, Lord, with the comforting assurance that You are still in control. Thank You for teaching me to let go of my own so-called wisdom and to depend completely upon You.

IT IS SO EASY TO BECOME INFATUATED WITH THE SOUND OF OUR OWN VOICES AND TO STOP LISTENING FOR THE STILL, SMALL VOICE.

THE RESULTS OF FORTHRIGHTNESS

Be still before the Lord and wait patiently for him; do not fret when men succeed in their ways, when they carry out their wicked schemes (Ps. 37:7, NIV). Read 2 Kings 23:1-29.

I praise Jehovah for the king
Who tore his clothes and wept in prayer
And then put action to his words,
Tore down the groves and places where
The people worshipped heathen gods
And smashed the idols to the ground.

—Huldah

Partially because of Huldah's forthrightness, King Josiah not only purged Israel of idolatry and paganism, but also moved aggressively to encourage spiritual growth and true worship. After destroying all traces of idol worship in drastic measures, he commanded the people to keep the Passover. Josiah had turned to the Lord "with all his heart, and with all his soul, and with all his might" (2 Kings 23:25).

How differently this story could have ended had Huldah been hesitant to speak out, afraid to pass on God's revelation. Huldah's forthrightness, combined with her purity of heart and her prophetic insight, enabled her to be used of God at a crisis point in Israel's history.

Help me, Father, to know when to speak and what to say. Help me to avoid empty words and fancy phrases; replace them with the simple beauty of Your wisdom.

BE SURE TO SPEAK WHEN GOD TELLS YOU TO!

Week 50

ESTHER: WOMAN AS SOVEREIGN

There is neither Jew nor Greek, slave nor free, male nor female, for you are all one in Christ Jesus (Gal. 3:28, NIV).

Nancy Tischler comments: "Though woman in Eden was granted, along with man, dominion over nature, history has seldom seen female sovereignty."[1]

What about Queen Esther? Was she truly a queen? Let's review the story. Vashti, Esther's dethroned predecessor, was a woman of very strong character and probably virtue as well, but she was deposed on the whim of the oriental despot, her husband King Ahasuerus (or Xerxes). The monarch and his advisors had decided that Vashti's lack of submission might cause other women to behave in like manner, so gutsy Vashti was given the royal ax (figuratively speaking, at least). At the same time the king issued the decree that every man would henceforth be ruler in his own household—a ruling that was definitely easier to make than to carry out!

Vashti's replacement, Esther (or her Jewish name, Hadassah), was certainly not a sovereign in her own right. Esther's role in the "beauty contest" (including the summons to participate) smells more of slavery than sovereignty. Probably Xerxes was mainly concerned with her physical appearance and her ability to delight him.

There is one more woman participant in this drama of the Persian palace. Zeresh, wife of Haman the new prime minister, may have had almost as much power—if indirect—as the queen. She seems to have been the mind behind the man.

Volumes have been spoken and written about the power struggle between man and woman, but seldom is the fact mentioned that it was Jesus Christ who offered Jewish and Gentile women alike a new sense of importance.

O. T. PASSAGE THIS WEEK: Esther 1:1—4:9

SPECIAL PRAYER NEEDS THIS WEEK:

ANSWERS TO PRAYER THIS WEEK:

THE FIRST WOMEN'S LIB CONVENTION!

'Come,' they say. 'We'll get some wine and have a party; let's all get drunk. This is really living; let it go on and on, and tomorrow will be better yet!' . . .And they are as greedy as dogs, never satisfied (Isa. 56:12, 11, LB). Read Esther 1:1-12; Proverbs 23:29-35.

> *That drunken king! I won't parade*
> *Before inebriated men. . .*
> *Their lips inviting me to share their cups,*
> *Their eyes suggesting other things.*
> *How can he make a toy of me!*
> *I won't allow it to be so. . .*
> *I'll show the king I am a queen,*
> *Not just another harem girl!*
>
> *—Vashti*

Queen Vashti's refusal to display herself before the king's drinking cronies (one commentator feels the king was asking her to parade in the nude) was an act of considerable courage. Did the queen come to this decision on her own, or was she encouraged to refuse the king by the women of the palace (for whose benefit she was giving a party)?

The men of the palace had been engaged in a monumental eating and drinking orgy for seven days. Prior to that, a six-month celebration of King Ahasuerus's wealth and the glory of his empire had stretched on and on. Can you imagine how disgusting the drunken orgy must have become—especially to the wife of this "glorious" king? She may have refused his request with self-righteous condescension.

Father, I know that You love the sinner (although not his sin). It's very hard for me to even love the sinner. Remind me, Lord, that I am only a sinner saved by grace.

"IF GOD JUDGED US THE WAY WE JUDGE OUR FELLOWMEN, WE'D ALL BE IN HELL; GOD JUDGES US THROUGH THE ATONEMENT."[2]

A NEW QUEEN

God protects the upright but destroys the wicked (Prov. 10:29, LB).
Read Esther 1:13-22.

I do not understand why I am here
And yet there is a purpose, I am sure.
Thank You for Hegai; he's been kind to me
And eased the fear and anguish I have known.
Jehovah God, please help me to remain
As pure in Your eyes as the day I came
And show me what You have in store for me.
My will is Yours; You are my sovereign Lord.
—Esther

Vashti had been deposed because of her insubordination, and Esther had been chosen as the new queen. Imagine Esther's feelings as she entered the harem for the first time! The Jewish girl had been raised by her cousin Mordecai (he had been captured when Jerusalem was destroyed by King Nebuchadnezzar and had been exiled to Babylon), and their home was probably very humble. Esther made such an impression on Hegai, the eunuch in charge of the harem, however, that he gave her the most luxurious apartment in the place!

Esther also received a special menu and frequent beauty treatments, as well as seven maids to administer them! And yet none of these advantages could produce—or change—the inner beauty that, out of all the contestants in Ahasuerus's beauty contest, only Esther possessed.

Thank You, Father, for Your special gift of spiritual beauty that is available to every woman.

"IF YOU ARE GOING TO BE USED BY GOD, HE WILL TAKE YOU THROUGH A MULTITUDE OF EXPERIENCES THAT ARE NOT MEANT FOR YOU AT ALL...THEY ARE MEANT TO MAKE YOU USEFUL IN HIS HANDS, AND TO ENABLE YOU TO UNDERSTAND WHAT TRANSPIRES IN OTHER SOULS SO THAT YOU WILL NEVER BE SURPRISED AT WHAT YOU COME ACROSS."[3]

THE PRIME MINISTER

How much better is wisdom than gold, and understanding than silver (Prov. 16:16, LB). Read Esther 2:1—3:1.

> *We're on our way—we have arrived!*
> *And Haman is prime minister!*
> *All the officials bow before him;*
> *He is next in power to the king!*
> *I am richer than I ever dreamed*
> *And yet I don't feel satisfied.*
>
> *—Zeresh*

Meet Zeresh, wife of Haman the prime minister! I imagine her as a squat, dumpy, pushy woman who was never satisfied with what she had, always nagging Haman on to positions of greater wealth and power, no matter what the cost in human lives or misery.

I'm sure you know women like Zeresh—unsatisfied, unfulfilled, infecting everyone around them with the contagion of their discontent. It's easy to slip into the fantasy that wealth or position would solve all our problems. . .but even Zeresh was realizing that neither was a panacea.

I know, Father, that through true worship and fellowship with You, I can find the security I need, and that in Your service I can feel significant. Help me to reach up and out—up to You and out to those around me.

REMEMBER: "THE TWO REQUIRED INPUTS FOR A SENSE OF PERSONAL WORTH ARE SIGNIFICANCE AND SECURITY."[4]

THE WOMAN BEHIND THE MAN HAMAN

Throw out the mocker, and you will be rid of tension, fighting and quarrels (Prov. 22:10, LB). Read Matthew 5:3-12.

This new queen I don't like at all!
Something about her turns me off.
She is too sweet, too pure, too good!
I like a queen who speaks her mind.
Oh, she is beautiful, it's true
But she's too sweet to handle power.

—Zeresh

Enter Esther, a "beautiful and charming girl" who "charmed all who saw her" (Esther 2:1, 15, NEB). . .except, perhaps, jealous Zeresh, who may have envied her potential power, and other jealous entrants in the beauty pageant. Can you imagine all the petty jealousies, backbiting, and open quarreling that would have existed in such a dead-end pattern of life?

Have you ever noticed the interaction between an easy-going, tolerant person and an aggressive, competitive Zeresh type? Often the aggressive personality dominates the scene—urging action, barking orders, chafing impatiently at delays, becoming exasperated with anyone who is patient.

Thank You, Father, for the contrasting temperaments You have given to us, Your creations. Put Your Holy Spirit to work within our individual personalities so that each of us might be conformed to Your image (Rom. 8:29).

REVIEW: "PROBLEMS DEVELOP WHEN THE BASIC NEEDS FOR SIGNIFICANCE AND SECURITY ARE THREATENED."[5]

PLANS FOR A POGROM

Pride ends in destruction (Prov. 18:12, LB). Read Esther 3:2-15.

So Mordecai will not bow.
Well, don't just sit there—do something!
Don't waste your time on just one man;
Get the whole race, those hateful Jews!
I never liked their wily ways.
They've been a nuisance far too long.
                                    —Zeresh

"Don't let anyone stand in your way, Haman! We've worked hard for this position and we're going to make the most of it! If old Mordecai won't give you the respect you deserve, get rid of him!" And so perhaps Zeresh went on. . . and on. . .and on.

Zeresh would have been a real pain to live with—for anyone but Haman. Perhaps he considered her an asset, because their goals were the same: power and wealth, no matter whom they trampled in the process. They deserved each other.

Help me, Father, to learn a lesson from this power-seeking couple. Thank You, Jesus, for being so much more concerned about people than power that You were willing to give up heaven and become a servant.

REMEMBER: "TRUE SIGNIFICANCE AND SECURITY ARE AVAILABLE ONLY TO THE CHRISTIAN, ONE WHO IS TRUSTING IN CHRIST'S PERFECT LIFE AND SUBSTITUTIONARY DEATH AS HIS SOLE BASIS OF ACCEPTABILITY BEFORE A HOLY GOD."[6]

REASON TO HESITATE

The king's anger is as dangerous as a lion's (Prov. 19:12, LB). Read Esther 4:1-9.

I hate this life I have to live.
My heart is with my people who
Will die before a year is gone.
My uncle says, "Go to the king—
This is the time to plead our cause."
But if I go without a call
I'm doomed to die.

—Esther

Esther had charmed everyone's hearts, including the king's. . .but now, five years later, it seemed the king had forgotten her. In the meantime, you remember, he had staged another beauty contest, and as the old saying goes, "out of sight, out of mind." Esther had not been called in thirty days, and if she incurred the king's disfavor by entering his presence without invitation, one snap of his fingers could mean death.

Some commentators have criticized Esther's reluctance, taking it as an indication of selfishness. But I think if we put ourselves in her royal slippers, we can easily understand Esther's hesitation. She was risking everything—her home, her reputation, her future, her life!

Father, am I willing to risk everything for Your sake? **GOD NOWHERE TELLS US TO GIVE UP THINGS FOR THE SAKE OF GIVING THEM UP. HE TELLS US TO GIVE THEM UP FOR THE SAKE OF THE ONLY THING WORTH HAVING—LIFE WITH HIMSELF.**

ESTHER: WOMAN AS SERVANT

Wesley Fuerst explains: "It is noteworthy that many Christians have had to struggle in order to justify the presence of the Book of Esther in their Bible. . . . To be sure little theology is present in Esther. . . . The book has a different purpose. Its message is nationalistic.

"Esther does not describe what should happen, but what *does* happen. Jews have been confined to ghettoes, discriminated against, and terrified and tortured by inquisitions, and all this for no other reason than for being Jewish. The Book of Esther cries out against this evil. . . . This book satisfied and helped generations who felt the hatred of their neighbors.

"But the book offers more. It speaks of a people who are moved, guided, and protected. Things work out satisfactorily for Israel, *because it is Israel.* Speaking with convictions born of a long history and centuries of faith, the author rejoiced in his Jewishness; he addressed times of threat and peril with a word of hope, which was built on confidence and faith in a very ancient promise."[1]

"I will establish my covenant as an everlasting covenant between me and you and your descendants after you for the generations to come, to be your God and the God of your descendants after you. The whole land of Canaan. . .I will give as an everlasting possession to you and your descendants after you; and I will be their God" (Gen. 17:7-8, NIV).

That promise, as we have seen, was made to Abraham by God. And, as we have also seen, God's promise was carried toward its fruition by some very human people.

O. T. PASSAGE THIS WEEK: Esther 4:10—10:3

SPECIAL PRAYER NEEDS THIS WEEK:

ANSWERS TO PRAYER THIS WEEK:

ESTHER'S DECISION

Commit your work to the Lord, then it will succeed (Prov. 16:3, LB).
Read Esther 4:10-17.

> *He hasn't called me for a month*
> *Or perhaps more—I don't keep count!*
> *I dread his touch, his coarse embrace. . .*
> *But now I wish he'd call so I*
> *Could go before him without fear.*
> *I will ask good Mordecai*
> *To fast and pray. . .and I will go.*
> *If I must die, then I will die.*
>
> *—Esther*

Esther fully realized the tremendous risk of her venture; she knew that the favor or disfavor of an oriental despot could not be counted on beforehand. Making use of her knowledge of human nature, she put on her royal apparel, making herself as attractive as possible to appear before the king. On the surface she was the charming, beautiful Esther; in reality she was shaking in her shoes!

The name of God is not mentioned in the Book of Esther, but I feel that Esther relied very heavily on the fasting (and prayer) of her cousin Mordecai to get her through this ordeal she had to face. What would have happened if Mordecai had not done as requested—and if Esther had not had three days of spiritual preparation?

Help me, Father, to be a Mordecai—the strong, dependable person who can always be counted on in times of emergency. Help me to be there when I'm needed, to pray when I can't be there physically.

"YOU DO NOT KNOW WHAT YOU ARE GOING TO DO; THE ONLY THING YOU KNOW IS THAT GOD KNOWS WHAT *HE* IS DOING."[2]

ESTHER'S PLAN

Many favors are showered on those who please the king (Prov. 16:15, LB). Read Esther 5:1-8.

The king has promised he will come
With Haman to a banquet that
I have prepared to sooth his mind.
I trust in Mordecai's prayers—
To our great God—to aid this plan.
                                    —Esther

Esther had a plan, but it required time and care to bring it to fruition. Had she presented her petition to the king in the court, Haman's friends would have reported her words to him; so very diplomatically she invited the king—and Haman—to a banquet. She would be able to judge better what to do when Haman was off guard.

Peace in the midst of panic—the secret of a heart at peace with itself and with God! During those three days of preparation Esther had been cleansed thoroughly. One shred of bitterness, one trace of resentment, one smattering of jealousy—any one of these are enough to disrupt peace.

I need Your peace, Father. So many petty emotions fight within me. Quiet my mind and heart with the gentleness of Your Holy Spirit.

"THERE ARE TIMES WHEN OUR PEACE IS BASED UPON IGNORANCE, BUT ONCE WE AWAKEN TO THE FACTS OF LIFE, INNER PEACE IS IMPOSSIBLE UNLESS IT IS RECEIVED FROM JESUS."[3]

A POWERLESS PRIME MINISTER

The wicked man stares into space with pursed lips, deep in thought, planning his evil deeds (Prov. 16:30, LB). Read Esther 5:9-14.

That man of mine! For all his power,
He doesn't ever use his head!
He banquets with the king and queen,
Yet fears to ask the king a favor.
But I'll make sure gallows are built
To hang my husband's enemy.

—Zeresh

Zeresh has no peace. She is still pushing, manipulating, trying to strike what she thinks will be the final blow at the man who blocks her husband's power. And yet she herself seems to despise her husband's lack of initiative, his impotent frustration. Haman is prime minister of all Persia, but he cannot be the leader in his home.

No one is unhappier than the man whose wife despises him—unless it is his wife! She may cater to her husband's wishes, even "baby" him, yet despise him in her heart. But how lonely and miserable both of them are!

Help me to cover relationships, Father, with Your healing love. Help me to be loyal when I feel betrayed, to show respect when I am not given respect, to be true when others are false. Teach me the meaning of Calvary love.

"THE MOST BASIC HUMAN NEED IS A SENSE OF PERSONAL WORTH, AN ACCEPTANCE OF ONESELF AS A WHOLE, REAL PERSON."[4]

PLANS GO AWRY

The whole city celebrates a good man's success—and also the godless man's death (Prov. 11:10, LB). Read Esther 6:1-14.

If Mordecai is a Jew,
You never will succeed against him.
You have already begun to fall
Before this strange and hated people.
They have a power we do not know
Nor will we ever understand.

—Zeresh

Zeresh and Haman's retaliatory plans against Mordecai boomeranged, and the prime minister returned home utterly humiliated after his highly frustrating day of honoring his enemy Mordecai the Jew. Looking to Zeresh and his friends for reassurance, Haman must have been totally disappointed by their discouraging responses. Nobody loves a loser.

Zeresh had at last realized that the Jews were simply not ordinary people. In effect, she was now telling her husband that he should have realized all along that he couldn't fight Mordecai! Notice that she took none of the credit for the plans that were now impossible to execute!

Thank You, Father, for Your faithfulness in the face of our fickleness. I sometimes find it so difficult to be loyal in my earthly relationships. . .but "great is Thy faithfulness." Thank You that Your promises are steadfast and sure.

"IS THERE A THOUGHT IN YOUR HEART ABOUT ANYONE WHICH YOU WOULD NOT LIKE TO HAVE DRAGGED INTO THE LIGHT?"⁵ IF SO, BETTER PRAY ABOUT IT.

ESTHER'S PLEA

From a wise mind comes careful and persuasive speech (Prov. 16:23, LB). Read Esther 7:1-10.

Please save my life, O gracious king!
I and my people have been sold
To be destroyed and to be killed.
If we were only sold as slaves,
I would have held my tongue, my tears. . .
But I am sold, to be destroyed
By a man who claims to be your friend.
                                                    —Esther

There has been no time for Esther to learn of Haman's humiliation, so her accusation and petition are made boldly in the face of what seems to be a most formidable opponent. For the first time she reveals her well-kept secret—her identity with the condemned—and thereby places herself in the balance with her people.

If you have ever experienced direct confrontation of a mortal enemy, as Esther did, you know the anxiety and tension that almost paralyze your body. Yet "we wrestle not against flesh and blood, but against principalities, against powers"—a greater force—each day of our lives (Eph. 6:12, KJV).

Help me, Father, to be alert, to keep an ear tuned for the criminals who seek to burglarize my spiritual life—the TV set, the superbusy schedule, the seemingly innocent activities that rob me of time to read Your Word and just to spend time talking to You.

"THE FINAL AIM OF SELF-SACRIFICE IS LAYING DOWN OUR LIVES FOR OUR FRIEND."[6]

SAVE MY PEOPLE!

We can make our plans, but the final outcome is in God's hands (Prov. 16:1, LB). Read Esther 8—10.

If it please my lord,
And if you love me,
Reverse the plans that Haman made.
He plotted to destroy the Jews,
And though he's dead,
His work goes on!
Reverse his plans and save my people!
                                    —Esther

We cannot read this passage without realizing the inner strength of the woman Esther. She knew how to plan and how to carry through on her plan. She knew when to hold back and when to go forward. She could fearlessly risk her life for a great cause.

The Book of Esther was written for people who were oppressed and persecuted, who needed encouragement and a hope for the future. It tells us that just one person who is listening to the call of God and is willing to obey—male or female—can be His instrument to accomplish a miracle.

"Lord, make me an instrument of Your peace.
Where there is hatred let me sow love;
Where there is injury, pardon;
Where there is doubt, faith;
Where there is despair, hope;
Where there is darkness, light; and
Where there is sadness, joy. . . .
                                    (St. Francis of Assisi)
"LORD, MAKE ME AN INSTRUMENT OF YOUR PEACE"

GOMER: LIBERATED BY LOVE

The word of the Lord that came to Hosea son of Beeri during the reigns of Uzziah, Jotham, Ahaz and Hezekiah, kings of Judah, and during the reign of Jeroboam son of Joash king of Israel: When the Lord began to speak through Hosea, the Lord said to him, 'Go, take to yourself an adulterous wife and children of unfaithfulness, because the land is guilty of the vilest adultery in departing from the Lord.' So he married Gomer daughter of Diblaim, and she conceived and bore him a son   (Hos. 1:1-3, NIV).

David Hubbard asks, "How would a man like the prophet Hosea have fared in our day?

"In a society where the public image is the thing, and the woman behind the man is thought to hold the key to his success, what would have been the fate of this upright citizen who suddenly married, of all people, a prostitute?

"In a generation that regards self-expression and self-fulfillment as the goals toward which the well-adjusted strive, how would this single-purposed man who relentlessly pursued the goal of obedience to God have been received?

"In a world that practices a kind of moral disarmament and assumes that truth, if it is to be spoken at all, must be diluted, sugared, and given in small doses, what would have been the response to this forthright man of God?

"The fact is that Hosea would not have been given a high rating on the Gallup Poll of any age; for, as Scripture points out, the heart of man is desperately corrupt."[1]

As you scan the Book of Hosea, ask the Lord to open your eyes and your heart to His message of love.

O. T. PASSAGE THIS WEEK: Hosea 1—7; 14

SPECIAL PRAYER NEEDS THIS WEEK:

ANSWERS TO PRAYER THIS WEEK:

LOVESONG

I don't want your sacrifices—I want your love; I don't want your offerings—I want you to know me. But like Adam, you broke my covenant; you refused my love (Hos. 6:6-7, LB). Read Hosea 1.

I loved you, Gomer, even though
You didn't know what loving meant.
I took you for my own, your bridal dowry paid.
I treasured, loved, and cherished you
And held you to my breast.

My love was not returned.
You left me for another man
And yet another. . .and again.

—Hosea

Hosea was a voice of God crying in the wilderness, and in his tragic marriage he dramatically demonstrated God's redemptive love for man. This poignant story tells of a one-sided love that continued unswerving through every possible discouragement, humiliation, and torture.

Gomer: the picture of adulterous Israel, forsaking her divine Bridegroom again and again for lovers and idols who held out only empty arms and empty promises.

Teach me Your lessons, Father, through this painful story. Thank You for the faithfulness of Hosea's love that is only a small-scale model of Your love.

"BUT I WILL COURT HER AGAIN, AND BRING HER INTO THE WILDERNESS, AND SPEAK TO HER TENDERLY THERE" (Hos. 2:14, LB).

BETRAYAL OF LOVE

She doesn't realize that all she has, has come from me (Hos. 2:8, LB).
Read Hosea 2.

And so you drifted downward. . .
Farther still. . .
Until one day you stood in chains,
A slave upon the block,
Your very life on sale.

I watched as others mocked your fate,
And then, my wanton wife, I bought you back.
I bid against the highest bids
Until your well-used body was my own again.

"Hosea's crazy!" people said.
"A fool!" the local gossips hissed.
They couldn't understand.

—Hosea

Can you imagine the lonely prophet wandering about town, looking through windows and into doorways, seeking for a glimpse of the woman who had once been the joy of his life? Finally he finds her—with another man—but in need, and in unbelievable self-sacrifice he supplies her with the staples of life.

But Gomer doesn't realize who is paying her bills. She continues her promiscuity until she no longer is desirable and is sold as a slave. In the master stroke of love Hosea buys a wife-turned-prostitute-turned-slave.

Have I ever realized, Father, just how much You love me? **"I WILL GIVE BACK HER VINEYARDS TO HER, AND TRANSFORM HER VALLEY OF TROUBLES INTO A DOOR OF HOPE" (Hos. 2:15, LB).**

CONSCIENCE-STRICKEN MISERY

Your deeds won't let you come to God again, for the spirit of adultery is deep within you, and you cannot know the Lord (Hos. 5:4, LB). Read Hosea 3, 4.

> How can Hosea want me back?
> The very thought of my past life
> Must turn his stomach.
> I've been told he paid my lovers, gave them gold
> So I could live.
> I never knew. I believed their lies.
> The one good man I've ever known I've cruelly betrayed.
> How can he love me still?
>
> —Gomer

What started Gomer on the path to prostitution? Was she rebelling against a superstrict home life followed by a lonely marriage to a misunderstood, unpopular prophet? Was Hosea always too busy for her needs? Or did she feel totally inadequate for her role as a pastor's wife?

We can blame many factors for a woman's immorality: a problematic home life complicated by abuse, incest, or rape; severe emotional problems; rejection by her father; physical problems—the list could go on and on. But what is meant in Hosea 5:4 by "the spirit of adultery"?

I have sensed that "spirit of adultery" within myself, Father—that desire to wander away from what I know to be right and good. Cleanse me of that spirit, Father, and replace it with Your Holy Spirit.

"SHE WILL RESPOND TO ME THERE, SINGING WITH JOY AS IN DAYS LONG AGO IN HER YOUTH, AFTER I HAD FREED HER FROM CAPTIVITY IN EGYPT" (Hos. 2:15b, LB).

I COULDN'T PLAY THE ROLE

Bring your petition. Come to the Lord and say, 'O Lord, take away our sins; be gracious to us and receive us, and we will offer you the sacrifices of praise (Hos. 14:2, LB). Read Hosea 5.*

How can I go back?
A prophet's wife must be above reproach,
And I'm below the lowest.
Can I tell him
I felt his standards were too high
Right from the start?
Those righteous-looking people
Who hang upon each word he speaks
Look down on me.
I couldn't play the role.
They wondered all along
Why such a man chose me.

—Gomer

Can you imagine Gomer's feelings when she saw Hosea bidding for her at the slave auction? Was she happy to see him, or too miserable to look into his eyes?

How do you feel about facing God after what seems to be an unforgivable sin? Can you "look Him in the eye" in prayer? How long has it been since you have made an honest, up-to-date confession of sin?

Father, I have sinned in Your sight. I am not worthy to be called Your daughter.

"IN THAT COMING DAY, SAYS THE LORD, SHE WILL CALL ME 'MY HUSBAND' INSTEAD OF 'MY MASTER'" (Hos. 2:16, LB).

THE POINT OF DESPERATION

Israel is destroyed; she lies among the nations as a broken pot. She is a lonely, wandering wild ass. The only friends she has are those she hires (Hos. 8:8-9, LB). Read Hosea 6; 7.

> *So to escape from righteous stares,*
> *The pain of worthlessness,*
> *I left for other worlds*
> *Where I could cope with life;*
> *Where little was expected of me,*
> *Where I could be myself.*
>
> *It lasted for a little while, my brand-new world,*
> *But soon it too turned sour.*
> *Again I ran. I couldn't admit*
> *I'd failed once more.*
> *From one man to another*
> *And to another still*
> *I ran and ran until—you know the end.*
>
> *And now Hosea's bought me back!*
> *He says he loves me*
> *Just as God loves Israel*
> *With an everlasting love. . . .*
>
> *I just don't understand.*
>
> *—Gomer*

God understood.
He knew her fickle heart, her hurts and hang-ups.
He also knew His power could change her life
If she would let Him lead.

O Father—may I call you that?—my life is so confused, so broken, so messed up. I too need Your power. . .and Your love. **"THEN YOU WILL LIE DOWN IN PEACE AND SAFETY, UNAFRAID: AND I WILL BIND YOU TO ME FOREVER WITH CHAINS OF RIGHTEOUSNESS AND JUSTICE AND LOVE AND MERCY" (Hos. 2:18-19, LB).**

REUNION AND REDEMPTION!

Then I will cure you of idolatry and faithlessness, and my love will know no bounds, for my anger will be forever gone (Hos. 14:4, LB). Read Hosea 14.

God understands your heart as well.
He speaks to you today:
 I formed your body long before
  you knew what life would hold.
 I stood by waiting patiently
  for you to turn to me in love.
 I waited while you turned your back instead
  to taste life's "greater pleasures."
 I watched while sin's chains bound you
  to the auction block.
And then I paid the price to buy you back—
 though you were rightly mine.

 I've loved you with an everlasting love,
 With gentle lovingkindness drawn you close.
 I claimed your tarnished soul a second time.

 Don't turn away again.
 I've called you mine.

O, Father, I too have been a Gomer—
Faithless, fickle, hurting deep inside.
Forgive me, Father, heal my past, help me to start anew.
You bought me from the auction block—
How can I not be Yours?
"I WILL BETROTH YOU TO ME IN FAITHFULNESS AND LOVE, AND YOU WILL REALLY KNOW ME THEN AS YOU NEVER HAVE BEFORE" (Hos. 2:20, LB).

SUBJECT INDEX

Since the days of the week rather than page numbers designate each devotional, the Subject Index uses the same designation. The Sunday readings are designated by the week.

NOTES

Preface

1. Eugenia Price, *The Unique World of Women* (Grand Rapids: Zondervan, 1969), p. 30.

Week 1

1. Bill Gothard, *Institute in Basic Youth Conflicts Syllabus* (Oakbrook, IL: IBYC, 1975), p. 1.
2. Charles F. Pfeiffer, ed., *The Wycliffe Bible Commentary* (Chicago: Moody Press, 1962), p. 6.
3. Lawrence J. Crabb, Jr., *Effective Biblical Counseling* (Grand Rapids: Zondervan, 1977), p. 70.

Week 2

1. Nancy Tischler, *The Legacy of Eve* (Atlanta: John Knox Press, 1977), p. 20.
2. Ibid., p. 21.
3. Gothard, *Institute in Basic Youth Conflicts Syllabus*, p. 2.
4. Howard Hendricks, *Heaven Help the Home* (Wheaton: Victor Books, 1973), p. 31.

Week 3

1. Tischler, *The Legacy of Eve*, p. 22.
2. Oswald Chambers, *My Utmost for His Highest* (New York: Dodd, Mead & Co., 1935), p. 325.
3. Bill Bright, *Discipleship and Evangelism Training Handbook* (San Bernardino: Campus Crusade for Christ International, 1975), p. 1.
4. Ibid.
5. Chambers, *My Utmost for His Highest*, p. 301.

Week 4

1. *The Wycliffe Bible Commentary*, p. 17.
2. Eugenia Price, *God Speaks to Women Today* (Grand Rapids: Zondervan, 1964), p. 19.
3. Chambers, *My Utmost for His Highest*, p. 344.
4. Gothard, *Institute in Basic Youth Conflicts* (Notes).

Week 5

1. Jill Briscoe, *Prime Rib and Apple* (Grand Rapids: Zondervan, 1976), p. 27.

Week 6

1. Matthew Henry, *Commentary on the Whole Bible*, vol. VI (Old Tappan: Fleming H. Revell, n.d.), p. 669.

Week 8

1. "Whatever It Takes," *100 Heart Warming Sacred Favorites* (Nashville: John T. Benson Publishing Co., 1976), p. 187.

Week 9

1. Hendricks, *Heaven Help the Home*, p. 59.
2. Ibid., p. 62.
3. Ibid., p. 39.
4. Dorothy Law Nolte, *Children Learn What They Live*, poem published by John Philip Co., 1963.

Week 10

1. Nolte, *Children Learn What They Live*.

Week 11

1. Gothard, *Institute in Basic Youth Conflicts Syllabus*, p. 2.

Week 13

1. Price, *The Unique World of Women*, p. 51.
2. Evelyn Christenson, *Lord, Change Me!* (Wheaton: Victor Books, 1977), p. 132.

Week 14

1. Chambers, *My Utmost for His Highest*, p. 261.
2. Christenson, *Lord, Change Me!*, p. 126.
3. Chambers, *My Utmost for His Highest*, p. 284.

Week 15

1. "Count Your Blessings," *Hymns of the Christian Life* (Harrisburg: Christian Publications, Inc., 1978), p. 200.

Week 16

1. Gothard, *IBYC*, (Notes).
2. Chambers, *My Utmost for His Highest*, p. 225.
3. "A Quiet Place," *He's Everything to Me Plus 103* (Waco: Lexicon Music, Inc., 1972), p. 7.

Week 17

1. Chambers, *My Utmost for His Highest*, p. 37.
2. Ibid., p. 270.

Week 18

1. Chambers, *My Utmost for His Highest*, p. 165.
2. Gothard, *Institute in Basic Youth Conflicts Syllabus*, p. 8.
3. Chambers, *My Utmost for His Highest*, p. 174.

4. Ibid.
5. Ibid.

Week 19

1. Miriam Neff, "Why I Question the Feminist Movement," *Moody Monthly* (Nov. 1980), p. 38.
2. Chambers, *My Utmost for His Highest*, p. 344.
3. Ibid., p. 232.

Week 20

1. Chambers, *My Utmost for His Highest*, p. 124.
2. Gothard, *Institute in Basic Youth Conflicts*, (Notes).
3. Chambers, *My Utmost for His Highest*, p. 76.
4. Ibid., p. 189.

Week 21

1. Chambers, *My Utmost for His Highest*, p. 161.
2. "Great Is Thy Faithfulness," *Hymns of the Christian Life*, p. 576.
3. Lou Beardsley and Tony Spry, *The Fulfilled Woman* (Irving, CA: Harvest House, 1975), p. 17.
4. Richard DeHaan, "Comment," *RBC Discovery Digest* (May 1980), p. 2.
5. Beardsley and Spry, *The Fulfilled Woman*, p. 21.

Week 22

1. Beardsley and Spry, *The Fulfilled Woman*, p. 11.
2. Hendricks, *Heaven Help the Home*, p. 30.
3. Ibid., p. 27.
4. Ibid., p. 32.
5. Chambers, *My Utmost for His Highest*, p. 132.
6. Crabb, *Effective Biblical Counseling*, p. 70.

Week 23

1. Leontine R. Young, *Out of Wedlock* (New York: McGraw Hill, 1954), p. 2.
2. Chambers, *My Utmost for His Highest*, p. 324.
3. Ibid., p. 261.
4. Ibid., p. 250.
5. Ibid., p. 105.
6. Ibid.

Week 24

1. John White, *Eros Defiled: The Christian and Sexual Sin* (Downers Grove, IL: InterVarsity, 1979), p. 61.
2. Scofield's Notes, Numbers 6:2.
3. Andrew Murray, *How to Raise Your Children for Christ* (Minneapolis: Bethany Fellowship, 1975), p. 87.
4. "I Am a Promise," (Alexandria, IN: Gaither Music Co., 1975).
5. Murray, *How to Raise Your Children for Christ*, p. 87.

Week 25

1. Crabb, *Effective Biblical Counseling*, p. 61.
2. Ibid.
3. Ibid., p. 69.
4. Ibid.
5. Ibid.
6. Ibid., p. 71.

Week 26

1. Clyde Narramore, *How to Handle Feelings of Depression* (Grand Rapids: Zondervan, 1975), p. 8.
2. Hendricks, *Heaven Help the Home*, p. 59.

Week 27

1. Price, *God Speaks to Women Today*, pp. 83, 86.
2. Chambers, *My Utmost for His Highest*, p. 155.
3. Ibid.
4. Howard G. Hendricks, *Elijah: The Battle of the Gods* (Chicago: Moody Press, n.d.), p. 8.
5. Ibid., p. 23.
6. Traditional spiritual.
7. Hendricks, *Elijah: The Battle of the Gods*, p. 39.

Week 28

1. Corrie ten Boom, "I'm Still Learning to Forgive," *Guideposts Magazine*, orig. prtg. (Carmel, NY: Guideposts Associates, 1972).
2. "Grace Greater Than Our Sin," *Hymns of the Christian Life*, p. 545.
3. "Take My Life, and Let It Be," Ibid., p. 225.
4. "Gentle Shepherd," *Hymns for the Family of God* (Nashville: Paragon Associates, Inc., 1976), p. 596.
5. "He Touched Me," *Hymns of the Christian Life*, inside back cover

Week 29

1. "Lead Me to the Rock," *Songs of Inspiration* (Nashville: John T. Benson Publishing Co., 1949), p. 246.
2. Chambers, *My Utmost for His Highest*, p. 232.
3. Ibid.

Week 30

1. Gothard, *IBYC Syllabus*, p. 16.
2. Amy Carmichael, *If* (Grand Rapids: Zondervan, 1980), no page designations.
3. Ibid.
4. Ibid.
5. Ibid.
6. Ibid.
7. Ibid.

Week 31

1. Carmichael, *If.*
2. Ibid.
3. Ibid.
4. Price, *God Speaks to Women Today*, p. 95.
5. Christenson, *Lord, Change Me!*
6. Carmichael, *If.*
7. Ibid.

Week 32

1. H. V. Morton, *Women of the Bible* (New York: Dodd, Mead & Company, 1956), p. 102.
2. Chambers, *My Utmost for His Highest*, p. 241.
3. Ibid., p. 231.
4. Ibid., p. 80.

Week 33

1. Chambers, *My Utmost for His Highest*, p. 323.

Week 34

1. "The Love of God," *New Songs of Inspiration No. 2* (Nashville: John T. Benson Publishing Co., 1955), p. 158.

Week 35

1. Author Unknown.
2. William M. Thackeray.
3. Chambers, *My Utmost for His Highest*, p. 202.
4. Hendricks, *Heaven Help the Home*, p. 132.

Week 36

1. O. Hallesby, *Prayer* (Minneapolis: Augsburg, 1931), p. 17.
2. Ibid., p. 18.
3. Ibid., p. 29.
4. Crabb, *Effective Biblical Counseling*, p. 106.

Week 37

1. Reuel Howe, quoted in: Joan Winmill Brown, *Wings of Joy* (Minneapolis: Worldwide Publications, 1977), p. 27.
2. Ethel Waters, *His Eye Is On the Sparrow*, quoted in: Brown, *Wings of Joy*, p. 119.
3. Chambers, *My Utmost for His Highest*, p. 124.

Week 38

1. William Smith, *Comprehensive Bible Dictionary* (Chicago: John A. Hertel Publishing, 1963), p. 787.
2. Chambers, *My Utmost for His Highest*, p. 114.

3. Ibid., p. 268.
4. Ibid., p. 272.
5. Ibid., p. 325.
6. "Great Is Thy Faithfulness," *Hymns of the Christian Life*, p. 576.

Week 39

1. Chambers, *My Utmost for His Highest*, p. 11.
2. Ibid., p. 12.
3. Ibid.
4. Ibid., p. 364.

Week 40

1. Chambers, *My Utmost for His Highest*, p. 257.

Week 41

1. Henry, *Commentary on the Whole Bible*.
2. Chambers, *My Utmost for His Highest*, p. 324.
3. Ibid., p. 2.
4. Ibid., p. 102.
5. Ibid., p. 9.
6. Ibid., p. 284.

Week 42

1. Hallesby, *Prayer*, p. 47.
2. Chambers, *My Utmost for His Highest*, p. 174.
3. "Take My Life, and Let It Be," *Hymns of the Christian Life*, p. 225.

Week 43

1. Chambers, *My Utmost for His Highest*, p. 50.
2. Ibid.
3. Ibid., p. 190.
4. Larry Christenson, *The Christian Family* (Minneapolis: Bethany Fellowship, 1970), p. 64.

Week 44

1. Edith Deen, *All the Women of the Bible* (New York: Harper Brothers Publishers, 1955), p. 131.
2. Ibid., p. 133.
3. Chambers, *My Utmost for His Highest*, p. 11.

Week 45

1. Nancy Tischler, *The Legacy of Eve*, p. 93.
2. Robert T. Boyd, *Tells, Tombs, and Treasures* (Grand Rapids: Baker, 1969), p. 121.
3. Chambers, *My Utmost for His Highest*, p. 235.

Week 46

1. Mildred Tengbom, *Sometimes I Hurt* (Nashville: Thomas Nelson, 1980), pp. 30-31.
2. Michael Quoist, quoted in: Tengbom, *Sometimes I Hurt*, p. 46.
3. Paul Tournier, quoted in: Tengbom, *Sometimes I Hurt*, p. 50.
4. Ragnar Bring, quoted in: Tengbom, *Sometimes I Hurt*, p. 36.

Week 47

1. Tengbom, *Sometimes I Hurt*, p. 30.
2. Ibid., p. 29.
3. Ibid.

Week 48

1. Chambers, *My Utmost for His Highest*, p. 176.
2. Ibid., p. 153.
3. Ibid.
4. Ibid.

Week 49

1. Chambers, *My Utmost for His Highest*, p. 91.
2. Ibid., p. 110.
3. Joseph P. Free, *Archaeology and Bible History* (Wheaton: Van Kampen Press, 1950), p. 215.

Week 50

1. Tischler, *The Legacy of Eve*, p. 86.
2. Chambers, *My Utmost for His Highest*, p. 174.
3. Ibid., p. 310.
4. Crabb, *Effective Biblical Counseling*, p. 61.
5. Ibid., p. 69.
6. Ibid., p. 71.

Week 51

1. Wesley J. Fuerst, *The Books of Ruth, Esther, Ecclesiastes, The Song of Solomon, Lamentations—The Five Scrolls* (New York: Cambridge University Press, 1975), pp. 89-90.
2. Chambers, *My Utmost for His Highest*, p. 2.
3. Ibid., p. 239.
4. Crabb, *Effective Biblical Counseling*, p. 61.
5. Chambers, *My Utmost for His Highest*, p. 259.
6. Ibid., p. 238.

Week 52

1. David Allen Hubbard, *With Bands of Love* (Grand Rapids: Eerdmans, 1968), p. 11.